WHY HONEST PEOPLE SHOPLIFT OR COMMIT OTHER ACTS OF THEFT

Assessment and Treatment of 'Atypical Theft Offenders'

National Library of Canada Cataloguing in Publication Data

Cupchik, Will, 1940-
Why honest people shoplift or commit other acts of theft: assessment and treatment of 'atypical theft offenders': an educational resource for professionals and lay persons, *First Revised POD Edition*

1st Revised Edition   P.O.D. version.
Includes bibliographical references

ISBN   1-896342-08-6

HV6652.C86 2001a   616.85'842   C2001-901264-0

1. Shoplifting - Psychological aspects.   2. Shoplifting - Prevention.
3. Stealing - Psychological aspects.   4. Stealing - Prevention
5. Behavior Modification   6. Kleptomania.
7. Compulsive Shoplifting   8. Compulsive Shopping

Why Honest People Shoplift or Commit Other Acts of Theft

A Resource for both Professionals and Laypersons

Dr. Will Cupchik, C.Psych.

Formerly Psychologist-in-Charge,
Forensic Outpatient Psychological Services,
Clarke Institute of Psychiatry, Toronto, Canada

Why Honest People Shoplift or Commit Other Acts of Theft

Table of Contents

Book Reviews for Original Print Edition

Book Review #1: From the CRIMINAL LAWYERS ASSOCIATION NEWLETTER:

"Dr. Will Cupchik offers a fascinating study of the atypical client (and) assists both the professional and lay person in learning how to identify and understand atypical theft behavior, ...(provide) specific assessment approaches, ...determine which judicial options are more or less likely to be effective with these cases, understand the prognoses in such cases and the factors upon which they depend, and generally how to be of assistance to the individuals who have committed these acts of theft. While the crimes themselves may be minor, the underlying factors that lead to these crimes are extremely important both in identifying and assisting the atypical offender. ...While defence lawyers are not social workers, we are still obliged to ensure that our client's problems are properly identified and responded to by the courts. Dr. Cupchik's extremely useful text will help both us and hopefully the judges meet that obligation."

Review #2: From Dr. J. D. Atcheson, Professor Emeritus, Department of Psychiatry, University of Toronto

"I wish you great success in the distribution of this important contribution to Forensic Science... I know it has been used in court many times... I hope that every lawyer and forensic service will have it in their library."

Review #3: From the NEWSLETTER OF THE ONTARIO PSYCHOLOGICAL ASSOCIATION (June 1998):

"This book... offers some tools for making appropriate responses or interventions. ... There are sufficient examples (of Atypical Theft Offenders) in our society to make understanding their dynamics ...important. ... I would

recommend this as a book which will add to understanding and assist in interpersonal interactions for a broad range of readers. "

Review #4: From Mary Derouard, editor, Source ReSource...

"...An easy read with important info that I hadn't seen in print anywhere else. ...The book is also friendly, engaging and informative. I am confident that it will be a great resource not only to the mental health practitioner but also to the individual struggling with the behavior. "

Review #5: from a loss prevention professional.

"I have been in the loss prevention business for almost 20 years and have arrested literally thousands of people in that time. I have always been amazed by the fact that a number of those theft offenders who have the means of purchasing the items they have stolen. I have listened to countless stories of losses by these people and have never made the connections before reading your book. Everyone was profiled in your book; the most intriguing was the information on the relationship between cancer and shoplifting. I can tell you from actual experience that you are right on the money. ...From now on I will pay closer attention to what is going on an attempt to get these people the help they may need. "
K.H., Oklahoma City

Other Responses to the First Edition of This Book

Progress in the recognition of the Atypical Theft Offender syndrome: Some gratifying feedback and interesting e-mails

More and more professionals and laypersons have become aware of the Atypical Theft Offender phenomenon and its implications since the publication of the first edition of this book, in 1997. In the past four years I have received hundreds of e-mails, telephone calls and letters from laypersons and professionals who have been relieved and excited to learn that this seemingly bizarre atypical theft behavior can be understood and that the individuals involved can be helped.

It may be of some interest to readers of this revised edition of "Why Honest People Shoplift Or Commit Other Acts Of Theft" to learn how other individuals responded to the information provided in the original edition of this book and the various articles and presentations I have made on this subject, including on my website, www.whyhonestpeoplesteal.com. Below is a representative sample of these responses.

Note: I have altered certain information in the material below to preserve confidentiality.

From a U.S. psychologist:
"Just want to tell you how much I appreciated your article on Atypical Theft Offenders in the last Forensic Examiner (the peer-reviewed journal of the American College of Forensic Examiners). At the time I read it I was doing a sentencing evaluation of a 75 year old, civically involved, family man, first time offender, who had had a few drinks, put on a child's Halloween mask and very politely robbed a Seven-Eleven in his neighborhood. He had just learned that his wife was terminally ill...Your article helped me to see the connection and write about it in a way that directly addressed the question on everyone's minds around here: Whatever possessed a man like him to do something like that? Thanks."

From an Atypical Theft Offender who came to Toronto for an intensive number of sessions over two days.

Hi there, Dr. Cupchik: I just thought I would drop you a message to let you know how I'm doing. I'm doing much better than ever before in my life actually. I never even experienced the desire to take anything since our sessions... However, I realize even that doesn't necessarily mean I might not want to do again.

The other day I bought something from a store and the sales clerk forgot to take the tag off. I left the store and the alarm went off. And for second, I felt a familiar sense of panic... However, it was such a wonderful feeling to be able to show the receipt to the security guard and just leave, knowing I had done nothing wrong.

But the best thing is, I feel good about myself. I'm doing well at work. I devote my extra energies to working out every day and I feel a lot better about my body than I did when I came to see you last winter, even though I haven't lost a pound. For the first time, I enjoy spending hours with myself. I don't hide from myself. And I like who I am becoming.

I understand that I will never be "cured". Believe me, I will never stop thinking about that part of me that stole and enjoyed it...

A part-time security guard's inclinations to shoplift

Dear Dr. Cupchik. I am writing this letter to let you know that reading all the information in your website has really stock struck a chord with me...   I am an honest person in almost all respects, yet I keep having these troubling thoughts about wanting to shoplift and steal things from people. I have not acted on any of these thoughts but things have gotten so bad that when I recently applied for a new job and I was in the employer's office I thought about taking some of the pens they put out for the applicants to use in filling out the job applications; I thought of putting them in my pocket and walking of the door with them. I had to restrain myself from not doing this.

While applying for another job I saw a bunch of pens in a container on the receptionist's desk and wanted to take them too. I have also have a part-time job as a security guard. I work in a shopping mall, and it is not an ordinary mall but a very upscale one. It is very hard sometimes for me to not take things."

From a US Commercial Airline Pilot

I recently was arrested for shoplifting four videotapes from a Target store in Toledo, Ohio. This is the first time though I have ever broken the law [other than two speeding tickets]. All of my life, I've worked extremely hard to get myself where I am currently at. .

I was brought up living on a farm in Idaho and learned early to be honest and work hard for the things I have. But, for some reason I can't figure out, this past weekend I decided it would be so easy to put the videos in my shopping bag and walk out of the store without paying for them. As soon as I passed through the door, I was stopped by the security police and asked into their office. I went with them, and was nice as could be to them, like it never happened. I still can't believe I would do such a thing. It's not like I don't have the money, or have a great need for these items.

A few years ago I finished college in just over three years, and it was all paid for by the military. I was accepted to go for USAF pilot training - my lifelong dream. And I graduated near the top of my group. For the past few years I have been employed as a 747 pilot for a major airline. But now, it seems I may have thrown every single thing that I have worked my entire life for away by this one stupid act that I never did before or even contemplated. I'm talking to an attorney but it turns out that shoplifting over $50 in this state is considered a felony. I am hoping to plead with the store company to see if they can drop the charges completely and let me make it up to them, but I highly doubt this will happened.

Email from a man whose wealthy father shoplifted from the same department store three times in a 'three strikes' state
Dear Dr. Cupchik: I want you to know that when my 88-year old father, a retired successful businessman, was arrested for the third time at a major department store (we live in a 'three strikes' state), I got on the internet and found your website and your book. I ordered a copy and found so much that sounded just like my father that I personally contacted the CEO of the department store chain, explained about the Atypical Theft Offender and loss-substitution-by-stealing finding and pleaded with him to please have the charge withdrawn. I explained to the CEO that my dad lost my mom a year ago, and then, two weeks later, one of his grandchildren died in an accident. Since then he has lost over forty pounds, cries almost daily and has stolen many small things he can well afford that he doesn't even need. The CEO he asked me to send him a copy of your book. He got back to me two weeks later and personally arranged to have the charges dropped.

Media Interest In This Subject

Since the original edition of this book was published in 1997, Dr. Cupchik has been interviewed by a great many television and radio programs, and magazine and newspaper writers. He has appeared on **NBC, ABC, Lifetime Cable Network,** and **CBC** and **BBC** programs; he has been quoted in the **Los Angeles Times, Denver Post, the Globe and Mail,** and **Allure, Self** and **Health** magazines, among others.

The kinds of cases with which this book deals:

- An outstanding law student from an upper middle class family brazenly attempts to pass a forged check at the very hour that his mother is being operated on for cancer...
- A highly decorated police officer, with a justly deserved and fine reputation, only one year from retiring with a sizable pension, risks it all by stealing a $3.50 door knob from his neighborhood hardware store...
- A nanny of modest means and requirements, over a three month period, steals over 150 dresses and keeps them in her closet, with the tags still attached. She has no intention of wearing, selling or giving them away. But she reports feeling much less anxious when she sits in her walk-in closet surrounded by the stolen merchandise...
- A lawyer earning over $400,000 per annum steals a tube of toothpaste from a drugstore in his firm's building on the very day that his child is undergoing chemotherapy at the Children's Hospital...
- A sincerely religious individual commits a series of break-and-enters at the times he knows that total strangers will be away from their homes celebrating the marriages of their relatives...

Following up on a ground-breaking 1983 clinical study of shoplifting as 'an occasional crime of the moral majority', Dr. Will Cupchik, a psychologist with over 17 years investigating such seemingly bizarre acts, provides the results of his latest study of nonsensical theft behavior, and reports important insights and unique approaches for professionals who have to deal with those he has termed **'Atypical Theft Offenders'**.

This 1st revised edition has been entirely re-edited, resulting in an easier reading experience. As well, additional information and updated clinical opinions have been inserted throughout the text, that brings the reader even more up-to-date on the author's clinical efforts and findings in this most interesting and important area. As well, some information about the three-day <u>Atypical Theft Offender Intensive Intervention Program</u> is provided.

About the Author

Will Cupchik, Ph.D. is a Registered Psychologist in private practice in Toronto. His office address is 250 St. Clair Avenue West, Suite G-3, Toronto, Ontario, Canada M4V 1R6   Ontario, Canada (tel: 416 928-2262; email: *wcupchik@aol.com*.)

Dr. Cupchik was formerly the Psychologist-in-Charge, Forensic Outpatient Psychological Services (1984-86), at the Clarke Institute of Psychiatry in Toronto. His clinical investigations of atypical theft behavior began at the Clarke in 1979. He was the senior author of the 1983 article entitled Shoplifting: An Occasional Crime of the Moral Majority published in the *Bulletin of the American Academy of Psychiatry and the Law, Volume 11, No.4.* He is also the senior author of an identically titled chapter that appeared in the book, Clinical Criminology: The Assessment and Treatment of Criminal Behavior, published by the Clarke Institute of Psychiatry and the University of Toronto, in 1985.

Dr. Cupchik holds full membership in the American Psychological Association. He has been awarded the designation of 'Diplomate of the American Board of Certified Forensic Examiners' by the American College of Forensic Examiners. Dr. Cupchik also holds full membership in the Canadian Psychological Association, the Ontario Psychological Association, the Canadian Group Psychotherapy Association, and the Canadian Registry of Health Service Providers in Psychology. He is a Registered Psychologist with the College of Psychologists of Ontario.

Dr. Cupchik has also been granted a Certificate of Professional Qualification in Psychology by the <u>Association of State and Provincial Psychology Boards</u> (ASPPB). On February 10, 2002 members of the ASPPB Agreement of Reciprocity included the states of California, Connecticut, District of Columbia, Idaho, Kentucky, Louisiana, Maryland, Michigan, Mississippi, Missouri, Nevada, New Mexico, Ohio, Oklahoma, Pennsylvania, Rhode Island, Vermont, Virginia, Wisconsin and Wyoming, as well as the provinces of Alberta, Manitoba and Ontario.

Dr. Cupchik obtained his Ph.D. in Counseling Psychology from the University of Toronto in 1979. He acquired his M.Ed. degree in Counseling and Guidance from University of Toronto in 1970, and his B.A. degree with a major in psychology from Carleton University in Ottawa in 1963. He also earned a Bachelor of Engineering (B.Eng.) degree in electrical engineering from McGill University in 1961.

Additional information about Dr. Cupchik and up-to-date materials about the subject of this book and the **Atypical Theft Offender Intensive Intervention Program** offered by Dr. Cupchik are all available on his whyhonestpeoplestealdotcom web site.

For Whom This Book is Intended

This book for primarily intended for the education and elucidation of professionals who have to deal with individuals who have displayed bizarre, nonsensical or otherwise atypical theft behavior, and whom this writer has termed "Atypical Theft Offenders" (A.T.O.s).

Among the professionals who will find this book of interest and use will be:
- **clinicians** whose task it is to provide effective assessment and/or treatment for such theft offenders;
- **lawyers** whose task it is to defend (or prosecute) them;
- **judges, probation and parole officers** who must process these cases;
- **loss prevention personnel** who often are the first professionals to encounter the Atypical Theft Offenders following their acts of theft;
- **police officers** who arrest and charge the Atypical Theft Offenders,
- **EAP (Employee Assistance Plan) and HR (Human Resources) personnel** who may need to deal with employees who have been charged with theft of their employer's property, as well as
- **students of psychology, psychiatry, social work and criminology** who are curious about the aberrant behavior of generally 'normal' persons.

This book will also be of interest to:
- **the theft offenders** themselves;
- **their significant others** (e.g., spouses, parents, etc...),and **laypersons** interested in understanding why good people do bad things.

Warning-Disclaimer

This book is designed to provide general information in regard to the subject matter covered. It is sold with the understanding that the publisher and author are not engaged, in this book, in rendering clinical, legal, or other professional services. The contents of this book may not be relevant or applicable to every theft offender case. If clinical, legal or other expert assistance is required, the services of a competent professional should be sought. The theft offenders themselves and the professionals who arrest, assess, treat, represent them and/or determine the disposition of their court cases, must take the responsibility for the uses made of this book.

It is not the purpose of this book to reprint all the information on the subjects covered that is otherwise available to the author and/or publisher. You are urged to read all the available material on the subjects, learn as much as possible about the subjects referred to in this book, and to tailor the information to your own personal or professional needs.

Theft behavior is an exceedingly complex human activity. Its motivations are frequently 'multi-determined,' that is there is often more than one reason why the individual theft offender has stolen. No claim is made or intended that the cases presented have described all of the possible motivations of theft offenders. Furthermore, all the case histories in this book are composites of two or more actual cases and have been significantly altered as far as identifiers are concerned. Therefore they cannot and should not be construed to represent any one actual person's behaviors or motivations, and should not be used to come to any conclusions about any particular case with which the reader may be familiar. Any similarities between the cases presented and those the reader is familiar with are merely coincidental.

Every effort has been made to make this e-book accurate in regard to the nature of the data that is presented. However, there may be mistakes both typographical and in content. Therefore, this text should be used only as a general guide and not as the ultimate source of information on the subjects. Furthermore, this book contains information only up to the printing date. New data, insights and knowledge are continually being derived, and are, of course, not necessarily represented in this book.

A Caution Regarding The Applicability Of The Material Contained In This Book To Any Specific Cases Of Interest To The Reader

In no way can the author know what may be clinically appropriate for any individual case in which he has not been formally and fully professionally involved. Much of the material in this book reports upon the findings of clinical investigations, assessment procedures, treatment modalities and exercises that he has developed and has found to be useful when dealing with certain theft offenders. Such information may or may not fit or be relevant or useful in any specific case that the reader has in mind. The responsibility for successful clinical assessment and treatment, legal representation and professional involvement by loss prevention personnel, police forces and others must lie with the client himself or herself and the clinicians, lawyers and other professionals involved in any particular case. Nothing in this book can or should be construed to indicate necessarily appropriate or applicable approaches in regard to any case the reader may encounter or have in mind.

Regarding Confidentiality And The Cases Presented In This Book.

In order to assure the confidentially of the persons from whom the data and details in this book are drawn, actual names, ages, gender (sometimes) and other identifying details of the 'cases' presented in this book have been substantially altered. Furthermore, all 'cases' described throughout the book are actually composites derived from at least two (and usually more) clients. It has thus been possible to effectively disguise the identity of those clients from whom such composite cases were formulated.

It should also be noted that care has been taken to make the sample 'cases' no more dramatic than those upon which they were based. Indeed, all of the case descriptions have been 'toned down'. Therefore, the reader can be assured that, as remarkable and bizarre as the 'cases' presented may appear, the original cases from which they were derived were even more so!

Acknowledgements

Our clinical investigations into the phenomenon of essentially honest people who shoplift were initiated in 1979 while I was on the staff of the forensic service of the **Clarke Institute of Psychiatry**, in Toronto. **Dr. Don J. Atcheson** (at the time, a senior psychiatrist on the same forensic service) and I began focusing upon these unusual cases when we recognized that certain commonalties seemed to exist. I gratefully acknowledge his colleagueship, integrity, good humor and friendship throughout our period at the Clarke Institute and afterwards.

I also want to thank the then staff of the forensic service of the Clarke Institute of Psychiatry, where I worked for twelve years, from 1974 through 1986. The period from 1974 through 1982, in particular, was highlighted by great interdisciplinary camaraderie, professional enthusiasm and mutual support.

Barbara Simmons has provided me with her steadfast encouragement for this and my other projects.

My friend, **Father Bill Hallahan**, of the Oblates Order, was one of my first colleagues to encourage me to write the original version of this book.

I am grateful to **Dr. Jack Birnbaum**, a psychiatrist and dear friend, whose oft-voiced enthusiasm for my finally producing a book that the lay public as well as clinicians and lawyers and other professionals would find valuable, has helped provide the impetus to get this long-time-in-the-birthing project out in its original and revised versions. Several years earlier my son, **Jeff Cupchik**, had also strongly suggested that this book should be done, and sooner than later.

Janis Foord Kirk and **David Kirk** most generously shared their personal experiences and accumulated knowledge about publishing, and David offered some particularly important feedback about the original version of this book. The Kirk's friendship and colleagueship are much appreciated.

I have the great good fortune to count as a dear friend and colleague, **Dr. Dvora Levinson**, a clinical psychologist who very kindly gave generously of her time and expertise in reviewing a nearly final draft of the book. Dvora offered many valid and helpful corrections and suggestions. This book is certainly more readable because of her efforts.

Mary Goulding offered some important comments about an earlier draft as well. I am very appreciative of her input, and as well, of her caring and kind words in regard to myself as well as the fundamental potential value of this project. The late **Dr. Robert Goulding** was a great teacher, major mentor and latterly, a dear, dear friend from whom I gained so very much over many years, and still do.

I thank **Doreen Adams** for her many years of encouragement of my writing efforts, and dear friends **Steve, Judy, David and Christine Adams** for their continuing and rejuvenating friendship and nourishing hospitality. I also very much thank **Barbara Barash Simmons** for reviewing an earlier draft of this book, and for her many constructive comments throughout its development.

My close friends **Jack Lin**, President and co-founder of National Technical Systems headquartered in Calabasas, California, and **David Martin**, architect extraordinaire in Monterey, California, have given me a great deal of support over the past several years, and have motivated me to do better.

Dedication

This first revised edition of the book is dedicated to those people I acknowledged on the previous pages, as well as the colleagues and clients who have helped me to gain further understanding and insight into the workings of essentially honest persons who have stolen in some fashion or another, either once, occasionally or even often, even though by doing so they have violated their own moral and ethical code.

Clients, in particular, who have come to Toronto to take the highly concentrated and focused three-day Atypical Theft Offender Intensive Intervention Program, have assisted me to further refine an efficient means of providing assessment and treatment for the category of theft offenders I identified and labeled as Atypical Theft Offenders over sixteen years ago.

List of Cases

CASE #	NAME	DETAILS
1	Bill	The Executive Who Lost A Lover And Risked His Career For $30 [p.72]
2	Mary	One Parent's Extreme Difficulty In Letting Go Of Her Child [p.75]
3	Victor	The Holocaust Survivor Whose Theft Was Classically Atypical [p.77]
4	Bert	The Lawyer Who Jeopardized His Career For Toothpaste [p. 80]
5	Alice	The Woman Who Stole Whenever Her Husband Had Another Bout Of Cancer [p.83]
6	Sylvia	Stealing As A Way Of Coping With Parental Loss And Emotional Distress [p.88]
7	Martha	The Nanny Who Stole 150 Dresses That She Kept In Her Closet With The Tags On [p.92]
8	Barney	The CEO Who Shoplifted Socks And A Steak [p.101]
9	Tony	The Cop Who Shoplifted To Avoid Getting Killed [p.105]
10	Alan	The Case Of The 'Wedding Day Spoiler'[p.111]
11	Betty Ann	The Shopper Who Stole An Item That Symbolized Her Cancer-Stricken Friend[p.115]
12	Steve	The Outstanding Law Student Who Broke The Law And Nearly Destroyed His Future [p.116]
13	Harvey	The Cop-Shoplifter Who Wanted To Kill Himself [p.119]
14	Sonny	The Engineer With The Repressed Depression [p.123]
15	Estelle	The Hard-Driving Executive Who Learned Of Her Possibly Malignant Tumor And Immediately Went Shoplifting [p.124]
16	Jim	The Man Who Lost His Common-Law Partner But Gained A 4wd Vehicle [p.128]
17	Marge	Who Lost A Husband But Got A Dog [p.131]

List of Tables

An Orientation of Some Terms

Throughout this book references to "our investigations" are meant to refer specifically to those that I carried out, over a seven-year period, from 1979-1986, with my co-investigator Dr. D.J. Atcheson when we were both working on the same clinical team and in the employ of the Clarke Institute of Psychiatry, in Toronto.

References to "my investigations" are meant to refer to those I have primarily carried out since leaving the Clarke Institute over eleven years ago (in 1986) and which I have conducted from within my private practice as a registered psychologist in Toronto.

I have attempted, for the sake of clarity, to indicate which of these two phases of my clinical work with Atypical Theft Offenders particular materials in this book refer. My apologies for any errors that may occur or be inferred in the body of this book in these regards. Any errors or erroneous inferences are unintentional.

Our initial investigation (1979-1983) involved only shoplifting events. However, as we stated in a chapter that I co-authored with Dr.Atcheson[i], in a book entitled Clinical Criminology: The Assessment and Treatment of Criminal Behavior [ii](1985), "the authors and certain colleagues have noted the similarities between some shoplifters and certain perpetrators of acts of fraud. We now use the term Atypical Theft Offender (A.T.O.) to refer to those perpetrators of acts of shoplifting and/or fraud who seem to belong to the same psychodynamic and psychofunctional categories."

In the course of my continuing clinical investigations over the dozen years since the above statement was published, I have concluded that acts of theft of any kind may be committed by Atypical Theft Offenders.

Definition of an 'Atypical Theft Offender'

An <u>Atypical Theft Offender</u> *is defined as* "an individual whose theft behavior was <u>not</u> primarily precipitated out of either need or greed, but rather was a behavioral response to usually subconscious or unconscious psychodynamic factors. The act of theft and/or the item(s) stolen have symbolic meaning."

Primarily, the item was not stolen for it's monetary or utilitarian value. Not infrequently, that which was stolen is of meager monetary value and/or is not of consciously recognized interest or merit to the offender.

Atypical Theft Offender Intervention Programs

The **Atypical Theft Offender Intervention Programs** are the product of Dr. Will Cupchik's clinical work of over a quarter-century with Atypical Theft Offenders and compulsive shoppers. It is offered in *two* formats:

i) The Atypical Theft Offender *Ongoing* Intervention Program, consisting of (usually) weekly clinical sessions aimed at providing both assessment and treatment for possible Atypical Theft Offenders and/or compulsive shoppers, as well as court-directed Psychological Reports, if and as required and desirable
    &
ii) the Atypical Theft Offender *Intensive* Intervention Program, involving 16 clinical [50-minute) hours] held over 3 days, usually entails six sessions on Sunday, another six sessions on Monday, and four sessions on Tuesday, that is usually held for out-of-town clients.

Both versions of the program are aimed at uncovering, within a relatively short time period, the underlying dynamics that are involved in the client's atypical theft behavior, and in making some psychotherapeutic headway in moving the client towards resolving his or her theft and/or compulsive shopping behavior.

The Intensive Intervention Program offers out-of-towners a time-manageable and efficient clinical experience comparable in many ways to the equivalent of four or more months of weekly sessions insofar as assessment and treatment effectiveness is concerned. Prospective participants should note that relative success in the program may be proportional to their willingness and readiness to participate fully in the experience.

Dr. Will Cupchik personally conducts both. For further information about the Intensive program please contact Dr. Cupchik directly at 416-928-2262 *or* through e-mail via wcupchik@aol.com.

Part One:

Understanding Why Honest People Steal

INTRODUCTION

What is going on here?

- According to a press release put out by the Republican National Committee, on February 6, 1996, in a special state legislative election in Minnesota, a Republican candidate defeated the Democrat for a seat that became vacant when <u>the former occupant, a Democrat, resigned after he evidently was caught shoplifting at J. C. Penny's.</u>[iii]

- In its May 7, 1996 edition, the Toronto Star daily newspaper reported that a "roadie" with the Bob Dylan tour stepped across the street from where Dylan was performing to a major hardware store "and promptly got himself busted for shoplifting....Seems the young stagehand was dispatched to pick up a few extension cords and such but is also alleged to have slipped a $20 measuring tape into his pocket... (At the time he was apprehended he had $800 US in his other pocket...".

- In 1991 actor Hedy Lamarr was arrested for stealing eye drops and laxatives from a drugstore in Florida.

- In 1988 media personality Bess Myerson pleaded guilty to shoplifting items worth about $44 from a department store in Pennsylvania.

And consider the following remarkable happenings:

- In 1994, the millionaire president of a large manufacturing concern, with top secret security clearance, nearly lost his security clearance and jeopardized his company's governmental military contracts, when he was apprehended as he walked out of a supermarket without paying for some underarm deodorant and a package of sausages which he had tucked into his inside overcoat pocket.

- The New York Times, in its Saturday, August 28, 1993 International edition, had an article headlined "Acting Secretary Accused of Shoplifting". The article said that the Acting Secretary of the Army, John W. Shannon, had been placed on administrative leave after been accused of shoplifting a skirt and blouse valued at about $30 from the Army post exchange at Fort Myers, VA. Pentagon officials said Mr. Shannon had been an early candidate for the post of Secretary of the Army but had been dropped from consideration a few months earlier.

- A world famous chemist was threatened with losing his job and his considerable pension after he was charged with stealing $1,000 of office supplies from his employer. Together, he and his spouse (a university professor) earned more than $270,000 a year. Furthermore, they had no debts and maintained a modest standard of living that they could more than easily handle with only one of their salaries.

Why would generally honest people who have worked so hard for so long risk so much for so little (and illegal) gain?

Why would persons who have been leading exemplary lives, and who receive excellent remuneration for their work, risk losing it all (frequently for so little possible gain) through stealing?

> **Losses due to thefts from North American retail stores alone amount to over $30 million a day. Theft is the most common crime in North America.**

Each day tens of thousands of people in North America are apprehended for committing acts of theft. An article in the March 9, 1996 Globe and Mail newspaper stated that "about 60 percent of all reported crime in Canada is against property, involving offenses such as theft, fraud and robbery.... (In 1993) victims' losses were $4 billion." Extrapolating conservatively to the United States situation, where the population is approximately ten times greater, theft offenses probably resulted in over $40 billion in losses to victims in the US in 1993.

3

In most cases we do not need to search very long to find likely motives for acts of theft. In the majority of cases, undoubtedly, monetary and/or material gain is the main reason for these thefts. In a substantial minority of cases, however, the motive is not very clear at all. In fact, sometimes the potential downside of getting caught has such dire consequences that these acts are described by the press (and even by some of the professionals who have to deal with them) as "nonsensical", "bizarre", or "downright dumb"! These theft behaviors seem all the more "weird" when they have been carried out by members of the 'moral majority' in society. Occasionally these nonsensical acts are even perpetrated by highly successful and prominent persons in the community who have more than adequate financial resources to have easily purchased the items that were stolen.

As you will learn in this book, so-called 'nonsensical' acts of theft do have underlying reasons that can be understood. Indeed, these reasons frequently provide some of the most interesting and illuminating demonstrations of the unconscious workings of the human psyche.

****

Incidentally, I want to acknowledge the various schools of psychology and psychotherapy that I have integrated into and otherwise made use of in my clinical work over the past 37 years, including Carl Rogers, Sigmund Freud, Carl Jung, Robert and Mary Goulding, and Albert Ellis. The ideas, approaches and basic underpinnings of their various approaches provide a variety of ways to consider and deal with different aspects of the human condition.

The clinical findings presented in this book are not garnered from, nor were they stretched or bent to fit any one 'school' of thought or theory. Rather, the findings presented themselves, and the understanding of these findings belong to more than one invested 'professional point of view'. As a former electrical engineering graduate some four decades ago, I learned how vital it was to form a hypothesis that might fit and help explain the evidence, and not the other way around. Similarly, in my psychotherapy work with clients, the 'engineer' who still resides in me is *not* welded to a single approach or set of 'techniques'. I believe that wisely selected different strokes and/or interventions really do frequently provide a better fit for different folks.

****

I also want to mention that since I introduced the term Atypical Theft Offender into the professional literature in 1985 it has clearly resonated with both laypersons and professionals in the clinical and legal fields.

The beginnings of my investigations into theft behavior

It was my privilege, from 1974 to 1986, to work on the forensic service of the Clarke Institute of Psychiatry, one of the major psychiatric facilities in Canada. Many of the patients who presented themselves to our facility had been charged with, and in many cases convicted of, assault, rape, murder and a very wide variety of other illegal and often, horrific acts.

The persons whose cases I found the most interesting, however, were those that are the subject of this book -- the Atypical Theft Offenders. These persons were usually members of the mainstream, not the margins, of society.

Over my 12 years on staff at the Clarke and in the 11 years since I left to be in full-time private practice, I have carried out assessments and treatment of hundreds of such theft offenders. I have dealt with them in specialized individual and group therapy sessions, and have developed a dedicated assessment and treatment methodology that I call **S.T.A.T.O.** (**S**pecialized **T**reatment for **A**typical **T**heft **O**ffenders), a program that is described in Part Three of this book.

An unusual opportunity presented itself in 1979

A major reason that Dr. Don Atcheson and I were able to uncover the phenomenon of the Atypical Theft Offender was that, from 1979 through 1983, defense lawyers in the Toronto area referred numerous clients whose theft behaviors could be best described as bizarre and/or nonsensical.

Having been presented with so many unusual examples of theft behavior in such a relatively concentrated period of time, there began to emerge in our awareness some patterns of likely motivations for the theft behavior of some of these clients. In 1984 I developed and led a specialized therapy group for Atypical Theft Offenders at the Clarke, which further helped me to determine which treatment approaches were more likely to yield positive results with this clientele.

My clinical sensitivity to the notion of a symbolic component to some shoplifting

I began working as a counselor 34 years ago, in 1963, some 16 years before beginning to seriously consider the issue of 'nonsensical shoplifting'. First, as a high school guidance counselor and later as a trained group psychotherapist and clinical psychologist, I learned some of the ways in which overt human behavior may represent hidden motives.

In addition, my doctoral dissertation, begun in 1976, was an experimental investigation of mental imagery. This study demonstrated that many people, while in a relaxed but awake state, naturally produce visual images that contain deep symbolic significance, without the creators of the images consciously recognizing their meanings.

The first murderer I ever assessed: learning about the true meaning of the expression "There but for the grace of ..."

I remember interviewing 'my first murderer' in 1976 when I was a Ph.D. student intern on the Clarke Institute's forensic service. My supervisor had assigned me the task of interviewing this person about her crime, and of giving her the Rorschach, the so-called 'inkblot test.'

I had never previously met a confessed murderer. I was not sure what I would encounter, but I did have many more of my middle class perceptions in place at the time, and I am sure that, at the very least, I had expected this person 'look like' a criminal! Imagine my surprise when a soft-spoken, highly intelligent, middle-aged, well dressed and articulate woman came into the room, tentatively offered her hand in greeting, and sat down opposite me with a look of what seemed to me to be immense angst! Out of the window went one of my stereotypes, that of a sleazy, mean looking 'gun moll-type' out of a gangster movie.

But! There was a much greater surprise --and learning experience -- awaiting me.

As we discussed her background there was nothing to suggest that this person had had an exceptional childhood. Indeed, she had not! Then, less than half way through the administration of the Rorschach, which involved me showing her each card, her telling me what she 'saw' in the cards, and me writing down every word she spoke, she suddenly became very distraught, and in between taking huge gulps of air and crying, tried to tell me what had caused such a reaction.

7

She told me that one of the cards had a color that was her favorite color for roses. She went on to say that her spouse had, throughout their marriage, almost always brought roses of nearly the very same color when he came home from work on Friday evenings. Then, putting down the card, and looking directly at me while I wrote down feverishly everything she was saying, she said, "Look! I know that I killed him, I've never denied it. I'm guilty and I deserve to be punished for what I did. But all these months that I have been in jail awaiting trial, I have been thinking, "What if?" What if we had not had a party that night? What if we had not both had too much to drink and gotten into such a heated argument? What if we hadn't fallen asleep on the couches in the living room, and I hadn't woken up in the middle of the night with too much beer in my bladder, and what if I hadn't gotten up to pee, and hit the coffee table, knocking over some wine and liquor bottles, and the ice bucket with the ice pick in it?

"And what if my husband hadn't woken up when the bucket and bottles hit the floor with such a loud racket? What if my husband hadn't started screaming at me, and confronting me while I stumbling in the dark trying to pick up the bucket and bottles? What if, when he got to me, I wasn't just at that moment picking up the ice pick? What if we both hadn't still been plastered? When he came at me and pushed me and I started to push back and I had the pick in my hand, I was so angry with him! If all that hadn't been happening, I am certain that I wouldn't have stabbed him with the ice pick! Never!... I just keep thinking, what if even one of those things that happened, had not happened? I think he would still be alive! We would probably still be married! I would be happy and at home instead of being here in jail, and on trial for murder."

As I listened to this woman recalling the events of the evening that ended her husband's life and forever altered her own, I found many of the remainder of my stereotypes about who might commit murder, severely challenged. I also thought of the many people walking around today, a hair's breadth away from some horrible result of the simultaneous occurrence of unfortunate events, rather like being in the wrong place at the wrong time in the wrong state of mind and with the wrong implements within arm's each. The same could be said, in numerous instances, with regard to those I have termed 'Atypical Theft Offenders'.

A case of mistaken identity that resulted in a loving husband killing his wife

Another case that I recall involved an honest and hardworking CEO who had started receiving threatening letters and ended up accidentally killing his spouse. The police had told him that they could not state with any degree of certainty that the threats were nothing for him to be concerned about. They did say that they would attempt to locate the source of the threats. However there was little they could do to protect him within his own house, since he was not willing to allow them to station an officer on site. So this person kept his hunting rifle in his bedroom, not quite believing that he would ever have to use it.

A couple of weeks after receiving the first threatening letter he was awakened out of a fitful sleep in the middle of the night by sudden sounds that he quickly concluded had been caused by someone bumping into and knocking over a vase and stand that were positioned at the top of the stairs, just down the hall from his bedroom.

He had been so nervous earlier that evening that he had taken a tranquilizer, and then, when he had difficulty getting to sleep so he had also taken a sleeping pill. Groggy and anxious, he reached for his rifle, and when he heard the bedroom door click open suddenly his finger almost instinctively pulled the trigger. His spouse, still holding the tray from which her glass of milk had dropped onto the marble floor in the hallway, took the bullet in her chest and died almost instantly.

These and other clinical experiences have made it abundantly clear to me that, when it comes to avoiding being involved in disastrous, or at the least highly inappropriate behavior and situations, there, but for good fortune -- or whatever gods or deities may exist, -- might go many more of us. The line that separates 'us' from 'them' may not be as well defined and stable as we might like to believe.

How our coping mechanisms help determine whether 'we' might become one of 'them'

As I shall discuss in more detail later, we have all developed our own idiosyncratic ways of dealing with life's difficulties. For example, when faced

9

with stress and trouble, some of us eat more, treating ourselves to an extra dessert, while others buy themselves a treat. The saying, "When the going gets tough, the tough go shopping" contains more truth for some than many others of us would care to believe. Still others attempt to distance themselves from -- if not drown -- their sorrows and stresses, with drink. And, of course, others of us -- especially professionals-- run towards our work in order to avoid our pain.

Still others of us steal when stressed! Why? Why, when stressed, does one person eat while another person drinks, and a third person steals? Why steal? And by "steal" I include here acts of shoplifting, fraud, and all other manner of thieving. These questions will be addressed, and at least partially answered, in the remainder of this book.

The notion of the 'Typical Theft Offender' (T.T.O.)
Certainly, there are persons who steal what they want to, when they want to, and have no remorse whatever about their theft behavior. These people are the sort that most of us usually think of as 'thieves' and this category of thief is undoubtedly in the majority. I have labeled these individuals Typical Theft Offenders (or T.T.O.s).

This sort of offender, of whom I have seen many examples, particularly in the dozen years that I was on the staff of the Clarke Institute. They are not as clinically interesting to me, however, as are those persons who do not generally steal and who are much more likely to be conflicted about, and not infrequently shocked and appalled by, their own theft behavior. I have termed these persons Atypical Theft Offenders (or A.T.O.s).

> **In this book we will primarily be dealing with Atypical Theft Offenders (A.T.O.s), those theft offenders who are generally honest, hardworking, and ethical; their illegal theft behavior is essentially an aberration from, and at odds with, the ways they usually conduct themselves in the world. These persons are often very uncomfortable and upset with their stealing, yet frequently do not seem able to stop themselves, and virtually never understand why they stole.**

Undoubtedly, these so-called 'Atypical Theft Offenders' are in the minority when it comes to the total population of people engaged in thieving activities. As I shall detail later in this book, many of these theft offenders are too often misdiagnosed as kleptomaniacs or, perhaps even worse, are considered to be 'just like the rest of those thieves'. Therefore they may be neither properly assessed nor treated. Consequently there is considerable likelihood that they will re-offend.

> **If they do re-offend, then unless most of the A.T.O.s are distinguished from kleptomaniacs, or the T.T.O. type of offender, they are at risk of being misdiagnosed. And so the cycle of offending --> misdiagnosis --> inappropriate treatment (if any) --> no meaningful long term change in underlying causative factors --> (re)offending .... may repeat itself -- again, and again.**

> **One of the main reasons that I have written this book is to help reduce the number of cases of individuals who are misdiagnosed and therefore mis-treated (if treated at all), and who may therefore unfortunately repeat the sad cycle described above, over and over and over again.**

This book aims to be of assistance to:

•**clinicians,** who need to identify, understand, assess and treat these persons but who -- if they are not cognizant of the Atypical Theft Offender phenomenon-- may misdiagnose and therefore mistreat them so that the offenders end up re-offending, all the while getting increasingly confused, dejected, depressed and desperate (some to the point of being actively suicidal);

11

•**lawyers,** who have a sense that there is something very bizarre going on when generally responsible, sometimes high profile, and frequently financially sufficient well-to-do persons with hundreds of dollars and several valid credit cards on their person at the time nevertheless steal a $5 or $20 item. When apprehended they almost universally cannot adequately explain to their lawyers what was going on in their minds when they chose to steal rather than pay for the item(s) involved. Their lawyers are especially befuddled when these clients further state that they may not even have wanted the items they stole. Without understanding the Atypical Theft Offender syndrome, it may then be exceedingly difficult to explain their clients' theft behaviors to the courts in ways that don't result in the presiding judges expressing considerable skepticism and impatience.

•**judges,** who frequently confront in their courtrooms not only those persons who have no qualms about taking what does not belong to them (these T.T.O.s are at least relatively easier cases to deal with) but also persons of either high or low station who are genuinely good citizens, hard working and ethical, who appear before the courts charged with what can only seem to the courts to be acts of nuisance, if not nonsensical, theft behavior. Too often the cases are defended by lawyers who attempt to convince the courts that their clients were merely depressed (as if that explains the behavior) and that they will never do such a thing again, (as if, in the absence of any concrete changes in the offender's inner or outer life, such a claim could be justified)!

The judges in such cases are often left to consider what may be in the best interests of society, and the matter may be disposed of without the underlying problems that precipitated the acting out behavior having been recognized, let alone understood and dealt with. When the same person next appears before another judge on another day, with their 'charge sheet' showing previous similar offenses, sentencing may be even less directed to preventing further occurrences than to mete out punishment. This book aims to inform the courts as to the underlying dynamics frequently at play in cases of apparently 'nonsensical' theft, and describes in detail, some ways of more appropriately treating these offenders.

•**loss prevention workers, police officers, human resources (HR) and employee assistance plan (EAP) personnel** who are usually among the first professionals involved in dealing with instances of shoplifting or employee theft. It is important that these professionals learn about the differences between

Atypical and Typical Theft Offenders, because treating the former as if they were the latter could result in the offenders taking self-destructive physical actions against themselves, and/or cause perhaps unnecessary additional future losses for the employer through either loss of a valuable customer's purchasing power or a heretofore dedicated (and already trained) employee's productivity.

Some Atypical Theft Offenders have been so embarrassed and self-punishing after being apprehended that they have suicided. In contrast, typical thieves almost never think of suiciding in response to having been caught stealing. Being caught is considered merely an occupational hazard to be avoided as much as possible.

•**Atypical Theft Offenders,** whose own theft behavior causes them great distress, in no small part because they consider themselves to be generally honest, ethical and contributing members of society. They may have been before the courts previously, and may also have seen a counselor of some type but to no evident benefit. They do not know why they are stealing and therefore they may repeat the behavior. Often their self-esteem is dangerously low.

•**family members and friends** who usually do not understand why their loved one did something so offensive as to steal, perhaps for the 'nth' time, thereby putting in jeopardy their good name and possibly their jobs, and their families' standings in their communities;

•**students of psychology, sociology, criminology and the human condition** will find much in this book that may be of interest. Many of these persons are particularly interested in misbehavior by persons who should, and do, 'know better'.

This book is divided into five parts, each of interest to one or more of the categories of readers described above.

The titles of the parts provide an obvious guide to the reader: in order to gain a thorough understanding of the Atypical Theft Offender syndrome, however, the reader is urged to read the entire book.

14

The Five Major Parts Of This Book

Chapter 1

STEALING OUT OF NEED, GREED, AND/OR CONFORMITY
(Or what this book is not about, mostly...)

Typical Theft Offenders

Most stealing in North American society is done deliberately by persons who do not view their stealing to be something about which to feel ashamed or upset. These individuals are frequently quite comfortable with their stealing; they view these behaviors as egosyntonic[iv]. Among such persons can be included professional thieves who do what they do 'for a living', acting primarily out of greed; their primary purpose is either, (a) to 'save money', by avoiding the cost of purchasing an item through stealing it instead of buying it, for their own or a family member's or friend's use, and/or (b) to 'make money' by first stealing and then selling the item to a 'fence' (middleperson) or directly to the end-user.

In the dozen years (1974-86) that I was a member of the psychology staff of the forensic service of the Clarke Institute I interviewed and assessed many of these typical thieves. However, they are not the main subject of this book. Such individuals usually consider their primary problem to be that they were caught; they do not view the stealing itself as a problem.

From a psychological perspective these persons are not especially remarkable, although it may be accurate to say they are frequently tragic examples of lives wasted. Often they were raised in a criminally-oriented subculture where it is not surprising when a former shoplifter or pickpocket 'graduates' to more daring and potentially violent acts such as armed robbery. Conforming to the norms of certain groups in our society can mean acquiring an apprenticeship in stealing. If one's friends or mentors steal, and one begins stealing also, then we might say that peer or authority influences may have been a major aspect of the initial motivation underlying such behavior. The study of these individuals and their theft behavior is not the primary focus of this book, although we shall refer to them many times, and address their differences vis-à-vis Atypical Theft Offenders.

16

Who else this book is not primarily about -- persons who steal out of need!

Unfortunately, there are persons who lack the funds to support themselves and their families, and whose prospects of finding work and/or suitable monetary resources are so poor that they are subsisting below what is termed 'the poverty level'. When such persons steal, while most honest members of our society would not condone such behavior, we can nevertheless, with compassion and concern, appreciate the distress that may have provoked them into stealing to provide food, clothing, or funds to obtain needed medical help for their loved ones.

Some portion of shoplifting that is carried out in department stores and supermarkets is done by persons in such dire straits. They are people who have fallen between society's cracks, so to speak, and we can sympathize when their stories are accompanied by reports of their previously having lost their jobs and/or homes, or family members, through little or no fault of their own.

The issue of poverty in our society is, of course, an important matter. Sadly, the hard economic times of the 1990's in North American and other 'modern' societies have undoubtedly increased the number of theft offenders who are financially distressed to the point of feeling -- and being -- desperate. The reader will understand that we will not say much more about this category of theft offender. The issue is quite simply outside the scope of this book.

From a clinical point of view such cases of theft behavior are rather cut and dried. The motivations are obvious; the offenders' needs clear. It does not take specialized training to understand the desperation and despair that might drive a parent to steal food or clothing for his or her child, when to not do so would mean the child would do without some of life's necessities. Sadly, the courts probably deal with hundreds, if not thousands, of such cases every day in the US and Canada. Some of these persons may be considered 'typical' theft offenders only to the extent that they stole what they *wanted* to steal and *intended to use or sell* the items stolen. However to place such persons in the category, let alone the same jail cell with those who steal 'for a living' and to not acknowledge or take into account their genuinely dire financial situations or recent traumatic experiences, may well lead to instances of justice denied.

Summary

When instances of theft occur which do not surprise or shock us in terms of *who* committed the act, and under *what* circumstances, then such cases may be considered to be rather typical acts of theft. In the remainder of this book the perpetrators of such acts are referred to as Typical Theft Offenders (T.T.O.s).

While we shall indeed be referring to T.T.O.s at many points throughout this book, they will usually be mentioned in comparison with -- and in contrast to -- the Atypical Theft Offenders (A.T.O.s), whose theft behaviors do cause most clinicians, lawyers, judges and laypersons much consternation and confusion because we have difficulty comprehending why this latter sort of perpetrator would have chosen to steal, given the nature of the theft and evidently positive circumstances of their lives.

Later in this book I provide two pen-and-paper tools[v] that will assist the offender, and those professionals and laypersons having dealings with them, in ascertaining the degree to which the offender might be considered a Typical or an Atypical type of theft offender.

Chapter 2

WHEN THE STEALING DOESN'T 'MAKE SENSE'

In contrast with the Typical Theft Offenders described in the previous chapter, whose motivations to steal are at least seemingly obvious (and who undoubtedly constitute the majority of theft offenders), there are ten of thousands of cases each day in North America where the theft behaviors of the perpetrators seem, at best, nonsensical if not downright bizarre.

Many interesting cases where the acts of theft 'do not make sense' are detailed in this book to give the reader the full 'flavor' of the phenomenon. I have created 34 composite cases from the hundreds of theft offenders whom I have assessed and/or treated. These cases both implicitly and explicitly elicit the same question, over and over again: "Why, for goodness sake, did this basically honest person who, in most instances, had more than sufficient financial means to acquire the item(s) taken -- choose to steal instead?!".

Consider, for a moment, the following cases:
•Case # 7, a variety store cashier who stole over 150 dresses over a five month period, which she kept in her basement closet, with the sales tags still on, without using or selling even one of them;

•Case # 8, a highly paid CEO who shoplifted a steak and a pair of socks from a supermarket; and

•Case #9, the brave veteran police officer who risked his reputation, and his substantial and (almost within reach) pension, by stealing a $3.50 closet door knob. His baffling behavior was even more bizarre considering that he had bought and paid for an identical item (he needed only one for the home repair he was doing) at the same store, earlier the same day!

Such cases obviously suggest that psychological, as opposed to monetary, motivations may have been at play.

> **A Reminder:** All the cases presented in this book are composites based upon actual cases assessed and/or treated by the writer, with details of age, marital status, life circumstances, items taken, number of previous offenses, and (sometimes) gender, altered in order to preserve confidentiality.

> The reader is also assured that the actual cases from which these composite cases have been derived are even *more* bizarre, in terms of their details, the offenders' assets, the items taken, etc... and would warrant even *greater* intellectual curiosity being directed towards them than do the composite cases.

There is a need for suitably trained clinicians to assess and treat these Atypical Theft Offenders, and for informed judges to be familiar with this syndrome so that these theft cases will be dealt with more appropriately and effectively.

In this book I will often make reference to the original clinical investigation carried out by me and Dr. Don J Atcheson, and the publication in 1983 of our article outlining the findings of this initial study. I shall write of "our" investigation when referring to these materials.

The findings of my more recent clinical study (referred to throughout the book as the '1996 study') are published here for the first time. The 1996 findings will be compared with those of the original 1983 study. Generally speaking, the results of the two studies are highly consistent with one another. When referring to my own clinical work during the past fifteen years since leaving the employ of the Clarke, I shall write of "my" clinical efforts.

In the four years since the original hardcopy edition of this book was published, my further investigations of a wide variety of cases, including not those involving not only minor shoplifting, but also instances of theft of hundreds of thousands of dollars, in both Canada and the United States, have further corroborated our and my previous theoretical and practical findings.

When professionals deal with apparently nonsensical theft

Experienced (and dare we also say, in some cases, jaded) professionals who work in the legal system can be excused for simply shaking their heads in dismay when they are presented with a theft case wherein mention is made of the:

- more than adequate on-hand resources of the perpetrator;
- obvious and self-defeating manner in which the theft was carried out by an otherwise intelligent person;
- relatively paltry sum involved had the offender chosen to pay for item;
- frequently, the unsuitability and/or worthlessness (to the offender) of the item; and/or
- the profound risk taken for such little potential gain.

There are many cases, as well, where the offender is back before the court for the sixth (or sixteenth) time, and where neither fines nor even incarceration has motivated the offender to cease what may be viewed as a sort of 'nuisance-theft' behavior.

What is going on in these sorts of cases, anyway? How can such behavior be understood? How can defense lawyers better represent such clients and not feel like they are resorting to fallacious arguments (or psychobabble) in order to minimize the court's response to the client? How can crown or prosecuting attorneys dispose of such cases in ways that does not tie up valuable and expensive court time, and that leads to appropriate rehabilitation?

Mistaking Atypical Theft Offenders for kleptomaniacs

There continues to be prevalent among many mental health professionals a lack of understanding in regard to apparently nonsensical stealing. It is therefore hardly surprising that laypersons who have committed such acts, or who may know someone who has committed an act of 'nonsensical' theft, would also be confused. **In 1991 Dr. Atcheson and I estimated that less than four or five of the hundreds of shoplifters we had assessed over a period of 12 years between 1979 and 1991 would legitimately qualify as suffering from kleptomania.**

Furthermore, it was clear to us that, at the psychodynamic level, the majority of such atypical acts of theft were not at all 'nonsensical'.

A major component in assessing a theft offender as suffering from kleptomania is that the offender *does not* commit the act of theft out of anger or vengeance. However, Dr. Atcheson and I have been entirely convinced that the vast majority of theft offenders we have assessed have been *very angry indeed* at the time of their offenses, and that there existed a strong *psychodynamic* relationship between the person's underlying anger and his or her subsequent theft behavior .

The psychodynamic elegance of atypical theft behavior

In this book I will describe the psychodynamics underlying dozens of cases of apparently nonsensical theft. It is hoped that the reader, after considering these cases and the 1983 and 1996 clinical investigations referred to in the chapters that follow, will concur that these cases are not only fascinating, but in addition, that they justify the following statement: **Many acts of supposedly nonsensical stealing by adults represent some of the most dramatic and revealing instances of the acting out, at an observable behavioral level, of subconscious and unconscious psychodynamics, usually in the absence of any conscious awareness by these perpetrators, of either the underlying psychodynamics, or the relationships between their behaviors and these underlying psychodynamics.**

Again and again the reader will be provided with what, at first glance, may appear to be a nonsensical action by a generally intelligent, law-abiding and hard working person. You will be able to follow along as the underlying dynamics are outlined. *Then these seemingly illogical acts of theft can be seen for what they are, namely, behaviors that emanate directly and often even elegantly, from the subconscious or unconscious of the perpetrator.*

By considering these cases seriously the reader will understand why:

- some persons steal in response to both current and much earlier traumatic events
  and situations;
- some persons steal when they, or persons close to them, confront cancer and other serious illnesses;

- there may be a connection between an individual's personal loss and his or her theft behavior;
- it is probably wrong to refer to most offenders of acts of 'nonsensical theft' as suffering form kleptomania, although they may be very atypical theft offenders, indeed.

Chapter 3:

A BRIEF MENTION OF THE 1983 STUDY

The original study of shoplifting that Dr. Don Atcheson and I reported upon in 1983 involved 34 cases of adult shoplifters selected at random from more than 90 cases seen by the forensic service of Toronto's Clarke Institute of Psychiatry between January 1979 and July 1982.

This sample ranged in ages from 26 to 60, with two age 'peaks' for the twenty-three females, the first between ages 26 to 35, and the second between ages 51 to 60. For the eleven males in the sample there were also two peaks observed, the first between ages 36 to 40, and the second, as was the case for women, occurring between ages 51 to 60.

Of the total sample of 34 cases, 33 were at least moderately depressed at the time that they were assessed. Of course, we initially saw them only after they had been arrested and charged with theft; therefore, the fact that they were depressed is not surprising. Most were likely also depressed prior their acts of theft as well, but we have no assured way of validating that hypothesis.

> **In 62% of the cases in the 1983 study a personally meaningful loss had occurred in the offender's life in close temporal proximity to the act of theft.**

We believe that this statistic is most important, and it led us to formulate the Loss-Substitution-by-Shoplifting Hypothesis.

From an analysis of the clinical data we also concluded that although personal loss is frequently a principal precipitating factor when honest people shoplift or carry out other acts of theft, *there is often more than one reason for their atypical theft behavior.* Indeed, their motivations are frequently multi-determined -- that is, there are several motivations prompting their behavior.

A listing of underlying motivations of Atypical Theft Offenders as derived from our original (1983) study

The Loss-Substitution-by-Stealing Hypothesis outlines what is likely the common factor that motivates most atypical theft behavior. Other psychodynamic factors may also be operating in such cases. A complete list of such factors includes the following elements:

- stealing as a reaction to stress
- stealing as a regressive, symbolic act
- stealing as unconscious retribution
- stealing as unconscious manipulation
- stealing as conscious manipulation
- stealing as a response to perceived actual or anticipated loss, where the loss any involve
...loss of a country, job, home
...loss of a significant other(s)
...losses due to separation or divorce;
...life-threatening illness --or death-- of a significant other, generally, and in particular the occurrence of cancer in a significant other, or in the offender.

In order to fully understand why essentially honest people steal it is important to consider each of the above motivations in turn; we shall do so in upcoming chapters where I shall be referring to both the 1983 and the 1996 studies. I shall attempt to make clear which data and conclusions relate to which study. Generally, the findings of the 1996 study corroborate those of the 1983 investigation. However, there are a few interesting differences as well as a number of important new observations that emerged from the more recent study.

Chapter 4

THE 1996 CLINICAL STUDY OF ATYPICAL THEFT OFFENDERS

The findings of this more recent clinical study have been drawn from a sample of 36 cases that I assessed, and in some instances provided treatment for, after 1984, which is to say after the initial 1983 study was published. In fact, the majority of the cases included in the 1996 study were assessed within my independent private practice, after I had left the employ of the Clarke Institute in 1986.

The 1996 study involved, strictly by chance, a sample comprised of an equal number of men and women. The cases selected were simply the first 36 cases for which at least partial assessments had been carried out.

Incidentally, it is my estimation that the gender ratio, i.e., males to females, that occurs in actual atypical theft cases, including shoplifting and fraud, is likely close to 1:1 as well. Slightly over half (56%) were born in North America, 25% were born in Europe, and 5% were born in Britain. The remainder came from an assortment of other countries.

Table One: Basic Demographic Data of the 1996 Sample
(N=36)

Age Range	of the 18 men: 17-69 yrs	of the 18 women: 26-61 yrs
Average Age	men: 43.8 yrs	women: 42.2 yrs old
SOCIO-ECONOMIC LEVEL (S.E.L.)	S.E.L. OF SAMPLE OF 36Ss, NUMBER	S.E.L. OF SAMPLE OF 36Ss, PERCENT
low	6	16.7%
low-medium	8	22.2%
medium	11	30.5%
medium-high	2	5.6%
High	9	25%
TOTALS --->	36 Ss	100%

From the data in Table One the reader can observe several facts. To begin with, the average ages of both males and females in the group were very similar; for men 43.8 years, and for women, 42.2 years. That the average person is over 40 years old is noteworthy; clearly we are dealing with many people in their prime years.

The data regarding socioeconomic level was of necessity approximate. The retired dean of the faculty of engineering was considered to be in the high category; the office-cleaning person was considered to be in the low category. **It is interesting to reflect upon the fact that fully ¼ (25%) of the entire sample consisted of persons who were at the high socioeconomic level; clearly, there was no major monetary reason for these persons to steal what they did. Indeed, they had much more to lose than to gain from their theft behavior.**

Also worth noting is the fact that over 60% of the theft offenders were of medium socioeconomic level, or higher. These persons had the financial capacity to pay for what was taken; their stealing does therefore seem quite nonsensical, in most cases.

Table Two: Criminal charges of the 36 theft offenders in the 1996 study

Total number of current charges of all the 36 theft offenders	72 charges
Average number of current charges per theft offender	2 charges
number of shoplifting only cases	25 cases (69.4%)
number of fraud only cases	6 cases (16.7%)
number of break, enter and theft cases	2 cases (5.6%)
number of employee theft cases	3 cases (8.3%)
================================	=================
NUMBER OF PREVIOUS CHARGES	# OF CASES
0 previous charges	15 cases (41.7%)
1 previous charge	6 cases (16.7%)
2-5 previous charges	8 cases (22.2%)
6-9 previous charges	5 cases (13.9%)
10 or more previous charges	2 cases (5.6%)

From Table Two we can see that the 1996 study included 25 cases (or nearly 70%) where the theft offenders committed acts of 'shoplifting only.' Yet fraud, 'break, enter and theft', and 'employee theft' cases were also represented.

Table Two indicates that in 15 cases (41.7%) there had been no previous charges. This statistic can be misleading to the professional since the majority of theft offenders I have assessed admitted in interview that they had committed previous acts of theft but were either not caught (in most cases) or they were caught but no charges had been laid. It is these first-time-charged theft offenders who, incidentally, may be at particular risk for suiciding, as they imagine the devastating effects upon their reputations and/or careers if their offenses are made public.

Which kind of theft the offender committed depended upon several factors, often including circumstance and opportunity, the particular stressors operating in his or her life at the time, and the offender's personal history. **The underlying psychodynamics in cases of genuine Atypical Theft Offenders are frequently similar, regardless of the kinds of thefts that have been carried out.** By paying attention to these factors the reader will become more adept in being able to distinguish the extent to which, the theft offender under consideration is likely more of the A.T.O. as opposed to the T.T.O. type, or not. Some individuals display *both* Atypical Theft Offender and Typical Theft Offender qualities, and probably are of the A.T.O./T.T.O. or 'mixed- type' of theft offender.

From Table Three below, the reader can see that there was a wide spectrum or degree of clinical involvement with the 36 theft offenders considered in the 1996 study.

Table Three: Clinical Tasks Carried Out With The Cases of the 1996 Study

Partial Assessment Only	Full Assessment Only	Full Assessment plus Some Therapy	Full Assessment plus Full Therapy	Totals
13 cases	8 cases	12 cases	3 cases	= 36 cases
36.1%	22.2%	33.3%	8.3%	= 99.9%

Regarding assessing Atypical Theft Offenders; the issue of psychological testing

In dealing with theft offenders I have learned that the optimal form of clinical involvement is to have a full assessment. Here I am referring to a full psychodynamically-oriented assessment, not necessarily including psychological testing. The reader may be surprised by this last statement; however, in the 12 years that I was on the forensic staff of the Clarke Institute of Psychiatry, where as a matter of routine we always did conduct formal psychological testing, plus full and separate clinical interviews carried out by a staff psychologist, psychiatrist and social worker, it was found that psychological testing usually did not offer much additional clinical value in understanding the factors that were influencing the theft offender. Certainly formal psychological testing is not an efficient use of resources when dealing with most Atypical Theft Offenders, unless the testing is done for very specific reasons, such as assessing further possible organic problems.

Atypical Theft Offenders and the MMPI

The reader may wish to note that for the 1983 study we *did* give the MMPI (Minnesota Multiphasic Personality Inventory) to all subjects. Not surprisingly, most of the men (57%) and women (53%) did have significantly high D (Depression) scales; this finding certainly corroborated our impressions that most of these persons were clinically depressed at the time of our assessments.

Also, 67% of the women and 43% of the men had significantly high Pd (Psychopathic) scales on the MMPI. This finding suggested that these individuals may have been inclined to act out without as much remorse as might the average person when subjected to excessive stress. This data may have been suggestive of a constitutional personality predisposition.

Table 4: Significant MMPI elevations in the 1983 study

		Depression Scale (D)	Psychopathic Scale (Pd)
Females	Number	8	10
(N=15)	Percent	53%	67%
============	============	============	============
Males	Number	4	3
(N=7)	Percent	57%	43%

These findings regarding elevations on the MMPI for depression and psychopathy in the findings of the 1983 study are interesting but not particularly helpful from an assessment and treatment point of view. The problem remains of understanding and explaining the choice of stealing as a behavioral response by these clients. A psychodynamically-oriented assessment is far more likely to acquire clinical useful data that can serve both the treating professional and the courts. I therefore do not carry out psychological testing with most theft offender clients, but readily arrange for the same when considered likely to produce useful information.

There have been a few exceptions to my general finding that psychological testing is not very helpful with such cases. In fact, of the 36 cases involved in the 1996 study I considered it both relevant and prudent *in two cases* to have full psychological testing done for specific reasons. In both these cases I had detected what I believed might indicate the presence of some possible cognitive impairment and/or learning disability and/or major psychopathic or psychotic process. I requested a full psychological and neuropsychological testing program in these two cases, and indeed, the suspected factors were involved, and my court-directed psychological reports referred to these matters. In one instance there was some organic brain damage, and in the other case there was a serious learning disability.

In most cases of atypical theft behavior however, my investigations indicate that these acts are generally perpetrated by otherwise highly functioning, intelligent and responsible members of society whose motivations for their theft behavior reside in the psychodynamic realm and can be ascertained by comprehensive and vigorous 'therapeutic assessment' procedures.

Full treatment with Atypical Theft Offender cases involves using the results of a comprehensive 'therapeutic assessment' to assist the client to deal with those underlying psychological issues that, until they are located and resolved, may continue to precipitate acting out by theft behavior at times of stress in the future.

> **A full assessment/full treatment regime typically requires a period of weekly sessions for several months; between 6 and 12 months is not uncommon.**

It is worthwhile noting that none of the clients who completed the 'full assessment / full treatment' program have re-offended, as far as I have been able to ascertain. I sincerely doubt that they will, although, of course, recidivism cannot be absolutely ruled for any client with regard to any criminal or non-criminal activity, especially if they revert to earlier and less adequate coping mechanisms when subjected to extreme stressors.

Table Five: Education Levels of Clients in the 1996 Study

Public school only	7 cases	19.4%
High school completed	**17 cases**	**47.2%**
University completed	**12 cases**	**33.3%**
Totals--->	**36 cases**	**99.9%**

A third of the cases in the 1996 study completed at least one university degree program. Included in this group were four persons with BA degrees, an MBA, two medical doctors, two engineers, and a chemist. That such highly educated individuals, all of whom held very responsible positions at the time of their offenses, would risk so much by committing acts of theft for what, in most instances, were paltry sums indeed, is testimony to the strength of the underlying psychodynamics in operation at the time of their offenses.

Who were the victims of these 36 individuals' theft offenses?

The assessments that were carried out with this sample of theft offenders indicated that:

- •75% of the cases stole from large department stores
- •25% stole from smaller retail stores
- 8% stole from their employers
- 5% stole from strangers whom they selected via some criteria,
- 3% stole from strangers who were truly random choices.

Some offenders stole from more than one kind of victim, hence the percentages add up to more than 100%.

What was stolen by these theft offenders and how much were the items worth?
- Money was stolen ....……........by 22.2% of the offenders.
- Goods worth less than $10 ....by 11.1%
- Goods worth between $10 and $100 ......by 38.9%
- Goods worth between $100 and $1000 ..by 19.4%
- One offender stole more than $250,000 of goods from his employer.
- Another individual stole more than $90,000 in money from her employer.
- A third person stole more than $20,000 in goods from people he knew to have suffered very serious personally meaningful losses just prior to his offenses.
- Of the property stolen, the main categories taken were (1) food; (2)clothes; (3) computer and other electronics equipment

The total worth of goods and moneys stolen by these 36 offenders was nearly $500,000.

The estimated 'symbolic meaningfulness' of what was stolen by the 'classic' or 'pure' A.T.O.s and T.T.O.s

In order to estimate the degree to which
(a) that which was stolen, or
(b) the place or person it was stolen from, and
(c) the circumstances that existed in the offender's life at the time of the offense, may have had some symbolic significance for the theft offender, a scale was created. This **Symbolic Meaningfulness Scale** was then applied to the available clinical data with a view to making such a determination.

No claim is made as to the vigorousness of the findings included in Table Six below; the findings should merely be considered suggestive, although an argument could be made for face validity in these cases. A more rigorous determination of 'symbolic meaningfulness' will have to await another study. The reader may note, however, that this writer's doctoral dissertation was an experimental investigation of symbolic meaningfulness[vi] in which the protocols of subjects who were administered an original mental imagery exercise were demonstrated to be 'symbolically meaningful'. The findings of symbolic meaningfulness in relation to the 1996 study of theft offenders, however, have not been nearly as rigorously determined as were those of the dissertation.

'Symbolic Meaningfulness' Scale

The scoring scheme used in estimating "symbolic meaningfulness' is as follows:

================================

Very Symbolically Meaningful	= 4
Moderately Symbolically Meaningful	= 3
Somewhat Symbolically Meaningful	= 2
Slightly Symbolically Meaningful	= 1
Not at all Symbolically Meaningful	= 0

Table Six: The Estimated 'Symbolic Meaningfulness'* (SM) of What was Stolen by the classic A.T.O.s and T.T.O.s

Total number of cases =	36	
number of classic A.T.O. cases	14 (38.9%)	Average SM of 14 A.T.O.s = 2.43
number of classic T.T.O. cases	2 (5.6%)	Average SM of 2 T.T.O.s = 0

About the data in Table Six

Of the 36 cases in this sample, 14 cases (or 38.9%) were essentially classic A.T.O.s, which is to say that these individuals demonstrated several of the features of Atypical Theft Offenders and virtually none of the features that we would associate with Typical Theft Offenders.

At the same time, there were only 2 cases (5.6%) that were classic T.T.O.s[vii]. These persons appeared to represent the kind of theft offender that most persons think of when they think of a 'thief.' Even though I would estimate the ratio of classic Atypical Theft Offenders to classic Typical Theft Offenders in the general population is probably of the order of 1 in 20 (5%), or at most, 1 in 10 (10%), in terms of my own clinical practice, especially in recent years, lawyers have not even bothered to refer clients to me for assessment unless they believed there was a genuine possibility that they were involved, at least some respects, in essentially nonsensical theft behavior. Therefore, the ratio of Atypical Theft Offenders to Typical Theft Offenders in my clinical practice is more like 20 to 1 (95%).

An unexpected yet prominent finding of the 1996 study: The issue of not having, not being able to conceive, or losing a child as a factor in Atypical Theft Offender behavior

A major finding of the 1996 study was that that not having, or not being able to conceive, or losing a child was a precipitating factor in a noteworthy proportion of those assessed.

Table Seven: 'Not having', or 'Not being able to conceive', or 'Losing a Child' as a Precipitating Factor in atypical theft behavior in the 1996 study

Total number of cases	Number of cases where not having, or not being able to conceive, or losing a child was a precipitating factor in the theft behavior
36	6 (16.7%) [4 men; 2 women]

In 1 out of every 6 cases in the 1996 study, not having, not being able to conceive, or losing a child was a very probable factor in the subjects' theft behavior. For many and perhaps most persons in our society, having children is a very highly held desire. For some women and men who do want to be parents, their not being able to (or being in a position to) have a child, may be experienced as a huge void in their lives.

In the 1996 study, there were four males and two female offenders for whom the issue of not having (or being able to conceive, or losing) a child appeared to have been the chief precipitating factor in their theft

behaviors. For one man, his wife's miscarriage appeared to be the trigger; for another man, the delivery of their stillborn child led to a bizarre shoplifting spree; for a third man, the death of his daughter just preceded the beginning of this very religious person's stealing activities; a woman shoplifted a day after her fertility doctor said that there was no point making further efforts in that direction, and that he was very concerned for her deteriorating physical and emotional state in response to their several previous, unsuccessful efforts.

For the sixth person, a male, his frequent shoplifting appears to have been precipitated by his sense of guilt and loss regarding his having convinced his wife to have an abortion when he was first starting out in his career and it turned out that she was thereafter not able to conceive, even though both very much wanted a child.

Theft behavior and its relationship to the menstrual cycle in some females

Over the past decade I have become increasingly aware that for some female Atypical Theft Offenders, their theft behavior appears to have been coincidental with the prominence at the time of the offense of the issue of 'not having a child'. Numerous examples could be related, including the woman who felt so alone, sad and empty whenever she realized, by virtue of the onset of menstruation, that she was not pregnant, that she was then very tempted to shoplift. Also worth noting in this last case is that this individual was a single woman with no current mate, and being a staunch Catholic she said she would never consider having extramarital sexual relations, let alone getting pregnant. So although she was not even 'trying' to have a child, her profound feeling of loss at the realization that she was not pregnant appears to have precipitated her theft behavior. She reported that she only shoplifted while menstruating.

Lest the reader misunderstand, this finding of the psychodynamic importance of not having a child, or not becoming pregnant, or not being able to become pregnant, or losing a child, did not emerge from any previously held theoretical position or hypothesizing by the writer. Indeed, it was only after several years of dealing with Atypical Theft Offenders that I became aware that, in some cases, the theft offender's acts of theft appeared to be related to the individual's menstrual cycle. I am indebted to one particular client, who, although essentially unschooled and most definitely not psychologically oriented, was nevertheless very acutely aware of the experience of her body's functioning and of her mental activity. She informed me in explicit terms that she was most inclined to steal only during the 36-hour interval that terminated with the beginning of her menstruation. She said that she desperately wanted to have children, and that every time she had her period, she would experience both a severe depression and a sense of loss, and would feel impelled to go shoplifting.

In another case, several months of our charting the client's theft behavior relative to her menstrual cycle revealed that she was most prone to steal about seven days prior to the onset of menstruation. Once she was menstruating her inclination to steal was virtually nil.

The timing of the inclination to shoplift relative to the person's menstrual cycle seems to be a very individual matter. For some female clients, the 'danger' period for stealing was prior to menstruation, while for others it seems to coincide with a particular day (first, second, etc...) of menstruation. I currently have no particular explanation of the reasons why the timing seems to be so idiosyncratic in nature. However, in all such cases, the psychodynamics underlying the Loss-Substitution-by-Stealing Hypothesis appear to be operational.

Table Eight: The Relationship Of Theft Behavior To Much Earlier Life Events In The 1996 Study

Total number of cases	Number of cases where the theft behavior was likely related to much earlier (usually childhood) events
36	30 (83.3%)

This finding, that in 30 of the 36 cases (83.3%), these persons' theft behaviors appear to have been related to much earlier events, usually in childhood, has major import in regard to understanding and dealing with Atypical Theft Offenders, including how courts handle such cases, the manner in which clinicians should attempt to carry out assessment and treatment, and the fashion in which loss prevention and human resources personnel, the police, and significant others should conduct themselves when dealing with possible Atypical Theft Offenders.

We shall have much more to say about this finding throughout the remainder of this book.

The 1996 study's data also indicates that:
• in two cases (i.e. 5.6%), substantial sexual abuse was experienced during childhood;
• in seven cases (i.e., 19.4%), loss of a parent through death or abandonment had occurred;
• in two cases, (5.6%), emotional abuse by spouses very likely played a significant part in the individuals' acting out via theft behavior.

Table Nine: Cases where Illness in General, and Cancer in Particular, was likely a Dynamic Factor in the Theft Behavior of Offenders in the 1996 Study

# of cases in which cancer in subject or 'Significant Other' (S.O.) was likely a dynamic factor	# of cases in which non-cancerous illness in subject or S.O. was likely a dynamic factor		Total # of cases in which any illness (including cancer) of Subject or S.O. was likely a dynamic factor
4 cases	8 cases	=	12
(11.1%)	(22.2%)	=	(33.3%)

We shall discuss the conclusions to be drawn from both the 1996 study and the original 1983 study in considerable detail throughout the remainder of this book. Suffice it to say that the most recent study supports the findings of the earlier one in all major respects. The Loss-Substitution-by-Shoplifting Hypothesis, first articulated in the earlier study, has been found in the 1996 study to have been strongly supported, and has been extended as a result of clinical studies subsequent to 1983 to include instances of other kinds of theft, including fraud, as well as break & enter & theft. I now usually refer to this hypothesis in its more general form, as the **Loss-Substitution-by-Stealing Hypothesis.**

Chapter 5

THE RELATIONSHIP BETWEEN PERSONAL LOSS AND THEFT

The purpose of this chapter is to discuss what is probably the most important finding of our investigations into the theft behavior of generally honest persons who have led predominantly law-abiding lives, and have been conscientious and contributing members of society.

In briefest terms, we learned that when such essentially honest persons committed their acts of theft, they were in most cases <u>acting out</u> (at least in large part<u>) in response to the recent occurrence of what they have perceived to be unfair, personally meaningful losses.</u> These losses had usually either just happened, or were being anticipated.

Why would some individuals be inclined to steal, when faced with actual or anticipated personal losses? What are the psychological mechanisms that would drive such behavior?

As mentioned previously, in order to assure the confidentiality of the persons from whom the data referred to in this book are drawn, all actual names and identifying details have been altered, and all 'cases' described throughout the book are camouflaged composites of two or more clients. It should again be noted that care has been taken to make the sample 'cases' less dramatic than the actual cases from which they were drawn.

The following composite cases may give the reader a keener sense of the sort of offenses we will be dealing with in this book.

*****

Case #1: Bill; An executive who lost a lover, then risked his career for $30

Bill, a 43 year old married engineer and $275,000 senior vice president of the firm where he was employed, returned from a week-long

39

business trip, landed at Kennedy airport at 10 p.m. after a 12-hour plane trip, and was back in his substantial suburban home about midnight. His spouse, Joanne, was already asleep; he only woke her to kiss her 'hello' and 'goodnight'. He fell asleep almost immediately.

The following day, after an extremely busy morning of meetings with his project teams, and the CEO, Bill left his office around noon and 15 minutes later, excitedly let himself into Sally's apartment in downtown Manhattan. Bill not only had a key to the place, he also had been paying the rent for the past year. His spouse still had no inkling of the existence of this place, or of Sally, or of the passionate affair that had been preoccupying him during this period. As he had been given a major promotion at about the same time that he became involved with Sally (a legal assistant with the same firm), his wife assumed that it was his extra work load that accounted for the late hours and lack of energy and enthusiasm for their home life.

On this occasion, however, Bill was not prepared for what he found when he opened the door to the apartment. True, Sally had been pressuring him for several months to leave his wife or she would call it 'quits' with Bill, but he had always been able to calm her by assuring her that the time was "almost right to make the marital break -- just not quite yet".

The note on the footstool (almost the only piece of furniture left in the place) was brief and to the point. Sally wrote that she had finally given up all hope of Bill doing what he had been promising to do ever since before she had moved into the apartment. The note also said that she had accepted an offer of another job in "another city, out of state. ... Two years of waiting, two years of lies, is long enough! Good-bye, Bill."

Up to now, Bill had convinced himself that her many threats to end their affair had been hollow. She would wait, he had been sure. As he reread the note again and again in disbelief, for the first time in years Bill actually cried, sitting on the floor of the now-empty apartment. After what seemed like a very long time Bill left the apartment feeling "confused, frustrated, and with what felt like a large hole in my gut". Once back in the skyscraper in which his office was located, Bill remembered something he had planned to do before getting back to the office. Moving frustratingly slowly through the pedestrian traffic on the concourse level, he entered a stationary store to buy wrapping paper and a card for his wife with whom he was to celebrate their twenty-fourth wedding anniversary on the weekend. He took some items, put them into his coat and suit pockets, and walked quickly out of the store without paying. He was stopped by a polite but firm security guard after he walked out of the store.

Once in the mall's loss prevention office, and at the security guard's request, he slowly emptied his pockets. From his suit jacket pockets he removed one anniversary card, a folded-in-half package of wrapping paper, a roll of ribbon of the type used to wrap presents, and a typewriter ribbon. (Bill didn't own a typewriter and didn't need such a ribbon.) The total value of these items was less than $30.

After being charged with 'theft under $1000' by the police officer who had been called to the store shortly after he was apprehended, Bill was permitted to make a phone call. He called his personal attorney and close friend, Trevor Hastings. Trevor's initial response to Bill's brief summary of the events was succinct; "Are you bullshitting me, Bill? Do you realize what this could mean to your security clearance rating, and to your job?!". Bill mumbled that "of course" he did, but could not say any more. That's all he had been thinking about since he had been caught. That... and Sally...and his wife and children.

Bill accompanied the police officer to the nearby precinct station. After he was fingerprinted, and the stolen items marked as evidence, Bill was released on his own recognizance to appear in court within three weeks to set the date for trial.

*****

Now, why would a very intelligent, well educated, and highly paid professional person with a fine job, one that required security clearance, risk his personal reputation and vocational ruin by stealing items of comparatively minuscule monetary value? Did the events that preceded his entering the gift store really trigger this behavior? And if so, why? Did he truly commit the act of theft because he was feeling angry, or depressed, or lonely, or abandoned?

We shall return to this case shortly. First, though, consider the following two additional cases:

*****

Case #2: Mary: One parent's extreme difficulty in letting go of her youngest child

Mary's youngest child, 23-year old Ruth, had been married the previous June day, in a lovely outdoor ceremony on the Long Island estate where she had grown up surrounded by the trappings of her father's highly successful real estate practice.

Mary and Ruth always had an extremely close mother-daughter relationship. 'Too close' a relationship, according to some relatives and friends, who mused that such excessive closeness was due to the fact that Ruth had been born nearly two months prematurely, at a time when being born that early usually had life-threatening consequences. Indeed, both mother and daughter had stayed in the hospital for the first four weeks following Ruth's birth. After Mary was released from hospital, Ruth had been kept in the maternity ward an additional six weeks, with Mary visiting her every day, to breast-feed and otherwise care for her. Eventually Ruth was allowed to go home, and the rest of her overprotected childhood, from a medical point of view, had been thankfully uneventful.

Ruth and her new spouse, Tim, had come by her parents' house the day after they were married to say good-bye before they started on their honeymoon, which was basically a cross-country motor trip. Their destination was Berkeley, California where Ruth would be attending graduate school, and where Tim would be working for a 'new economy' company.

"This is really the end of my little girl's childhood!", her mother later tearfully told me that she recalled having thought to herself as the excited newly-weds pulled away from the curb and began their drive out west. Even as their car disappeared around the corner, Mary decided to change her plans for the remainder of the afternoon. She had intended to spend several hours helping her live-in maid clean house and putting away the extra chairs, dinnerware, and so on, that she had used to entertain the out-of-town guests during the three days leading up to the wedding. Now she decided that what she really wanted to do, and right away, was to go shopping!

Within an hour she was in the women's wear section of the high-end department store at the local shopping mall. She found herself drawn towards what she later would to describe to me as "a very large, very ugly, very heavy, fall overcoat." She said that she did not know why she even picked it up. Not only was it was a truly unflattering style, and of a color that she would never consider wearing, but it was also definitely several sizes too large for her petite build! Nonetheless, a few minutes later, without buying anything else, she casually walked out of the store wearing the large, heavy coat into the very warm, sunny June day! She was apprehended by security personnel just as she got to her car.

When she arrived at my office for the first time some two weeks later, Mary expressed total dismay, self-disgust, and extreme embarrassment that she could have ever stolen anything. "And, of all things, that huge, ugly thing!!!" She was unable to offer me the slightest reason for her actions.

As the spouse of a very prominent and highly successful businessperson, Mary was used to being immaculately dressed. Her credit card invoices were invariably promptly paid by a loving husband who appreciated his wife's good taste, and for the important role she played in their social life, helping him to make and maintain important business contacts. She had carte blanche for virtually any purchases that she might possibly wish to make.

*****

Why would Mary jeopardize her own (and her husband's) standing in the community by stealing? And why steal so blatantly, wearing such an ill-fitting and obviously much-too-large winter overcoat out of the store where she was very well known to the sales staff, and into the hot midday summer sun? Might this behavior have something to do with the leave-taking of her child? And if so, what was the connection?

The next case to be described is that of Victor, a 65-year old survivor of the Holocaust. In Victor we observe a particularly remarkable (in its clarity) and classical case of A.T.O.-type shoplifting in which the "personally meaningful losses" occurred 'in a different world', a half life-time earlier.

*****

Case # 3: Victor; The Holocaust survivor whose theft was classically atypical

Victor was apprehended in the spring of 1995 for shoplifting $15 worth of goods. What made the offense particularly ridiculous, at first blush, was the fact that Victor was a very wealthy person. As is true of probably most Holocaust survivors, Victor was an individual who had overcome incredible odds and horrific personal tragedy, had strived and succeeded in becoming very successful in his chosen business (as a manufacturer) and as one for whom life was carried on surrounded by an aura of lingering memories filled with terrors and sadness.

Everyone in his family, including both parents and five younger siblings, had been exterminated in the Nazi concentration camps. He recalled with profound emotion how, after they had tumbled out of the cattle car which had stopped just inside the gates of Auschwitz, his best friend had physically held him back from joining the line into which the Nazi soldiers had herded the rest of his family, including his parents and much younger siblings, and had told him to "stand up straight and look very strong", so the German soldiers might think him potentially useful.

Victor was charged with shoplifting on May 5, 1995. He could not provide me with any reason or excuse for his theft behavior. He only recalled having entered a drugstore on the way to his office, having placed an object in a shopping bag, and then had proceeded to walk out of the store, at which point he was apprehended.

Later in our interview, as I was taking his early history, and he was describing his years in the concentration camps, he recalled for me his day of liberation. The inmates in his concentration camp were awakened at 3 a.m. and had been marched off in the dark outside of the camp's perimeter and along a rock-laden rail line vaguely lit by the moon. They were sure that they were being marched to their deaths, probably to be shot in the woods and buried in a prepared pit, as had so many other thousands before them. He recalled that few of the inmates were wearing shoes, or any other foot-coverings, and that his own feet were bruised and bleeding as he staggered along. Those prisoners who fell down and could not walk further were immediately shot. Victor kept on his feet and kept moving.

After several hours of marching they suddenly arrived at a border and with no ceremony were released. They were informed that the war was now over for them, and that they were free. The Germans soldiers then ran away. Red Cross marked trucks appeared soon afterwards, and the prisoners' immediate needs were attended to, including the application of salves and bandages to their injured feet.

The date of liberation, he mentioned in passing, was May 5, 1945. A few minutes later, I realized what he had said and interrupted his continuing description of these events to ask, "When did you say you were liberated?" "May 5th, 1945." he said. And then as he heard what he had said an expression of shock followed by one of amazement flashed across his face. "Why, it's the same date that I stole!", he exclaimed, and he began to sob heart wrenching tears. "Now,", I inquired, "can you guess why it was that on May 5, 1995, you entered a pharmacy and stole a package of Dr. Scholl's insoles when you had no need for the product, and could have easily paid for it, or for new shoes for that matter, if you really needed them?"

After another minute or two of now quieter crying, Victor softly replied, "For my feet, I suppose. My feet that were hurting so much... in 1945!"

Incidentally, Victor expressed his certainty that he had not consciously recalled on the morning of his act of theft that it was the anniversary of his day of liberation. He claimed to never allow himself to "waste time" thinking about his war experiences, and he never, ever discussed them with his friends, or his children. It is virtually certain, in my clinical opinion, that his unconscious had recognized the date as the 50th anniversary of his liberation and that he had had a severe 'anniversary reaction' which manifested as an act of (definitely atypical) theft behavior, on May 5, 1995.

*****

Why did these intelligent, successful and usually honest persons commit these acts of theft?

Why did Bill, Mary, and Victor commit such apparently needless, senseless acts of theft? For what reasons would these people have jeopardized their financial and social standing by stealing items for which they could easily have paid, items they may have not even wanted or needed?

How are we to understand such behavior? And if we can come to an understanding of such apparently bizarre acts, then how might these people be helped, by family and friends who care and would like be supportive, by the clinicians who are asked to assess or provide treatment, by the lawyers who are attempting to represent them, by the judges who preside over their cases and whose courts are often inundated by people who have been charged with theft? Courts often have great difficulty distinguishing thefts that occur out of greed, from those that occur primarily due to unconsciously driven, or neurotic motivations, especially when appropriate clinical formulations or distinctions have not been fully articulated in so many of the psychological and psychiatric reports that are presented to the courts by defense attorneys!

And lastly, how can the offender be helped to understand his or her own behavior, and be assisted in dealing with the underlying causes of the behavior, so that the likelihood of such inappropriate acting out in the future will be minimized?

It is important to note that in many cases similar to those described above, the perpetrators have committed other rather similar theft offenses during their adulthood.

Our clinical investigations have definitely concluded that until and unless the underlying psychodynamics that precipitate these individuals' theft behaviors are uncovered and dealt with, usually through the assistance of effective psychotherapy, then there exists a substantial ongoing probability that additional offenses may be perpetrated by the same offenders at some times in the future.

In fact, in approximately 75% of the cases I have dealt with over the past dozen years, there had indeed been previous similar infractions of the law by the same individuals for similar offenses.

During the first four years of our investigations, from 1979 to 1983, an attempt was made to find some plausible and probable explanations for the atypical theft behavior of these primarily ethical and successful and socially responsible persons. And, indeed, when all the data was gathered, there did emerge an unexpected common theme in the lives of many of these clients.

Stealing and Personal Losses

Perceived, actual or anticipated, personally meaningful losses preceding the acts of theft were the common thread! These losses were almost invariably, were much more meaningful and valuable (in terms that *really mattered* to the offenders) than the monetary worth of the items they were charged with stealing!

But, to paraphrase and modify Winston Churchill's statement, we might well ask: **"Why would so many persons risk so much**, in terms of potentially disastrous personal, social, vocational or professional consequences, **for so little** monetary gain?" Often. the items taken were of relatively little monetary value! Time and again, at the time they were apprehended, these offenders had more than enough cash or credit available via the valid credit cards they were carrying, to easily and painlessly purchase the stolen items. Also, very often, the items stolen were not required, or even desired!

Often, as in the case of Mary, the clothing stolen could not even be used because of its inappropriateness. In other cases, items taken were either not needed, or were the exact duplicate of an item already owned (where only one such item was required)!

Another client, Alice (Case # 5, discussed shortly) stated about her most recent shoplifting episode, "I'm not sure what you call the tools I took. I think you call them wrenches. I wouldn't know what to use them for. I just took them, and then threw them into the Goodwill box near our home."

Now consider another case of exceptional risk taken for meager gain.

*****

Case # 4: Bert: The highly successful lawyer who jeopardized his career for a tube of toothpaste

In the mid-1980s a prominent attorney, Bert, who had amassed a fortune of over two million dollars through his own real estate holdings and business investments, called me. Imagine my surprise then when I learned that the client he was referring to me was himself. Bert had been apprehended in the

47

mall on the lower level of a 40-story downtown office tower known as the "Legal Needle". This building was occupied by many major legal firms, including his own.

On the first floor of the building is a major department store. The manager of the department store's loss prevention department personally dealt with Bert immediately after he was apprehended by an employee. This manager demonstrated both wisdom and compassion when he said to Bert, "Sir, my most reliable plain-clothed operative reports that you picked up this tube of toothpaste, took it out of its box which you dropped on the floor, then simply shoved it into your pocket and directly left the store, at which point he apprehended you. I have to tell you that I recognize you from seeing your picture in the newspapers and on TV. Sir, even I know that you must have a very serious personal problem, to have risked your professional reputation and even your license to practice law, for $2.95. We prefer not to charge you with theft on this occasion, but will require a letter from a psychologist or psychiatrist indicating that you have sought out professional help!"

Bert reported the manager's comments with tears of gratitude in his eyes. When he first attended my office he warned me that he was not interested in my offering him "any bullshit psychobabble-type excuses to explain away such totally abhorrent and entirely unacceptable behavior on my part. I had always assumed that I was an honest person who would never, could never, steal anything, regardless of the reasons. Now I have been shown that I am nothing better than a common thief, and a hypocrite to boot. As far as I am concerned I deserve to be punished to the full extent of the law. I just wish I knew why I did such a stupid, irresponsible and illegal thing."

(As I discuss in detail in a later part of this book, some persons with genuinely high moral values, who may (or may not) have a high public profile, and who are caught shoplifting, are substantial suicide risks. I had such a concern in this case, and was reassured by Bert in this regard when he said that he would not escape his due punishment by harming himself, for moral, ethical and religious reasons.)

Later, when we had uncovered the likely reasons for Bert's theft behavior, he said that he was still very uncomfortable with the notion that "there was probably an understandable 'excuse' " for his behavior. It turned out that he had stolen the items in question on the day his four-year old son had been scheduled for his first round of chemotherapy at the Children's Hospital.

Eventually Bert found himself revising his previously unequivocal and automatically harsh attitudes towards all persons found guilty of acts of theft.

*****

The wisdom of a gift shop proprietor regarding theft behavior

The major underlying issues to be addressed in this book were best articulated for me over 30 years ago by the proprietor of a modest gift shop in the province of New Brunswick on Canada's east coast, just up the highway from the sixty-foot tides that are the main claim to the Bay of Fundy's fame. This gentleman said to me while we were chatting, "You know, some days rich folk in their expensive clothes and fancy cars come in just to look at the sea shells (present in the thousands, in the plain bins overflowing the store's limited space), and I'll see the odd one of them put a couple of shells in his or her coat, and then walk out without paying."

"Do you stop them, then?", I asked.

"Son," said the proprietor, "If, with all their fancy cars and money and such, they feel a need to steal some shells from a small one-man shop, they must have some kind of serious problems in their hearts or heads already. I figure they deserve some compassion and need someone's love. I don't think of them as bad people and I'm sure that most of them are not really thieves." After several years of investigating this sort of behavior, I can attest to the soundness of the points that this proprietor made; many of those persons he was referring do indeed "have some kind of serious problems in their hearts or heads".

Its far easier to answer the question, "Why did that person take something?" than "Why that *particular* item?"

I occasionally still find it difficult to uncover the reasons that a certain individual stole the particular items in question rather than other, equally accessible items. A reasonable explanation of why the particular item was taken has been forthcoming in about 60% of the cases. On the other hand, some plausible understanding as to why an individual stole *some*thing at that particular time has been forthcoming in over 90% of the cases assessed.

Occasionally the reasons why a particular kind of item was taken has been sadly and painfully obvious, as for example, in Alice's case, as described below.

*****

Case # 5: Alice: the woman who stole whenever her husband had another bout of cancer

Alice telephoned my office at the Clarke Institute of Psychiatry in the early 1980's. She was very tearful and seemed highly anxious. She told me that she had kept a local newspaper report published the previous year about our investigations into shoplifting. She said that this article had provided her with the first plausible explanation of why she had occasionally shoplifted over the previous 8 years. She was now highly distressed because, even though she had never been caught, she said; "I'm doing it again! Ever since my husband's cancer came back last month. This time I didn't even know what I was taking. I think you call the things I stole wrenches, or something like that. Why did I do that? I don't need anything! I just throw the stuff out into the Goodwill box anyway."

When Alice came in for a session later that month, I asked if I could tape record the interview. She agreed, and a remarkable (for its classic, blatantly clear psychodynamic elements, and only somewhat edited) transcript of our session was later a part of the chapter I and my co-investigator wrote for the book Clinical Criminology: The Assessment and Treatment of Criminal Behavior, published in 1985. A modified version of this transcript is reproduced in this book in Chapter 21.

It is notable that each new bout of her husband's cancer was followed, within a day or two, by another theft episode. This desire to steal had first and suddenly come upon Alice after her husband's initial treatment for cancer. Without any understanding on her part as to why she stole, and why she stole what she stole, she first stole some lingerie. Interestingly, she did not usually wear anything in bed and so she could make no sense of why she would choose to steal lingerie. In our interview, however, she revealed that her husband's treatment for cancer of the prostate had left him impotent, and she noted that her sexual frustration increased as her sense of herself as a sexual being diminished. It seemed highly likely that the choice of lingerie was related to these factors.

It is probable that Alice's resentment, frustration and depression in response to being 'robbed' of a normal sex life by the advent of the cancer and its treatment's side effects had led to her acting out in a symbolically significant way. But neither at the time of her offense, nor afterwards, had the cause-effect connection been recognized by Alice. For this person, her theft behavior had remained a nonsensical, upsetting aberration, until we addressed the matter in our interview.

*****

Before leaving this case it is important to point out that the theft offenders we described in this chapter had <u>no conscious awareness</u> that there may have been any connection between the personally meaningful losses they had experienced (or were anticipating), and their theft behavior. This is generally true of Atypical Theft Offenders. And because they do not recognize these connections, and therefore do not understand their own theft behavior, it is all the more upsetting for them.

Why some people shoplift following losses

Conscientious effort is often required to ferret out the nature and extent of these individuals' recent loss experiences. Clients frequently do not provide complete answers to the initial queries regarding this matter, not because they are being consciously and deliberately evasive, but because they usually do not have a mental set that has sought out such connections prior to the interview. After all, to the person who has just been charged with theft, the theft event and the fact that he or she may have recently experienced upsetting circumstances or personally meaningful losses almost never seem related.

> **It is now a part of my standard procedure during initial assessment interviews with theft offenders, to doggedly inquire as to the events which had been transpiring in the offender's life just prior to the time of the onset or recurrence of his or her theft behavior.**

Patient and astute questioning will usually yield a reasonably full picture of the events, and in particular any losses, which may have occurred in the perpetrator's life at about the time of the offense.

Essentially the answers to the question, "Why did this basically honest person steal?" are likely to be found by considering in detail, with the theft offender himself or herself, the following hypotheses:

1. that the theft offender may have reacted by shoplifting, fraud, or other kinds of theft, to some recent traumatic event which had occurred, or had been anticipated, just prior to the act of theft;

2. that the theft offender had not coped adequately with the recent traumatic event; and

3. that the recent traumatic event involved the individual experiencing (or at least anticipating) some personally meaningful loss.

A thorough examination of the offender's background is very likely to yield psychodynamically relevant information that may relate to reasons why the person chose, at least on an unconscious level, to act out by stealing as opposed to committing some other kind of inappropriate behavior such as abusing food, alcohol, drugs, or another person.

In order to access the relevant information, consider also the following additional hypotheses:

1. that in childhood the theft offender may have experienced some major trauma, including what would likely have been perceived by that child as a major personal loss. Most likely this loss was experienced as involving unfair rejection and/or abandonment.

2. that this childhood trauma was not appropriately dealt with, at a psychological level, neither at the time, nor since.

3. that, as a result of this earlier childhood loss, the individual who is now an adult, has remained particularly vulnerable to perceived loss, and especially loss that can be interpreted, at least at an unconscious level, as representing unfair rejection, and/or abandonment.

The possible effect of childhood losses, on the now-adult who experiences a major loss was exceptionally well articulated by Judith Viorst, in her excellent book, **Necessary Losses**[viii]. She suggests that while we may not consciously remember early childhood loss experiences, they nevertheless can leave the individuals who have experienced them very sensitive to losses that may occur later in life. Furthermore she indicates that such a person's response to the loss of a job, a spouse, or a loved one may be the kind of response that which would more likely expected from a angry or helpless child.

In her book Ms. Viorst states that the manner of our mourning -- and its longevity --depends upon our prior experiences, especially those related to our earlier losses. Viorst quotes Hemingway as stating, "The world breaks everyone, and afterward many are strong at the broken places." Viorst then immediately adds a qualification: "Some are (strong at the broken places). Some aren't (Italics mine). "

This writer agrees with Viorst on all the above points. Some individuals respond to losses as Hemingway described, with apparently great and exemplary resources, indeed becoming stronger "at the broken places." Consider, as an example, the assassinated former Prime Minister of India, Rajiv Gandhi, who had himself emerged from the loss, also by assassination, of his own mother, Indira Gandhi, in 1984. A former airline pilot, he had no interest in pursuing politics, until pressed to do so in the throes of his personal tragedy.

Many of us marvel at the strength and courage of those who, like Mr. Gandhi, appear to have responded so admirably in such abominable circumstances. And we are left to wonder how we would respond in such a comparable situation.

At the same time, however, most of us do personally know two or more individuals who grew up, as siblings, in the same troubled home or surroundings, perhaps were even close in age, yet reacted as adults so very differently to, for instance, the loss of one or both parents through illness or misfortune. Why one person reacts to a similar situation so differently than another, even when they are siblings, we can only conjecture. Those of us who have grown up with brothers or sisters know only that individuals are indeed individualistic, with some reactions, attitudes, behaviors that are so similar, and other responses that are so different from one another.

I believe, on the evidence accumulated from more than thirty-seven years of functioning in the role of counselor and psychotherapist, that very few persons escape entirely unscathed from especially traumatic childhood experiences. One sibling may become a workaholic, another an alcoholic, and yet another a social deviant, while a fourth may become a social worker. Most people do pay a price in emerging from the mixed bag that was their childhood. We pay in different currencies, and in different amounts, and at different times. The persons we are examining in this book have paid in part by reacting to losses via stealing.

In 1983, in our original article we formulated this finding in terms of a Loss-Substitution-By-Shoplifting Hypothesis. As I mentioned earlier, in response to the findings of my clinical investigations of the past fifteen years, I have extended this hypothesis to include all manner of theft behavior, not merely shoplifting or fraud.

Before taking a close look back at our original investigations, let me state our hypothesis in close to its original form, as follows:

The Loss-Substitution-By-Shoplifting Hypothesis:

"Individuals may attempt to replace or substitute for an unfair (as perceived) actual or anticipated loss of a significant person, place, or object by unfairly taking another object, usually without any conscious awareness of the psychological relationship between the perceived (as unfair) loss and the (unfairly obtained) acquisition."

In order to emphasize the key elements of this hypothesis let me repeat it again, breaking it up into its key elements by reprinting it as follows:

"Individuals may attempt to replace or substitute for an <u>unfair</u> (as perceived) actual or anticipated <u>loss</u> of a significant person place, or object...

by <u>unfairly</u> taking another object,...

usually <u>without conscious awareness</u> of the psychological relationship...

between the perceived unfair personal loss ...

and...

the unfairly obtained acquisition."

For the mental health professional or lawyer who desires to understand the shoplifting behavior of an essentially honest, and generally socially responsible client, this hypothesis may represent a helpful starting point. If one begins by making the assumption that the hypothesis might apply to the case at hand, then no matter how seemingly far-fetched or bizarre the act, the professionals involved in the case (and the client) may well gain insight into the underlying reasons for the act having taken place.

The professional reader should note that reluctance on the part of theft offender to spontaneously present key data (as in the case of Sylvia, described below) may suggest that the client is still having considerable emotional difficulty dealing with the traumatic event that may have precipitated the behavior, and/or an earlier loss in childhood.

*****

Case # 6: Sylvia: Stealing as a Way of Coping with Parental Loss and Emotional Distress

A recent example of this loss-substitution phenomenon was provided by a 26-year old client, a management consultant, who described how, when doing her grocery shopping in a downtown 'food boutique', she had attempted to shove a two foot long French bread into her one-foot deep purse. This action was carried out in full view of a security television camera after she had seen the camera and had read the two foot-square sign posted below it that stated that surveillance to stop shoplifting was in force in the store.

It was only during the fourth interview that the client offered, in response to persistent questioning on my part, that she had carried out the theft behavior on the very day, indeed at the very hour, that her father was being remarried, an event to which she had not been invited. She told me that she disliked her new step-mother intensely, and had expressed to her father her strong resentment of the fact that her own mother had died of cancer less than six months before he announced his intentions to re-marry. When I inquired why she thought she had not been invited to the wedding, she replied without any trace of emotion in her voice that, "They didn't invite me because they really wanted to keep the ceremony and reception small and informal. I was fine with that."

*****

It soon became clear that Sylvia had very strong, unresolved feelings in regard to both her mother's death and her father's remarriage. Her theft behavior was an anti-cupid-like arrow aimed at the happy couple's love by a grieving daughter who was having great difficulty coming to terms with the loss of first one parent, and now (as she perceived the matter), her other parent as well.

Sylvia is typical of many clients who initially state that "nothing special" was happening in their lives at about the time they offended. Clinicians and lawyers alike should be prepared, regardless of initially dismissive comments by some clients, to gently but firmly continue the questioning tack recommended above. Hundreds of clinical assessments of such cases has conclusively demonstrated to me that some disturbing events in their lives that helped to precipitate the acting out behavior, very likely *did* occur.

What is the dynamic relationship between the theft behaviors of the cases referred to above and the issue of loss?

It is now possible to review some of the above cases in greater detail, and to provide reasonable explanations of what must otherwise appear to be bizarre and nonsensical behaviors. Lets deal with each of these cases in turn.

Case # 1 revisited: Bill, the executive whose lover left town

In Bill's case the loss of his lover was the precipitating factor in his acting out. When he then stole items presumably meant to be used to wrap an anniversary gift for his wife he was likely expressing his resentment towards both himself and his wife for being unable or unwilling to extricate himself from a deeply unhappy marriage.

Special Note: Shopping for a present for someone towards whom the shopper feels some resentment may be dangerous, *for the shopper*!

A birthday or anniversary or other supposedly happy occasion which, due to the prevailing situation or state of the relationship, is not, in fact, a happy circumstance, but rather one in regard to which that the individual feels obliged to "come across" with a gift of some sort, can be the very sort of situation that could precipitate a theft offense in some persons.

My usual advice to any person who has previously been charged with theft and who is intending to go shopping for a present for someone with whom he or she is currently seriously displeased, is that the individual should be on guard for the possibility of committing any 'small indiscretion' which may be viewed as an act of theft. It is undoubtedly better -- if more uncomfortable -- to admit to oneself that the card or gift is being given under duress. The feelings in regard to the person or the event being 'celebrated' need to be examined honestly and handled with care.

Case # 2 revisited: Mary, the mother who mourned her daughter's getting married and moving out west.

Giving birth to Ruth had been a very traumatic experience for Mary. The attending physician fully expected that neither Mary nor her daughter would survive, due to the serious complications that occurred during and immediately after the premature birth. Fortunately, and some believed miraculously, they both survived with no long-term medical repercussions.

Mary's extreme over protectiveness during her daughter's childhood had been a subject that her spouse and some relatives had tried to discuss with her, but to no avail. Mary considered herself merely a mother who was totally devoted all to her children. Now, suddenly (or so it seemed) Ruth had married, and Mary's last child was gone from the family home!

No matter that Mary knew the day was coming! No matter that she had helped Ruth prepare for the wedding day with real joy and pride. While she was sincerely happy for her daughter, she had not anticipated the powerful, sudden emergence of heretofore un-dealt with, painful emotions related to the birth trauma that Ruth's marriage and leaving would trigger. For, at the moment that her lovely daughter and her fine new son-in-law pulled away from the driveway on their trip out west, Mary experienced a state of profound loss and deprivation.

Now she was no longer an involved mother who could relish in her active daily role in her daughter's life. This loss of role function and intense involvement with her daughter, and Ruth's moving to the west coast, was nothing less than traumatic.

The fact that Mary stole a coat several sizes too large for her probably had symbolic import. She would only have needed a coat that size if she were at full term pregnancy, and was ready for the child to be born (and therefore, of course, leave Mary's womb)! Yet this was something that had just happened, symbolically, less than an hour before the act of theft. The 'full-term' coat may have represented both her birthing of Ruth, and an unconscious desire to have a immediate symbolic replacement.

Not surprisingly, since Mary and her husband were unaware of the loss-substitution-by-stealing phenomenon, neither of them had understood that her act of shoplifting was related to any current, let alone previous, events in her life.

Case # 4: revisited: Bert the lawyer

Bert had a great respect for the law. At the same time he had a somewhat rebellious streak. This streak lurked beneath his apparently straight-ahead, somewhat officious manner, emerging on occasion when he walked through supermarkets sampling the fruit bins. His spouse had commented on this behavior but he had sloughed her comments off as "her rigidity." He did not view this sampling behavior as theft, but as a customer's legitimate right.

On the other hand, at no time did Bert ever previously shoplift. When we examined what was happening about the time of the offense I learned that his four year old son was about to begin chemotherapy. Understandably, Bert was extremely distressed by this situation.

The law had always provided Bert with a sense of order (and control) in his life. He had been an only child since he was thirteen years old, after his five year old sibling had died of cancer. Here was an event with déjà vu qualities. His own mother had never recovered from the loss of her youngest child. For reasons he never understood Bert had felt guilty most of his life, and had always attempted to make things safe and secure for his parents, and more recently for his own family. His son's cancer occurred in spite of his hyper vigilance and best efforts.

Case # 6: revisited: Sylvia

Sylvia's was a relatively difficult case. This young person was grossly overweight. She told me in our first session that she did not like dealing with the topic of feelings. She seemed to understand that she had, at some primal level, stuffed herself with food as a means of drowning out other possible sensations, such as tense stomach muscles. Her body might have provided her conscious awareness of such sensations, if only the feeling of being 'stuffed' had not intervened. It was only after many sessions that she began to feel comfortable enough to relate the effects upon her of her mother's two-year-long, on-again, off-again struggle with cancer. She had depended upon her father for emotional support, just as she always had in the past. When her father had become involved with "that woman" she suddenly felt terribly alone, anxious and angry.

By shoplifting at the very moment her father was being remarried at another place in the same city, Sylvia was making a psychologically powerful statement. She felt enraged that "that woman" had 'stolen' her father's affection. At the same time she was attaching a negative situation, i.e., her blatant theft behavior, to what might have been a happy occasion. Also, of course she was getting something (however minor) for herself by shoplifting, even as she felt she was losing something so precious to her -- her father's primary attentions. That the French bread was also phallic-like in shape may also have been relevant.

Findings of the original study pertaining to the matter of loss and shoplifting

The reader will note from the accompanying table (Table 9), that actual or anticipated losses were noted and identified in nearly three quarters (actually 74%) of the cases that were part of the original study. In 65% of the cases, we were able to isolate actual losses that had occurred just prior to the offense, while in another nine percent of the cases, we found instances in which the patients had been anticipating meaningful losses.

Table Ten: Shoplifting, Losses and Carcinoma in the Original (1983) Study*

*(Total number of cases =34: Age range 16-70)

	Number of Ss	Percentage % of all 34 cases
At least moderately depressed	33	97%
Less than 6 previous offenses	19	56%
Six or more previous offenses	15	44%
Actual losses experienced	22	65%
Only anticipated having losses	3	9%
Shoplifting occurred in close time proximity to losses	21	62%
Shoplifting occurred in *very* close time proximity to losses	7	21%
Occurrence of cancer in self or 'Significant Other' in close proximity to shoplifting	10**	29%

** Six of these Ss had been the cancer victims

Table Nine indicates the 1983 findings in regard to 34 cases. The following data are particularly noteworthy:

- 33 of the 34 subjects were at least moderately depressed.

- in nearly 3/4 of the cases (actually 74%) the investigators were able to ascertain that these subjects had experienced or anticipated experiencing personally meaningful losses   just   prior   to   the commitment of the offense.

- in 65% of the cases the losses had already actually happened to the offender:

- in the remaining 9% a serious personal meaningful loss was being anticipated.

- the shoplifting offense had occurred shortly after the loss   in 62% of the cases.

- in about 20% of all the cases the offense was in startlingly close temporal proximity to the loss event.

Our findings indicated that the Atypical Theft Offenders were very angry indeed about their perceived-as-unfair losses (whether actual or only anticipated). In most cases these persons had not handled either their losses or their anger well. Through their atypical theft behavior the offenders symbolically expressed their feelings about their losses by unfairly gaining something else as a replacement for the losses.

Chapter 6

SOME CLINICAL ISSUES WITH A.T.O.s

I--Regarding the finding of clinical depression in A.T.O.s

It should be noted that nearly every person whom I have assessed who has been charged with theft was clinically depressed at the time of the testing procedure. *Small wonder!* Many of them were facing court, as well as the possibility of public humiliation as a result of media coverage. In some instances the prospect of vocational disaster or even a jail term were also possible consequences.

It is true that in many instances, the probability is that some of these individual were also depressed just prior to the time of their offenses. It is my clinician impression, however, that some were consciously experiencing depression in response to having been charged. Also, some of the Atypical Theft Offenders were much more angry than depressed when they committed the acts of theft, and then, *after* they were caught and charged, more depressed than angry.

The use of depression as a justification or explanation of atypical theft behavior is not very satisfactory or helpful, in my view, in most cases. The clinically important issue is not that the person was depressed anyway, but *why* was the person depressed? And did the depression cover anger towards some other person or circumstance or event? Clinicians are well advised to go deeper; depression is often a sign on a door that opens to a room filled with potentially relevant data that should be explored during the assessment – especially if the intent is to also assist the person to not be so prone to acting out by stealing in the future.

II--The likelihood of recurrence of theft behavior by A.T.O.s

All that is needed for further offenses to become likely is for circumstances to again press the individuals' psychological 'buttons' related to their earlier traumatic experiences. In other words, the offenders' family, social and working lives may continue to be threatened, until they uncover, and come to terms with, the underlying causes of their theft behavior.

In the past several years in particular, many offenders have made their way to my office only after repeated charges and convictions. They have frequently presented with a sense of frustration and futility, and are often afraid that there is no way of stopping what they experience as their "out of control" behavior. Usually within a single session, however, they begin to experience relief and reassurance that there are genuine and understandable reasons behind their acting out, and that these reasons can be confronted and dealt with, thereby very significantly reducing the likelihood of further acting out theft behavior.

They are invited to learn new and decidedly different ways of coping with life's stressors, which is the best means of ensuring that they will cease their theft behavior. They are also made aware that unless they do face and deal with the aspects of their personal lives that require attention, they may well remain at risk of acting out again.

The statistics given for the occurrence of losses in proximity to the acts of shoplifting (Table Ten) only referred to those cases in which we were actually able to determine that such losses had occurred. It is entirely possible that in some cases there were losses that were not uncovered. My own methodology of conducting inquiring assessments has certainly improved in the eighteen years since the original article was published. The better trained and more experienced the clinician, the more likely it is that relevant material will be uncovered. To assist both the offender and the clinician in locating the relevant data, the Cupchik Theft Offender Questionnaire[ix] has been developed and is presented in Chapter 17.

The reader is granted permission to use the Cupchik Theft Offender Questionnaire when dealing <u>with any one particular case only</u>. If the reader wishes to use the questionnaire in dealing with more than one case, then permission must be gained, in writing, from the publisher, Tagami Communications.

The more open and insight-oriented the client, the more likely it will be that the relevant information will be uncovered. I inform clients in the first session that although my intention is to be of assistance, they do not have to comply with any of my requests for information, nor answer all of my questions. However, I also make clear that it is crucial for my assistance to be maximally beneficial, that they not tell me anything they know to be an *un*truth. I ask that they simply inform me that they do not wish to respond to any particular question(s). Most clients readily comprehend that they will be wasting their money and our time unless they are forthcoming, and since most of them are anxious to put an end to their self-destructive behavior, it seldom happens that clients refuse to answer appropriate questions.

Let us look at one additional case, a classic in fact, in order to better appreciate the complexities that may be involved in dealing with theft offender clients. Martha was a day-time nanny whose honesty and dedication had so impressed her lawyer-employer and his family, that when she was arrested for shoplifting the lawyer sought my professional help and offered to pay for her assessment and any treatment that I might recommend.

*****

Case # 7: Martha: The nanny who stole 150 dresses that she kept in her closet with the tags still on

Martha was an attractive person in her fifties when she appeared for assessment. A woman of little formal education, she had worked as a day-time nanny for a wealthy family for over a decade. The family members thought of Martha as a treasured member of the household. Deeply religious and highly moral, she had agreed to an assessment because she believed there must be something fundamentally and terribly wrong with her as a human being.

The short version of her story is that she had been apprehended by the police at a shopping mall while she was making a third trip to her employer's station wagon, struggling to carry two large shopping bags filled to overflowing with some articles of clothing. The security person reported that she had seen Martha take a dress off the rack and place it in a large shopping bag, and then do the same with several other dresses. The police obtained a warrant and upon searching the small house that Martha shared with her husband, a taxi driver, they found more than 150 dresses, with their tags still on them and obviously unworn, in a walk-in closet in the basement.

Martha was at a complete loss to provide some plausible explanation for what she had done. Subsequent investigation led the police to conclude that she did not steal the dresses for purposes of resale. The neighbors described Martha and her spouse as retiring people who were regular church-goers, and ready volunteers at the local community center on Sundays. This hard-working couple had come to this country in the 1960s and had worked steadily ever since.

Martha related that she found herself going into the basement on numerous occasions over the previous few months. On those occasions she would place a chair in the middle of the walk-in closet where she had placed the dresses, and would simply sit for hours (while her husband was out working) surrounded by the dresses, finding their mere presence strangely soothing and peaceful.

Initially we were very much at a loss to understand Martha's shoplifting behavior. Of lower socioeconomic level, she certainly did not need most, if any of the rather upscale dresses she had stolen. Her employers had periodically gifted her some clothing that had been worn on only a few occasions but which were quite acceptable for Martha to wear, even to church.

Martha told me that all the dresses had been taken over a five month period. She said that she had never done such a thing before, and never intended to wear the clothes! She could not bring herself to even try them on in her own home. She could offer no reasonable explanation for her shoplifting behavior or the curious calming effect that being in their presence had upon her.

In our next interview she told me that she had discussed with her husband our conversation of the previous session. When I had asked what was happening in their lives back at about the start of her shoplifting spree, she had replied that their lives never changed, but had been, as usual, filled with work, church, and their volunteer activities; in short, nothing special. She said that her husband had been shocked to learn that she had not mentioned to me the death of their twelve-year old household pet, a small dog, which had occurred just prior to the onset of Martha's stealing activities. This new information was the thin edge of a wedge that allowed us to pry open the cover of her encapsulated memories and emotions regarding this recent loss, and an even more traumatic one that had occurred decades earlier.

Martha explained about the more recent loss first. It seemed that there had been an accident in the kitchen in their home when she was preparing dinner and the pet had been badly burned with cooking oil. The veterinarian could only put the poor thing out of its misery. A shaken and guilt ridden Martha had held the animal while the vet gave it a lethal injection.

For Martha and her spouse, Louis, it was a devastating loss. Unable to have children, they had had the dog since it was eight weeks old. Their friends would kid them about the child-substitute aspect of their relationships with the dog. Martha and Louis did not mind the joking. They readily acknowledged that the dog played such a role in their lives. Having to put the animal down was extremely painful for them both.

Of course this information hardly explains why Martha had shoplifted. It is true that she blamed herself for having left the kitchen for several minutes while the cooking oil was heating in the pot on the stove. But why the thefts? Why dresses? And why so many dresses? Why not shoes or dog collars or magazines or shirts or food?

It was during our third interview that the answers to these questions emerged. Like many children in Europe during the Second World War, Martha lived with her mother while her father went off to soldier. One day she was out in a field gathering potatoes when she saw a soldier staggering towards her in his rain-soaked and bloodied uniform. When he got closer, she saw that the soldier was her father, He had left the fighting at the front days earlier and had almost made it all the way back to their extremely modest home. He literally died in his daughter's arms. Other farm hands helped her to bury her father under the welcoming branches of a large tree.

Martha's mother, a seamstress, had been sick for months, and now there was almost no money left to see them through this horrible period. Before she got so ill, her mother used to made fine dresses for the rich ladies in the town nearby, and had been in the habit of making her dearly loved daughter gorgeous, finely embroidered dresses with the bits of material left over from her work for the wealthy townsfolk. Now those fine child's dresses became their currency of survival. One by one the mother required that her daughter part with yet another dress. Martha was instructed to go into the town carrying a bag containing one or two dresses. She was to knock on the wealthy women's doors and barter food, or a little money, in exchange for her lovely dresses. Thanks to her mother's handiwork, and the ample supply of dresses, only some

67

of which Martha had outgrown at the time, they were able to make it through the remaining months of the war.

*****

To the little girl residing inside the now-adult Martha the equating of dresses with survival, and the horror of having had her father die in her arms, had remained unrecognized and undealt-with for over four decades. When her dog was injured, and had to be put down, she had held it in her arms while the vet gave it a lethal injection.

Martha's acting out was very likely triggered by the loss of the dog. Moreover, the manner of the dog being put down most likely reverberated through her unconscious and activated the at least suppressed memories and undealt-with feelings regarding the much earlier traumatic loss of her father. When she had been a child, having a collection of dresses made survival possible in the face of painful and horrible loss. To this woman's unconscious mind, the death of the dog, and its manner of dying probably triggered a desire to compensate herself for this unfair loss of her child-substitute by acquiring that which meant hope, security and survival -- dresses!

III--The not uncommon phenomenon of A.T.O.s who had traumatic wartime experiences in childhood

I have had numerous clients with war-time traumatic experiences whose atypical theft behavior appears to have been psychodynamically related to these earlier events. As we shall discuss in the section of this book which deals with treatment, success in working with these offenders involves confronting <u>both</u> (a) the more recent, and (b) the distant past losses and/or traumas.

Success in working with Atypical Theft Offenders almost invariably involves dealing with the recent as well as the distant past losses and traumas.

Other examples will also be presented which illustrate this principle. That this is a phenomenon of universal import will be made clear, as well as the need to understand that such theft offenders are atypical and need be dealt with very differently from those who steal for profit.

First let me describe one additional case of present anticipated loss and abandonment bringing closer to conscious awareness similar feelings from a much earlier, undealt-with event from childhood.

*****

Case #8: Barney, the CEO who shoplifted socks and a steak

One of the more remarkable scenes of my twelve years on the staff of the forensic service of the Clarke Institute of Psychiatry occurred when a well known CEO of a major corporation slumped down into a chair in my office in a state of profound sadness and dismay and proceeded to describe for me his disbelief and disgust at his own actions of earlier that week. He had been apprehended as he left a large supermarket for having not paid for a pair of socks and a rib steak that he been observed stuffing into his overcoat's inner pocket. After he paid for some other items he walked out of the store and was promptly apprehended. A deeply religious man, he had been involved in working for various religious charities over the years and had been known locally as one of the most generous high-profile persons who could be counted on whenever the community required help to promote a worthy cause.

He could not explain to himself, his lawyer, or to me, why he had deliberately and knowingly carried out a flagrant act of shoplifting, an act that (as far as he could recall) he had never done before. He also was not aware of ever previously having had any desire to carry out such behavior. Certainly his $470,000 annual salary (not including incentives and stock options) did not require any financial shortcuts being taken regarding such items as socks and food. Furthermore, both the substantial home that he and his wife jointly owned, and the large country property they had used as a weekend retreat for the past ten years, were fully paid for and they had, some two years earlier, finished paying for the university education of their now-grown children.

When we discussed his marital relationship and its problems, he divulged that his spouse had told him the night before the offense that she wanted a divorce. He knew that things were hardly going well in their relationship but her statement about wanting to end their marriage had taken him entirely by surprise. The next morning she had gone to New York City for a business meeting, and he had been ruminating all day about the possibility that she was having an affair with her boss, who was also in New York City for the same meeting.

The next day, Barney recalled, he had also thought about his mother's death when he was nine years old, and his subsequent unhappy childhood living with his father and stepmother. He experienced a profound sense of abandonment that escalated throughout the day even though his spouse had said that she was not intending to separate immediately. In fact, having anticipated his shocked response, she had determined to stay for at least a few weeks so that they could discuss the matter thoroughly until he was hopefully resigned to the loss of their marriage.

*****

> **Just as an old sports injury can be reactivated by a new, relatively small stress to a particular joint, so too can a recent emotional injury reactivate an earlier pain that had been covered up or repressed for years, or even decades.**

IV--Considering atypical theft behavior in relation to all kinds of theft

Since 1985 I have become increasingly aware that not only shoplifting and fraud, but all other kinds of theft may be carried out by Atypical Theft Offenders as well as by Typical Theft Offenders. It is not so much how much was taken but why the act was carried out, that often distinguishes A.T.O.s from T.T.O.s.

V--The Loss-Substitution-By-Stealing Hypothesis

The Loss-Substitution-by-*Shoplifting* Hypothesis can now be restated as the Loss-Substitution-by-*Stealing* Hypothesis:

The Loss-Substitution-by-Stealing Hypothesis:

"In response to experiencing (or anticipating) what is perceived to be an unfair, personally meaningful loss some individuals, whom we have termed Atypical Theft Offenders, may carry out acts of theft, by which they cause other persons, places or institutions to suffer unfair losses.

Such acts of atypical theft behavior are almost always carried out without the conscious awareness on the part of the perpetrator, of the relationship of the act of stealing to the (experienced or anticipated) loss."

In such instances of stealing, what has been stolen may or may not be readily seen as having a symbolically obvious or relationship to what the perpetrator may have either lost, or anticipated losing. Regardless, the *act* of taking something in an unfair fashion (i.e., without paying for it, or asking permission to take it) is inherently symbolically meaningful at the subconscious and unconscious levels.

VI--The case for inclusion of this category of theft offender, and indeed the entire Atypical Theft Offender continuum in a future American Psychiatric Association's Diagnostic and Statistical Manual (DSM)

At the time of publication of this book's first edition in 1997, and in spite of the fact that (a) our original article appeared in the Bulletin of the American Academy of Psychiatry and the Law in 1983, (b) many clinicians and lawyers have utilized the findings of our investigations in court, and (c) other investigators[x] have since confirmed our major findings, it is probably still true that most acts of atypical theft behavior are continuing to be misunderstood and mislabeled as cases of kleptomania.

Many Atypical Theft Offender clients have contacted me only after they have been dealt with by other clinicians who have not recognized the 'Atypical Theft Offender' aspects of their difficulties, and who therefore may have not provided the psychotherapeutic treatment that would minimize the likelihood of recidivism.

71

On many occasions over the past twenty-plus years I been approached by television producers, magazine editors and newspaper reporters who have decided that the matter of bizarre theft behavior was one that would be of interest to their viewers or readers. They have often begun our conversations by asking if I would be interested in being interviewed for a program (or article) on 'kleptomania'. To their credit (in many instances), the subsequent direction of such programs or articles have been substantially altered after I have had an opportunity to discuss the matter in detail with the callers, and have provided them with some of the data included in this book, at which point the misconception and danger of continuing to refer to Atypical Theft Offenders as kleptomaniacs usually became obvious. It is to the credit of these media professionals that helpful information has consequently been passed along to their viewers/readers.

(Unfortunately it is also true that some in the media have been so wedded to the use of the term kleptomania (perhaps because it is so 'popular'), that, in spite of the distinct likelihood that it was being erroneously applied to the particular cases they had been calling about, they were not open to a likely more fruitful, and valid, interview regarding the more likely reasons for the theft behaviors involved.

Chapter 7

SHOPLIFTING AS A REACTION TO STRESS

Case #9: Tony; the cop who shoplifted to avoid getting killed

Tony was known among his fellow police officers as one particularly tough, courageous SOB. As the head of the Emergency Task Force (ETF) response team, he was known for leading (not merely directing) his men in difficult situations. He had always been that way, from the time he was a young person growing up in an extremely well to-do German family. Everyone had assumed that since he was the oldest (and brightest) son, that he would take over the family's manufacturing business. Even when he joined the air force it was assumed that he was just getting rid of his rather excessive need for adventure, and that when that 'bug' was out of his system, he would surely sit next to his father at board meetings. That was twenty-five years ago. Most of his family never understood his decision to become a career police officer.

As a teenager, Tony had adopted the motto from a childhood fiction action hero: "Live hard, not long". On his 50th birthday, while running some errands for his wife, and getting materials with which to build some shelves on the weekend, he stole a door knob from a hardware store, in full view of the manager, "while Tony was staring right at me", the manager would later testify!

The Clarke staff psychiatrist found Tony to be clinically depressed, highly stressed and very angry. I found him, as well, to be very 'typical' of classic Atypical Theft Offenders. At the age of 50 Tony had finally become conscious of being afraid of losing something -- namely, his life. This was new! In fact, this was paralyzing to a person who had previously 'handled' his fear, without flinching, for all of his adult life. But then he always knew, or thought that he knew, that he was bound to "live hard, not long", meaning certainly dying before age 50. Since he always believed that this was the scenario he was meant to live, he took life-risking challenges with relative ease, and didn't worry about dying: he simply expected it.

On his fiftieth birthday he remembered thinking, "Wait a minute! I might just live a long time and even grow old!" He had never, in his entire life, expected to grow old and lose his legendary energy and vitality. But now he admitted to himself, it was already happening. He was not quite as fast or as fit as the young officers under his command. It was scary. Damn scary! And he remembered thinking, "Say, that wouldn't be so bad, after all, retiring to our farm with my wife, having the (now married) children visit with our grandchildren in tow – now and then."

Tony had never expected to live long enough to see any of his grandchildren. Now his oldest daughter was pregnant. He might just be around long enough to be a grandfather. He realized for the first time that he rather liked that idea!.

Or, he might miss out on that experience. He suddenly realized, on his 50th birthday, at a profoundly felt level, that he did not want to miss out on the joys of being happily retired, of being a grandparent, of spending time with his hobbies..

The dangers inherent in his job made it distinctly possible that he might not make it to retirement, now just five years away. The threat of more emergencies involving ever more lethal weapons was growing. Everyone, especially Tony himself, relied on him to take an active role in leading his men. The odds of getting out alive and well had been getting worse the longer he continued to answer those emergency calls and avoided being seriously hurt.

"This kind of thinking isn't what you talk about with the men under you!" he told me during our initial interview. Or, for that matter, with your superiors either. "You were considered to be turning into 'chickenshit' if you talked that way."

His shoplifting of the $3.50 closet doorknob resolved some of these matters virtually instantaneously. He was hauled before the department 'shrink'. He was removed from his position at the head of the ETF response team, and given a desk job at headquarters. His superiors simply could not have someone who had done something so stupid, so... well, 'nutty', at the head of such a critical team, one that required clearheaded, 'un-nutty' thinking at the top.

<u>Tony's unconscious had creatively manufactured a way to get him out of the line of fire,</u> although it nearly cost him his job and his pension, until the

charges were dropped. If he had recognized his feelings of dread earlier and/or had discussed his growing anxiety over the increasing probability of his being wounded or killed he might have been transferred earlier.

But most police officers don't discuss their fears very easily or often, and in fact, usually suppress or repress them so that they can continue in their jobs. The price they pay is higher alcohol and drug abuse, destroyed marriages, and sometimes suicide. It is very unfortunate indeed that many police officers may feel unable to discuss their fears and concerns, in confidence, with an appropriate counselor.

*****

A.T.O.s and their unconscious motivations.

In our initial investigations of Atypical Theft Offenders we noted that there were several apparent categories of motivations operating in various instances of theft. In most cases the motivations were found to reside in the perpetrator's subconscious or unconscious.

It is my clinical experience that only in a minority of cases do Atypical Theft Offenders consciously and deliberately pre-plan their theft behaviors.

This is of course in sharp contrast to Typical Theft Offenders, i.e., those persons who steal primarily for monetary or material gain. T.T.O.s know well, and have full conscious awareness, of what they are about to do. They know it, intend it, desire it, plan it, and then do it! <u>And when they have committed their theft offenses they do not experience regret or remorse concerning their actions.</u> Nor do they experience shame, self-disgust, or suicidal thinking. On the contrary, they usually experience good feelings, including (however misguided) pride at having 'pulled off' their acts of theft, and they may even have a desire to brag to their friends about their exploits.

The A.T.O.s' terrible secret of stealing and their fear of exposure

'Classic' Atypical Theft Offenders virtually never brag about their stealing activities. It is their shameful secret. They are, in fact, deathly afraid (sometimes literally) of being found out - by 'the public', or worse by their friends, or worst of all, by their family members. They may anticipate their relatives' disgust, and even outright rejection.

What actually does happen when relatives find out about their theft behavior, and what are the possible effects of their relatives' reactions upon the likelihood of successful treatment? We shall discuss later these matters in more detail later.

> **Suffice it to say at this point that the reactions of relatives upon learning of the theft behaviors of family members are very important, and can be either a major positive contribution, or an inhibiting factor, in regard to the probability of an ultimately successful treatment of the offender.**

In our society committing a theft is sometimes viewed as worse than causing a death

Consider the judgment of US and Canadian courts in cases of persons who have caused injury or death when driving a vehicle while inebriated, and compare their sentences with those often issued to individuals who are convicted of shoplifting or other kinds of theft. In North American and many other 'civilized' societies, those who committed acts of even minor theft are often given the relatively harsher sentences.

> In one case that I assessed, a **29** year old individual was given a three month jail term for stealing an **8** ounce bottle of apple juice from a supermarket! <u>Three months in jail ... for eight ounces of juice!</u>
>
> In contrast, in the same province at about the same time, an intoxicated young man followed, in his car at night with his car lights off, a group walking along a suburban street. <u>He received a six-month jail term for deliberately having run down and killed two of the pedestrians.</u>

In North American society at the beginning of the 21st century, authorities sometimes seem to be more concerned with severely punishing minor crimes involving property than handing out relatively more substantial sentences for serious crimes against persons. Consider the sometimes shockingly brief jail sentences that are often handed out to persons convicted of rape; compare their sentences with those sometimes given those who have shoplifted or committed acts of employee theft involving relatively few dollars.

<u>Isn't a major discussion of these matters beyond the scope of this book? Indeed it is! I merely mention this issue to invite the reader to think about the judicial treatment of theft offenders compared with offenders of serious crimes against persons in jurisdictions with which the reader is familiar.</u>

Chapter 8

ATYPICAL THEFT BEHAVIOR AS A RESPONSE TO ILLNESS IN SELF OR 'SIGNIFICANT OTHER'

Illness generally, and cancer in particular, occurring in close proximity to acts of atypical theft behavior
In the initial (1983) study, where only cancer (and no other illness) was considered, <u>29% of the subjects had shoplifted in close proximity to the occurrence of cancer in themselves or a significant other.</u>

<u>In the 1996 study there appeared to be a relationship of illness to theft behavior in 33.3% of the cases.</u> In 1/3 of these cases (or 11% of the total 36 offenders) the illness involved was cancer.

<u>A psychodynamic/analytic hypothesis of how the unconscious may interpret the actions of cancer cells in relation to the human body as analogous to the act of retail shoplifting by Atypical Theft Offenders:</u>

Shoplifting may be described as *the unfair invasion of a host body* (such a department store) *and the stealing away of that which belongs to the host body* (e.g., material goods).

This scenario is analogous to what happens when the disease process of cancer occurs; the *individual's body can be viewed to have been unfairly invaded by malignant cancer cells, and these invaders attack and 'steal away' that which belongs to the body, namely healthy cells,* and thereby the very health of the person.

While the reader can be excused for being skeptical when first introduced to this hypothesis, the findings of the original 1983 clinical study, the more recent 1996 study, and a very many anecdotal reports provided by offenders and their relatives over the past 23 years of investigation lend major support to it.

Throughout this book we discuss cases where cancer specifically, and illness more generally, appears to have played a major psychodynamic part in the acting out theft behavior. At this point let us discuss one additional case where this phenomenon was present.

*****

Case # 10: Alan; The Case Of The Wedding Day Spoiler

Alan, educated, 53 years old, and divorced, was apprehended after police stakeouts were set up to cover the homes of individuals who were attending the marriages of their adult children. The Wedding Day Spoiler (as he was labeled by the media) seemed to target these persons with uncanny accuracy, and after opening the sliding back doors of their homes, would make off with jewelry, silverware, and assorted other items.

After several months of such break-ins the police determined that the houses that were 'hit' were those of persons who had placed notices in the newspaper announcing the dates, locations, and times of their sons' or daughters' marriages and wedding receptions. In all, over a seven-month period, more than $50,000 in goods and money was reported stolen.

When the police stakeouts netted a suspect, he readily admitted to several other similar crimes that had occurred during the previous year. Formerly an accountant with a large multinational corporation until he was let go due to downsizing, Alan felt very ashamed and humiliated as his name and details of his recent downturn in his life circumstances were published by the media..

During his assessment I learned that Alan had lost his fiancé to cancer two years earlier, the days before their planned wedding day. He had initially seemed to handle her death reasonably well, but within a few weeks had become increasingly angry and reclusive. His job performance worsened and the downsizing in his company's head office resulted in his being let go. His

79

break- enter-theft behavior of families who were celebrating marriages began shortly thereafter.

His personal financial worth, according to the prenuptial agreement he had signed a short while before his fiancé was diagnosed with cancer was in excess of $1,500,000.

*****

Helping Atypical Theft Offenders understand their behavior

It is my hope that some offenders will read this book before they act out or are caught, and that after reading the material presented here, they may realize that they could have some serious personal issues that need to be addressed with appropriate professional help, before their theft offenses damage or destroy their careers, social standing, or worse.

It is now part of my standard assessment procedure, in the initial interview, to tenaciously inquire as what events and situations may have transpired in the individual's life at, or just prior to, the offender committed the act of theft. Conscientious effort is required to ferret out the full answers to this inquiry.

Clients frequently do not provide complete answers to the initial queries regarding what noteworthy events or circumstances existed or transpired at or just prior to their committing their offenses. This is not usually because they are being deliberately evasive, but rather because they do not have a mental set that has sought out such connections prior to the interview. However, persistence will usually provide a reasonably full picture of the events in the perpetrator's life at about the time of the offense.

The answers to the question, "Why did this person steal?" usually include one or more of the following factors:

(1) the person may have reacted by stealing to some traumatic event which occurred just prior to the act of theft;

(2) The individual had not coped adequately with the traumatic event; if she or he had, then the theft behavior would not have occurred;

(3) The traumatic event, our investigations showed, usually involved the person experiencing (or at least anticipating) some personally meaningful loss;

(4) Much earlier in the theft offender's life, usually in childhood, he or she experienced some very serious and unusual stressors and/or major personal losses. Furthermore, this childhood trauma was not appropriately dealt with at the time, nor since; and...

(5) As a result of item (4), the individual, now an adult, has remained particularly sensitive and vulnerable to perceived or actual loss, and especially loss that can be interpreted (at least at an unconscious level), as representing rejection, and/or abandonment.

Reluctance by the client to spontaneously offer important data may be due, on occasion, to psychological blocking on his or her part because of continuing emotional difficulty dealing with the traumatic event that may have precipitated the behavior.

As mentioned previously, birthdays, anniversaries, as well as Christmas and other supposedly happy and memorable occasions may, in the then-prevailing circumstances of the offender's life, not --in fact-- be happy events. Indeed, the offender might wish to forget the occasion altogether but feels obliged to "come across with a gift or acknowledgement of some sort." These are the sorts of conditions in which atypical theft offenses are particularly prone to occur.

My usual advice to persons who are going shopping for a present for someone whom they are currently seriously displeased with, is that they should be on guard for possible 'small indiscretions' that may be perceived as acts of theft. It is undoubtedly better -- if more uncomfortable -- to admit, at least to oneself, that the card or gift is being given under duress, and that the feelings in regard to the person or the event being 'celebrated' need to be examined and dealt with in a constructive and psychologically healthy manner.

81

Shoplifting and depression

It should be noted that nearly all the persons we assessed for shoplifting offenses were at least somewhat depressed at the time of the testing procedure. Small wonder! Many of them were facing court, and the distinct possibility of public humiliation at best, and in some instances, the prospect of a vocational disaster (such as disbarment, as was the prospect in the case of the lawyer, Bert, Case # 4).

It is worthwhile noting that in many of the cases I have dealt with, the offenders have made their way to my office only after repeated charges and convictions. They have frequently arrived with a sense of frustration, and even futility, afraid that there is no way of stopping what they experience as their out-of-control behavior. When they have begun treatment they usually experience, in short order, a relief and reassurance that there are reasons behind their acting out, that these underlying reasons can be successfully uncovered, confronted and dealt with.

Through the use of specific psychotherapeutic techniques and methods, they learn new and decidedly different ways of coping with life's stressors. These measures offer the most promise for stopping their inappropriate and illegal coping approaches.

CHAPTER 9

THE CONNECTION BETWEEN CANCER, LOSS AND THEFT

A not uncommon case of atypical theft behavior related to the occurrence of cancer in a 'significant other' follows:

*****

Case # 11: Betty Ann; The shopper who stole an item that symbolizes her cancer-stricken friend

Forty-year- old Betty Ann, a business consultant, had felt so very sad as she flew into New York City to visit her friend, Susan, -- a 36 year old accomplished photographer -- now with a cancerous tumor whose prognosis was very serious. As she flew into La Guardia airport, Betty Ann thought of how beauty, success and virtually everything, no matter how seemingly secure, could be brought down by that 'damned disease'. As her mother had been brought down when Betty Ann was 8 years old. As her grandmother had been brought down when in her sixties, but only after a long, hard -- and oh, so painful --- fight. Now Susan had terminal cancer and Betty Ann was losing her, too.

After a valiant but sorrowful afternoon with Susan, trading stories about and looking at pictures Susan had taken over the years of their "good old times," and thereby probably saying good-bye to one another while acknowledging how much they meant to one another, Betty Ann decided to stroll through some of the shops she loved to visit whenever she was in New York City. A particular department store was her happy favorite, and it was there that she decided to buy a lovely black blouse for $175. As she left the premises she was stopped by a loss prevention person and arrested for possession of a pack of three rolls of 35-mm film.

Betty Ann did own a Polaroid camera and a camcorder, but not a 35-mm camera. Of course, Susan mainly took pictures with her array of 35-mm. cameras.

*****

83

Now consider the case of Steve, a law student who nearly destroyed his intended career because of having forged his mother's name to a check for $150, made out to himself.

*****

Case # 12: Steve, the outstanding law student who broke the law and nearly destroyed his future

At 23 years of age, and near the top of his class in final year law at an Ivy league university, Steve should only have been looking ahead to his final exams, the enriching experiences he would have at the prestigious law firm that had accepted him for clerking (articling), and finally being able to afford to move out of his mother's home and into a downtown apartment. They were a team, he and mom. She, a research biologist, had put him through law school: he gave her the comfort of love and some remaining semblance of family, and the knowledge that she had done some things right, after all, in moving her small family (consisting of herself, Steve and his younger sister, Cynthia) to America from England fifteen years ago shortly after her husband's death.

Five years ago Cynthia had suffered very serious injuries in a bike accident, she was rushed to the local teaching hospital and operated on in a desperate attempt to save her life. She died on the operating table. Steve's mother was never the same afterwards.

A month ago, Steve's mother learned that she had cancer. Her operation was set for a month later, and at the very hour she was in surgery, Steve's image was being captured by a bank branch's TV camera while he attempted to pass a crudely forged check on his mother's bank account. The virtual ruins of Steve's almost completed law studies were recorded for posterity on the bank's video tape.

*****

In the years during which I have assessed persons who have acted out, what were for them, atypical acts of theft, again and again the issue of the occurrence of cancer in a loved one or in the offender, has emerged. As indicated in the previous chapter the proportion of cases in the original study in

84

which such circumstances prevailed was nearly 30%. In the more recent study the figure was 11%.

Of course, it might be argued that cancer is such a prevalent disease in our society that the likelihood of its occurring in proximity to any one person is rather substantial. But the point is that *the theft offenses have often been noted to have occurred in very close temporal proximity to the occurrence of cancer.* It is not just that the offender knows someone who has or had cancer at some point in his/her life. But rather, the key point is that the act of theft occurred very shortly after the cancer was diagnosed in the offender or a significant other, or after the cancer had taken a body part, or a significant other's life.

More about the relationship between Loss and Theft

As explained in the last chapter, we had come to understand that shoplifting was in some cases an apparent response to actual or anticipated personally meaningful losses. We noted, also, that the unconscious mind seems to make a meaningful connection between losing something and wanting to fill the void left by what was lost. We observed, in case after case, that some persons responded to losses, especially what they perceived to be *unfair* losses, by causing 'someone/something else' to experience unfair losses.

> It is this element of <u>perceived unfairness</u> that may be the most essential aspect of the phenomenon we are examining.

After all, why not just simply go shopping when experiencing an unhappy or deprived period. Isn't that precisely what many of us do, certainly in enough numbers as to have brought into being a supposedly humorous saying that proclaims, "When the going gets tough, the tough go shopping!" Perhaps an addendum to the above line could be: "... and the excessively loss-reactive may go shoplifting!"

Why the connection between cancer and theft?

Why cancer, then? Is there something unique to cancer that would precipitate shoplifting? If the Loss-Substitution Hypothesis is valid, then don't people shoplift when their close ones experience other diseases, such as heart attacks or loss of limbs? Of course, some clients have acted out by stealing when these and other diseases have touched their lives, or those of their friends! I have assessed many cases where shoplifting followed a variety of non-cancer physical illnesses.

I opinion is that there is no restriction or limitation on the *kind* of perceived losses that may be reacted to by atypical theft behavior. And yet no other disease was as prominently represented in the original study's findings. And so it is worthwhile, I believe, highlighting the matter of the occurrence of cancer in cases of atypical theft behavior, in part to hopefully prevent some future atypical theft behavior by introducing this possible connection into the literature. If enough people become aware of this potential relationship, then perhaps they will become more sensitive to the possibility of their acting out by stealing when dealing with the issue of cancer in themselves or significant others, and by being self-vigilant may *not* steal.

The case of a friend's wife who caught herself in the act

In fact, a lawyer-friend with whom I had shared the finding of the cancer-shoplifting connection, called me to thank me for my work because, she said, on a recent visit to a shopping plaza following surgery for removal of a cancerous lump in her breast, she had found herself on the verge of putting a lipstick into her purse without paying for it. She said she could distinctly feel a strong desire to "just take the item and leave the store". At that moment she thought of my comments about our investigations into shoplifting, and she put the tube back on the display counter, with a sense of what she described to me as a combination of "shock and amazement," realizing that she had been on the verge of possibly becoming 'a statistic' in our investigations.

She said that whereas she had initially thought our findings were fascinating but related to the kinds of persons she had trouble personally identifying with, she now knew precisely what it actually felt like to want to take something in a compensatory fashion.

It is hoped that this book will be at least as valuable as a preventive device as it hopefully is a resource for understanding and dealing with such cases where the thefts have already occurred.

The Suicidal Potential of Atypical Theft Offenders

A few years ago I read of a police officer who suicided after having been apprehended for shoplifting. This had been his second offense. When he had been caught the first time, he apparently had been suspended pending an internal investigation. Eventually he was reinstated. He shoplifted again two weeks later, was apprehended and charged. He shot himself in the head with his service revolver later that same day.

I sent a letter to the chief of police of that city, along with a copy of our original article, and urged that any future cases be dealt with in the light of our findings, with an awareness that there may be a genuine suicidal potential present, regardless of how little the stolen item was worth in monetary terms.

*****

Case # 13: Harvey, The Cop/shoplifter who wanted to kill himself, and a telephone call that probably saved his life.

It was a few years after the above-mentioned police officer's suicide that I saw an article in a major American newspaper about another police officer who had been suspended following his being apprehended for shoplifting. The extremely thorough article mentioned that this man's mother had died after a long fight with cancer, two days before the shoplifting incident. The article went on to give the man's name (an unusual one) and even his street address.

With the memory of the earlier suicide of a policeman who had been charged with theft still fresh in my mind, and with the knowledge that most people were still not aware of the possible relationship between shoplifting and loss, and of the suicidal potential of some Atypical Theft Offender cases, I became very concerned for this police officer whose conduct and identity had been revealed to a potential two million readers of a large city daily.

Having dealt with a number of police officer –Atypical Theft Offenders over the twelve years I was on staff at the Clarke Institute of Psychiatry, I was familiar with the self-punitive and suicidal potential of some members of this highly stressed profession. I considered calling the person referred to in the article, yet I hesitated. I wanted him to be aware of our investigations; I wanted him to understand that he may have shoplifted for reasons having to do with his loss of his mother, and that regardless he should be very careful about drawing any negative conclusions about his self-worth from his behavior. Most of all I wanted him to not kill himself.

For approximately 20 minutes I debated with myself about my proposed action. What if I did call him? Would it be an unwarranted, and unwanted intrusion? Would he, or some of my colleagues possibly even consider that I was 'soliciting' a potential client by calling and offering to send this man a copy of our original article?

I also kept thinking about the other police officer who had suicided. I considered the risk of being misunderstood as to my intentions if I called, and compared that risk with how I would think and feel if I did nothing and this man was to suicide. So, I called him.

We spoke for about 10 minutes. No, he had not known of our clinical investigations. Yes, he would appreciate a copy of the article. I sent it, and then heard nothing more from or about him.

***Three years later** I received a call from the officer. He said that he was calling to let me know that my phone call was made exactly at the time when he was walking around his home looking for the keys to his police cruiser. His intention was to go for a drive into the country, away from his spouse and children who were at home, and kill himself. My call had provided him with information that countered directly what he was telling himself about what a fraud he must be since his theft behavior clearly indicated to him that he was at the least a hypocrite and would be the talk, and joke, of his precinct. It turned out that his lawyer had used the article to assist this officer in court, and the officer had then gone into treatment with a caring and competent clinician who was familiar with our study's findings.*

*****

How Atypical Theft Offenders and the courts have reacted to these findings

Persons learning about our investigations' findings for the first time might understandably predict that most clients would enthusiastically embrace the Loss-Substitution Hypothesis. Especially if they thought that the courts might be more lenient with them if the judges involved were to believe that there were serious personal psychological difficulties impacting on the offenders at the time of their offenses.

My experience is, indeed, that the courts are usually very receptive to the formulations that I have made in many theft cases. In fact, the judges involved in such cases are typically relieved and appreciative to have a report that provides a plausible explanation that helps them comprehend why it is that the 'solid citizen'-type persons appearing before them would possibly risk so much for usually so little gain, by having stolen perhaps a wrench, a few rolls of film, or a door knob.

<u>Actually, the courts are sometimes more receptive to the findings of my assessments than are the offender themselves.</u> Some offenders, perhaps about 60% to 75% of them, readily digest the findings of my assessments and do use them to assist themselves in acknowledge and deal with the underlying reasons for their actions.

<u>However, the other 25% to 40% of the clients I encounter have somewhat more difficulty with my findings.</u> These persons are often disbelieving, or at least rather doubtful, when I present them with my clinical assessment. As Bert (the lawyer, case #4) told me, *"Sir! I have always had the highest regard for 'the law.' I have never been too kindly disposed to those individuals who pleaded some sort of excuse to explain away why they stole, or in any other fashion, broke 'the law.' And now, here I am, having done something for reasons I admit that I do not understand, and here you are, some shrink-type person -- pardon me for saying so- --trying to give me some psychobabble to explain away my absolutely inexcusable conduct. I won't allow that to happen!"*

"I appreciate that you are trying to help, Dr. Cupchik. But do you know what it will mean to my perception of other offenders if I accept the possibility that my theft is explainable in such a way as to lessen my responsibility or guilt! Sure, I don't want to lose my license to practice law. But I believe that what I did was wrong, and that I deserve to be punished. So there you have it, sir. Excuse me, but it will be very difficult for me to accept any explanation for my behavior, other than I am not really as ethical, or honest, or honorable a person as I had previously thought."

Well, he was an ethical, honest, and honorable person who had been dealing with a terribly distressing situation, namely the possible terminal illness of his child, and, in my clinical opinion, he had acted out in response to these psychological pressures and the anticipation of the terribly unfair and all too possible loss of his son!

Many of the Atypical Theft Offenders I have assessed have several similarities in personality and perceptions:

(1) these persons are often **very psychologically naive**. They tend to not think in terms of subconscious or unconscious thoughts, feelings, or motivations. They fail to appreciate the breadth and depth of their own mental functioning, in other words. And, what follows from this lack of psychological awareness is usually another feature they have in common, namely...

(2) they frequently exhibit a harsh **self-punitiveness**. These persons often do not appreciate that they may continue to react strongly to a disturbing event at an unconscious level, even if they manage to block out much conscious thinking about the event. For example, if a loved one's life is lost, it takes considerable time and effort and experiencing painful emotions to work through, that is, to complete the mourning of the loss.

Just the fact that the individual may control his or her conscious mind in such a way as to avoid thinking about the loss does not mean that the unconscious mind is similarly distracted or blocked from ruminating about the subject. Indeed, their night dreams frequently take on the nature of nightmares, thereby signaling that their psyches are striving to deal with the disturbing issue. While there is some truth to the maxim that "Nothing is but thinking makes it so!", the individual is advised to consider that the term 'thinking' includes *unconscious* and *subconscious* as well as *conscious* thoughts (and feelings).

As an illustration I mention below the case of a person who hid from himself the fact that he was both extremely angry and severely depressed. (Sonny, Case # 14)

(3) Not infrequently, **they display a rigidity and defensiveness in regard to their thoughts, feelings and behavior**. Stemming in part from their naiveté, they are not used to examining their motivations or entertaining the notion that their behavior may sometimes be precipitated by some subconscious or unconscious motivations of which they are not aware. They may be quite

defensive and averse to changing their views when these new possibilities are discussed. A case in point follows.

*****

Case # 14: Sonny; the engineer with the repressed depression

Sonny was a 43 year old senior engineer with a large aerospace company who had been charged with shoplifting and presented with the sole symptom of experiencing extreme and chronic tiredness. He reported that he was frequently so tired, even after a full and evidently good night's sleep, that he had taken up the habit of closing his office door and having half-hour long 'snoozes' in the middle of both the morning and afternoon. Comprehensive medical tests had indicated that there was no apparent physiological or other medical reason why this previously energetic and productive professional should have become chronically tired.

Any personal questions about Sonny's home life were usually responded to in a cheerful, smiling manner. "Of course, everything at home is fine. I live with my mother and she and I get along very well. No, I don't feel any pressure to leave home. Yes, I know most men my age live on their own. No, I am not afraid to leave the house! I just simply enjoy living with my mother; also, I can save money and I don't see anything wrong with that!"

Sonny was sent to for a full psychological assessment. The results were most interesting. The assessment report noted that certain tests aimed at uncovering subconscious and unconscious material clearly indicated the presence of a marked depression in this client as well as a great deal of resentment towards his mother. What was particularly noteworthy was that this person was not consciously aware of his depression, let alone his resentment. His was a repressed depression. Any attempt to query him in this area was fruitless, as he vehemently denied experiencing depression, and certainly had no awareness of any anger towards his mother. All he felt, almost all the time, was great tiredness.

This client was a member of a weekly therapy group that I led. One evening I gave the group members an original mental imagery exercise[xi] that I had created (and which was the subject of my doctoral dissertation[xii]), one that assesses the status and psychodynamics of a significant interpersonal

91

relationship. Sonny client had a profound breakthrough via this exercise, getting in touch with both his heretofore repressed depression and his marked resentment towards his mother. The psychological effort he had to expend in order to keep those feelings repressed had seriously depleted his energy level. This was evidently why he had been so tired much of the time.

As he worked in therapy on his deeper feelings towards his mother, his depression, resentment and tiredness rapidly lifted. Within six months he had moved out of his mother's apartment and had bought himself a condominium.

*****

We shall now consider one more case that also illustrates the issues we are discussing in this chapter.

*****

Case # 15: Estelle, the hard-driving executive who learned of her possibly malignant tumor and immediately went shoplifting

In 1984, Estelle was a person in her early forties, a church-going person who had been happily married for over 18 years, with two bright and healthy teenage children. She was also a highly regarded senior executive with a software firm. On one particular afternoon she left her gynecologist's office after her annual checkup, having been told, to her total surprise, that she had what might well be a cancerous tumor in her ovaries.

Estelle had earlier arranged to meet a girl friend at a restaurant in the shopping mall near her doctor's office. She had not been at all prepared for any troublesome diagnosis. Yet she had greatly feared cancer during the past few years. Her mother had died of cancer six years earlier. Then her aunt Monique (twelve years older than Estelle) had gotten cancer of the stomach two years ago. Monique's disease was now in remission. Estelle and Monique looked somewhat alike, to the point that they were used to strangers who saw them together often assumed they were sisters.

Estelle was especially proud that she had exceptional blue-green eyes. These she usually highlighted with expert use of an eye pencil, eye shadow, and mascara. When she passed a mirrored wall in the plaza a few minutes after leaving her doctor's office, she was shocked to see a reflection of herself with streaks of black and blue coloring cascading down her cheeks. She only then realized that she had been crying, probably from the time she had left the doctor's office clutching the card bearing the time of the appointment he had made for her with an oncologist at the teaching hospital downtown for the following week.

Now Estelle ducked into a washroom and sat in a cubicle crying uncontrollably. "No, damn it, not me! Not now! No, no!" she cried aloud. Her tears flowed unabated. After about ten minutes they subsided, only to be replaced by a trembling that she could not suppress. Eventually she made her way to the sink and washed away as much makeup as she could from her now puffed up and incredibly frightened looking face.

On her way to the restaurant at the other end of the mall she went into an upscale department store and moved quickly to the cosmetic counter to obtain a new eyebrow pencil. Her old eyebrow pencil was unusable, she had discovered in the washroom when she checked her purse. She was now frustrated to learn that the store had run out of her choice of pencil (an expensive make).

She left the store feeling scared, angry and very shaky, her mind turning over her physician's words, and thinking about how and what to tell her spouse and children. She next passed a drug store that sometimes carried an acceptable, though definitely less desirable, make of eyebrow pencil. She entered the store, found the appropriate aisle, picked up an eyebrow pencil, as well as a copy of Newsweek, and then paid for them on her way out of the store. She also recalled thinking to herself as she had stood in line waiting to pay for the items that she really should, one of these days, stop using aerosol-type cans of hair spray.

When she was stopped (once she had exited the drug store) by "the rather rude little man" who identified himself as a loss-prevention employee, and was told that he thought she had something in her purse that belonged to the store and that she had not paid for, she began to protest in no uncertain terms. He was 'wrong, ridiculous, and should be careful how he spoke to her, for she would surely see the manager about his bizarre accusation! Nevertheless, she did hand him the plastic bag containing the eye pencils and the magazine as he requested. When he insisted that she open her purse, and then proceeded to extract an apparently unused can of non-aerosol hair spray with the store's price tag still on it, she was completely taken aback.

She was positive that there was no way that item should have or could have gotten into her purse. She became unnerved and verbally abusive, accusing the loss prevention person of having planted the can in her purse through some sort of 'sleight of hand' trick. He requested that she accompany him to the security office. After an initially shouted "No way!", she noticed other shoppers looking at her with that special, quizzical yet disdainful, glance reserved by some honest shoppers for those who are apprehended by security personnel in shopping malls. She then decided that she would go along and certainly straighten things out with the manager, who "this rude person" had assured her, she could speak to if she would only accompany him to the office.

When Estelle first came into my office, a week or so after the incident, she was still in a highly defensive and resentful state of mind. The only reason she had come along was because her lawyer had insisted that she do, so that a proper clinical assessment might be conducted. He had told her that I specialize in such cases, and she had told him that she had not taken the item. Now, a week after the unpleasant incident, she was certain that the man had planted the item in her bag.

This was a case of someone charged with a theft who sincerely believed that she had not committed the act of which she was accused. At last she calmed down and complied with my request that she tell me, in a chronological fashion, just what had happened on the day she was apprehended.

When she came to the part about the man finding the can in her bag she again insisted that she would have known if she had taken the item, and that she most certainly had not.

When I attempted to explain to her that our investigations had found cases where a provisional diagnosis of cancer had evidently precipitated acting out behavior of the sort with which she had been charged, she was hardly receptive to the information. "That's ridiculous and far-fetched, don't you think?", she asked sarcastically? "Nevertheless," I responded, "that is what we have found has happened in many cases." She assured me -- and on this point I did believe her -- that if she had consciously knew she had taken the item in question, (and, she further assured me, she had never done such a thing in her life before, and certainly had no financial need to do now, given her six-figure salary), then she would have admitted it to me.

I have to acknowledge that I missed the significance of what turned out to be one of the most important things she told me in the first interview, and only caught it as I reread my notes while waiting for her to arrive (late) for her second appointment.

<u>According to my notes, she had told me that she had thought, while she had been in the drug store, of switching to a non-aerosol type of can of hair spray.</u> Why would she, or anyone want to do such a thing? One major answer, of course, is that most of us are now aware that some aerosol sprays of the type used in the 1980's were found to be a major source of depletion of the ozone layer, and that such a depletion was thought by scientists to be a principal cause of the drastic increase in (skin) cancers.

When I queried Estelle about her thinking at the time she was in the store she denied having ever thought of the reasoning I have outlined above. She had not thought about the ozone layer! Or skin cancer! Only that she should switch to non-aerosol cans. No, she did not know why!

*****

I believe that it is very likely that at some level of her psyche Estelle had been immersed in thinking about the possibility of her having a malignant growth, and that by association the matter of non-aerosol vs. aerosol cans had emerged, at least in her subconscious or unconscious mind, as she passed through the store. Apparently the entire sequence of associated thoughts dealing with why she should bother switching, either was not brought into consciousness, or was not remembered. This explains why she may have taken the item.

Chapter 10

THE PSYCHOLOGICAL RELATIONSHIP OF LOSSES TO COMPULSIVE SHOPPING, GAMBLING AND SHOPLIFTING

In this chapter we shall consider, firstly, two *non*-theft offender cases of 'normal' persons, and their behaviors after having experienced personally meaningful losses. Many of us can relate to their actions as ways in which losses are often reacted to by people in our society (although perhaps not in as grandiose a style).

*****

Case # 16: Jim; The man who lost a common-law partner but gained a 4wd vehicle

When Louise told Jim that she was moving out his feelings ranged from rage to relief. After months of feuding over nearly everything (or so it seemed), she had finally carried out her oft-repeated threat. When Jim came home from the office on Friday afternoon, every stick of her furniture, her clothes and books, etc... were gone.

For a few days following, Jim fully expected Louise to call and -- according to his main fantasy-- she would ask him to "please, lets work it out, Jim. Tell me you'll go into therapy, alone or with me, and lets give it a chance, Hon!" He had even decided that his answer, for once, would be, "OK, if that's what you really want, dear," a major departure from his "I don't need a damn shrink!" Well, he thought, she was probably just staying with her folks in upstate New York for a week or so and then she would be back.

When the letter with the so familiar handwriting arrived a couple of weeks later, Jim's heart raced with excitement as he impatiently waited for the crowded elevator to finally get to his floor. But when he glanced again at the envelope he had the sense that something was not right. He finally noticed the post mark -- "San Francisco, for Pete's sake!".

When he got into the apartment, he poured himself a scotch and opened the envelope to discover a very brief letter. Now he received another shock. Louise informed him that the company she worked for had agreed to a request she had evidently made three months earlier, "for a transfer to another city. Good-bye, Jim. If you ever wake up to what you have missed out on, and only after you have gotten professional help for yourself, you can call. If I'm not otherwise busy at that time perhaps we'll talk."

"Damn! Damn!!!" For a few hours Jim was dazed. He had recently told her that he saw no reason to get married. They had lived together for nearly three years, and things had been "okay," as far as Jim was concerned, at least until she had started pushing for marriage -- and babies!

It was Friday evening. Jim went for a long walk, uptown, past the fancy stores, most of which were open late. Further uptown, past the car showroom dealerships. He now consoled himself with the thought that at least the second parking spot he had purchased at his condo (for $25,000 extra) for Louise was now vacant. Maybe he would put up a sign in the condo office and try to rent it out.

The hell he would! So she was gone, huh? Okay. So, that meant there was going to be more time to travel up to his cabin that she never liked all that much anyway, and that he loved! So he would just go up there more often. These were some of the thoughts he recalled having as he walked past the Mercedes dealership, past the Jag dealership. When he got to the Lexus dealership he stopped dead in his tracks. A huge sign that listed the extras on a new four-wheel-drive SUV, with a bottom line of $55,000, stuck him to the spot. An extravagance, of course! Not strictly necessary, true! But the attraction was undeniably immense. Jim walked into the dealership, took a test drive, and by the end of the week the second empty parking spot was no longer staring at him as he wheeled in at the end of a long day. Instead, his new 'mate' was there to greet him... "Hi, Hon, welcome home!"

*****

Compensation-by-Substitution

Lest any readers be too inclined to consider the above story farfetched they are hereby asked to recall whether, when they were children, their caregivers had ever attempted to compensate them for a loss by saying, "That's

97

okay, dear. We'll get you another one." Or, "Come on, we'll go buy you a new toy car (or doll, or baseball mitt, etc...)", to get your mind off some loss, or leave-taking of a friend, or a pet.

Compensation--by-substitution (of a person, object, or place) by acquiring some *other* 'thing', whether similar in function or not, is included in some of our earliest experiences. Freudians might suggest that the introduction of pacifiers to compensate for the absence of the desired breast may have also greatly promoted the compensation-by-substitution theme in many peoples' lives.

Such replacement even works, to some extent!

Decades ago, the psychologist Harlow[xiii] experimented with baby monkeys who were removed from their mothers and who were then given the choice of (a) a wire form in the general shape of a larger monkey, or (b) an identical wire form in the shape of larger monkey, but one that had been covered with foam rubber and a terry cloth, making it softer and more "cuddly." The test subjects showed a clear preference for the terry-clothed mother substitute. Those monkeys who had been placed with the (a) type wire form soon became agitated and anxious. They calmed down, however, and seemed generally reassured and comforted by the physical proximity and soft tactile experience of contact with the then introduced terry-cloth covered shape.

Lets face it! Pacifiers do work, more or less effectively. As do our own thumbs. As do, apparently, cigarettes, pipes and cigars (even unlit), toothpicks, gum, candies, any other foods, and some drugs. Some are just much more or less adequate and/or dangerous and/or expensive than others.

Imaginary playmates also may have provided compensation-by-substitution when we were children. One of the main functions of what we call 'toys' and 'pets' is that they provide us with objects in the real world upon which we project or identify certain personal qualities and capabilities ("good, dog", "eat your food, Barbie and Ken," etc...as well as psychological or interpersonal attributes; "No I can't go to camp without my teddy bear. *It* would miss *me* too much!"

When, as adults, we lose something meaningful to us, the desire to compensate ourselves for our losses can be very powerful indeed! If the loss is also considered to have been *unfair*, then this tendency to compensate ourselves may be very intense, indeed. Just as a two or three year old child will reach out for *almost anything else* to play with or hold when something else he or she had been playing with (such as a cigarette lighter, or an empty glass) has been taken away, an adults may be inclined to reach for compensatory 'things' as well. Furthermore, if the individual perceives his or her loss to have been unfair or unjust, there is a certain degree of retribution to be relished in acquiring the compensatory item in an unfair, or unjust (read illegal) fashion.

Now, consider one other case of compensation-by-substitution...

*****

Case # 17: Marge; Who lost a husband but gained a dog

Marge was a physician whose marriage had broken up three years before I met her at a conference in San Diego. When I saw her talking in what appeared to be a casual manner with a colleague of mine I walked up to join them. As I patiently listened while they were conversing, I realized that Marge was speaking about someone named Robert, who was very meaningful to her. She spent most weekends with him, and they apparently really enjoyed going for long walks and rides together. Robert was a great comfort to her; they had evidently met soon after her spouse had left. When I innocently piped in with the thought that I was sorry Robert couldn't make it to the conference, they both looked at me with expressions of shock, followed by laughter and a speedy explanation on Marge's part that Robert was a horse whom she had bought (and renamed) within weeks of the time that her husband Thomas had left.

Marge was quite aware that she had given the horse what was usually a human being's name, but she said that that was merely coincidence. Nevertheless, as she spoke further about him, it became clear that her preoccupation with Robert, grooming, feeding, housing, maintaining, running and training with, traveling to competitions with, spending days with, talking about, etc...left her little time for a more orthodox social life. She was vaguely aware that the horse took the place of a good human companion, which, she readily said, he was better than in many ways, anyway. She also said that she felt more comfortable around him than most of the men she had met in the past couple of years.

*****

Jim and Marge are but two examples of persons who have found themselves inclined, probably temporarily, to replace an interpersonal human-human relationship with some*thing* else (a 4-wheeled vehicle), or some*one* else (albeit a member of a different species). Most persons, when they lose a relationship, find another relationship -- of some sort! Jim and Marge did.

The point is that frustrations and tensions of life are often reacted to by many 'normal' persons by their going out and getting themselves "a little (compensatory) treat"; an ice cream cone, a shirt or blouse, new underwear, something that says "Hey, it's okay! Enjoy! Here's something to feel good about--or with."

Some people may be inclined to get themselves more expensive items. Regardless, the 'name of the game' is obtaining some compensation-by-substitution for losses. The expression, "He got her 'on the rebound,'" comes to mind, as well, in this context.

An undoubtedly smaller number of people may go on major spending sprees when highly stressed, or distressed. For some of these persons, those we call **compulsive shoppers**, large bills may be accumulated as a result of their having engaged in massive spending orgies in response to experiencing deprivation and/or losses. For a not insignificant number of persons however, losses and stressors are responded to by acts of shoplifting.

If they know its wrong and bad for them, and they want to stop, then why don't they simply stop?

I believe that it was Albert Sweitzer who said that "The problem in life is not what we don't know; it's what we won't do!" Substantially overweight persons, who know that their high blood pressure, high cholesterol levels, or their families' histories of heart disease make it imperative for them to reduce their food consumption, lose weight and to increase their exercise regime, nevertheless sometimes have trouble doing so. There are specialized clinics, best-selling diet authors and weight loss practitioners galore who receive hundreds of millions of dollars every year in the US and around the world to assist people to lose weight, i.e., to do what they know they should do, for their own sake. These clients say they "want to lose weight" but in spite of their best intentions, continue to overeat and endanger their health and well being. Yet in our society it is not illegal to overeat; just wrong, undesirable, unhealthy, and in certain instances, plain life-threatening. Many of these intelligent, ill, and overeating persons consciously want to stop yet have immense difficulty doing so.

So it is with Atypical Theft Offenders. They know what they should do, for their own sake, and they are generally sincere when they say that they "want to stop shoplifting," but in spite of their best intentions, they continue to shoplift and endanger their livelihoods, financial resources, lifestyles, and even their freedom.

But surely everybody suffers 'unfair' losses! Why doesn't everybody shoplift, then?

This is of course an important question! Certainly nearly everyone, at some time or other, experiences extreme stress and decidedly unfair losses. Why is it then that we all do not shoplift, at least some of the time?

Well, for one thing, we know that not everyone reacts the same way to the same kind of stress, or distress. Some persons, as indicated above, overeat (or under eat) in response to stress. Other people drink too much and/or smoke and/or overwork and/or become violent.

Why would person A do one thing while persons B and C choose other ways of acting out in response to stress or loss? No one, and certainly no professional, can answer these questions, in every case for every person. In the 12 years during which I was on staff at the Clarke Institute, I assessed and attempted to treat people who had stolen, from, assaulted, raped, or murdered their spouses, children, friends, or even total strangers. Sometimes we were not able to determine, to a sufficiently satisfying degree, why many of these persons had carried out the particular acts they did (rather than doing something else).

On the other hand, as a team, we psychiatrists, psychologists, social workers, and psychiatric nurses, with the help of other professionals, *were* able to determine plausible answers in most cases. It is true that people are different; we react differently from one another to similar events. And yet, of course, there are some commonalties among many of us.

There are also commonalties among Atypical Theft Offenders (as listed previously), which is why it is possible to categorize them and refer to them as a group.

> **The major underlying common feature of most Atypical Theft Offenders appears to be the existence of unresolved earlier losses (usually in childhood), including those that involved major rejection and/or abandonment.**

Stealing as a Response to Losses in Childhood

Some children, whether for purposes of obtaining symbolic compensation, and/or as a means of expressing their resentment, may take things from peers, parents, or from stores, in response to experiencing personally meaningful losses. Stealing, or any other behavioral response pattern for that matter, to the extent that it provides some experienced momentary solace, or security, or tension release, may become a preferred response set for that person. Then, when that child becomes an adult and is then faced with an analogous (from a psychodynamic perspective) circumstance, he or she may respond somewhat similarly. (Recall Case #7, Martha, the person whose mother was a seamstress, and whose father died in her arms in a field during the W.W.II, and who did not steal until her household pet (and 'child substitute') was injured and had to be put down. Almost immediately thereafter she began shoplifting dresses, until she had accumulated over 150 of them.)

As children most of us suffered losses of varying degrees of severity. Some of us, however, experienced what must be considered relatively major personal losses that may have had a genuinely traumatic aspect; for instance, the loss of one or both parents due to death or divorce. Others have experienced separation from the family home for extended periods of time (due to having been sent away to boarding school, or to another country for safe-keeping, or for the sake of greater opportunities). Adoption, also, is an experience that may have involved many if not most of the above elements -- that is, separation, loss and trauma.

In response to the occurrence of life's disturbing events many if not most children seek out an object that will serve as a symbolic substitution. Like the 'Peanuts' cartoon character, Linus, many of us, have gone through a 'security blanket' phase. (Arguably, our society's acquisitive aspect may reflect our never having left that phase entirely behind.)

> Having something, or in some cases, anything to hold onto may give us some (albeit erroneous) sense of security.

How may such an early orientation to acquiring and holding onto compensatory objects influence later behavioral responses to stressful circumstances?

Not All Atypical Theft Offenders Stole As Children

Already in this book we have discussed cases in which the theft behavior appears to have been classical, Atypical Theft Offender type acting out in response to then-recent losses, where no major childhood losses nor childhood theft behavior evidently occurred. See Case # 1, Bill and Case #4, Bert, for examples. For the sake of completeness in this regard, we shall now consider one additional such case.

*****

Case #18: Dora; A 60-year old who went on a shoplifting spree after her spouse told her that he was leaving their marriage for his 35-year old lover

Dora had been brought up in an essentially normal, happy household, one in which she was much loved and cared for by both parents and two older siblings. As a child she did not experience major loss nor did she exhibit theft behavior. Apparently well married, she and her spouse, Tony had operated a successful and well-known retail business for 25 years, selling at an opportune time and retiring while in their mid-fifties. They had worked hard, long hours together over many years to build their business. Having carefully and wisely invested their savings, and with luck on their side, they had profited in real estate and the stock market, and now could look forward to an enviable retirement with homes in both the Northeast and Florida. Sun, warmth, golfing, boating, good friends, almost everything appeared to have gone according to the ideal North American middle-class script.

It is difficult to describe the excruciatingly pained presentation of the emotionally shattered person who, within the first few moments of our initial meeting in my office, let loose a torrent of tears that continued unabated for several minutes. What a profound state of sadness and devastation this woman was experiencing!

She slowly, and with obvious embarrassment explained to me that, just less than ten months after they sold their business and retired Tony announced to Dora that he was leaving her for Maggie, their former bookkeeper 25 years Dora's junior. Tony claimed with insensitive bravo that Maggie had been his mistress for the past four years.

For Dora, at a conscious level at least, there had been not the slightest warning, not the least little clue. Tony left the marital home the very day he told Dora of the affair. Later that day she went to a mall and went on a shoplifting binge that involved stealing from eight stores in the space of two hours. When she was arrested she was attempting to put a four-foot tall teddy bear into the already full (with stolen goods) trunk of her car. (Incidentally, she had no children or grandchildren.) Over $3000 in stolen goods were recovered by the loss prevention person who had followed her as she moved back and forth from the mall's stores to her car at least three times.

A list of the stolen merchandise taken by Dora included two full set of dishes, three nightgowns, a combination engagement and wedding ring set, three sets of expensive sheets and pillowcases for a queen-size bed (hers was a king size), a cloth coat three sizes too small for her to wear, and (from the supermarket located in the mall) four rib steaks and a pork roast: Dora was a vegetarian. According to the police report Dora said that she suddenly "just felt like taking" the items in question; she had not put any deliberate conscious thought, as far as she was aware, into deciding which items to take before shoving them into shopping bag.

When our assessment was complete, it was my conclusion that in response to the fact and manner of her husband's leave-taking, Dora had suffered a profound shock, not only to her self-esteem but, as well, to her expectations of what the remainder of her life would likely be like. It seemed highly probable that she had experienced a major regression in response to her husband's announcement and leave-taking, and that her shoplifting behavior was an acting out component of her seriously regressed and grossly inadequate coping response.

*****

In an instance such as this, where the shocking and sweeping nature of the losses are profound, such circumstances seem to be sufficient, in some people, to result in A.T.O.--type behavior, without any major losses in childhood having been experienced by the theft offender.

The impact of war upon its victims, and the relationship of this experience to subsequent theft behavior

Of course, not every person who has experienced war or who has found it necessary to steal under extraordinary conditions in order to physically survive, thinks that stealing is henceforth a permissible and morally correct mode of behavior, especially in peacetime. Nevertheless, readers can understand and even sympathize with theft offenders who, as children, lived through terrible wartime conditions, and who, perhaps decades later, found themselves again in severely stressful circumstances, and have acted out via theft in response to these new circumstances. After all, that which since childhood has been associated within one's psyche with survival -- such as stealing food or goods -- can be a powerful 'response set' indeed when the psyche again experiences extreme stress at some time in the future.

Several years ago I assessed an accountant who, over a four year period, stole over $200,000 of *obsolete* computer hardware shortly after he nearly lost all his hard-earned savings in a Savings and Loan bankruptcy.

For the boy that still resided within the man who had worked hard and frugally saved for over three decades, the loss of most of his life's savings was a terrifying experience. This man's father, during W.W.II, had repeatedly sent him above ground between air-raid warnings to scrounge whatever he could (potatoes in the fields, lumps of coal, anything made of metal or wood, etc...) to help the family survive until the next bombing run, and the next, and so on.

His monetary loss in the S&L debacle was the new enemy that threatened his very survival. Under this great stress he regressed, and again stole and hoarded 'things' (in this case, computer hardware). This he did even though, at the mature, adult level of his psyche he understood that stealing and hoarding outdated computer software and hardware would not provide much protection during his retirement years.

Compulsive Gambling

Compulsive gambling has been an issue for some recent clients who have also shoplifted. It appears that compulsive gambling, like compulsive shoplifting, when carried out by persons who are hard-working and usually ethical individuals, acts as an albeit inappropriate means of expressing frustration and anger to perceived unfair losses. It is as if the individual has decided to risk a great deal in order to gain some monetary advantage, even when he or she has come to realize that the financial losses from the gambling have become prohibitively large. The thinking accompanying such activities is often filled with illogical self-rationalizations that may become even more extreme as the gambling losses mount. Even when the gambler wins a modest or substantial amount, rather than 'walking away from the table', he or she may risk it all in a last gasp effort to 'make a killing'.

The compulsive gambler, like the compulsive shopper or shoplifter, tends to avoid facing and dealing with the really important –and frequently quite painful—issues in his or her life – namely the serious loss that has been suffered.

Compulsive shopping involves spending a great deal of much money on too many items; there is a feeling of being unable to resist carrying out the activity.

Compulsive gambling involves risking a great deal of money against too great odds; there is a feeling of being unable to resist carrying out the activity.

Compulsive shoplifting involves risking reputation, livelihood and freedom for usually very little material or monetary gain; there is a feeling of being unable to resist carrying out the activity.

Clearly, excessive risk or expense for monetary or material gain, and a feeling of being unable to resist carrying out the activity, help describe and define all of these activities. As neurotic behavior has sometimes been defined as 'stupid actions carried out by intelligent persons', these three different kinds of activities very likely qualify. Neuroses are best treated with the assistance of a competent, experienced professional.

Chapter 11

ATYPICAL THEFT BEHAVIOR AS REGRESSIVE AND SYMBOLIC ACTS

The ingredients of symbolic encoding[xiv]

The term "symbolic encoding" (or "symbolism") can be defined as the representation of one or more ideas or images by other ideas and/or images. It may occur consciously intentionally, as during the creation of a corporate logo by a public relations artist, or less consciously unintentionally, as in dreams, fantasies and other occurrences.

Symbolic encoding can come about through one (or more) of three mental processes; condensation, displacement, and symbolization. There is value in discussing each of these briefly, since the reader will then be in a much better position to appreciate the cases presented in this book insofar as understanding why the offenders stole the particular items that they did. In the brief discussion to follow we shall consider these three mental processes as they are often manifested in our night dreams. The point that will be made here is that these same mechanisms operate in certain acts of theft as well.

I--Condensation is a mental symbolic process resulting in the fusion of two or more images or ideas. For example, such is the current connotation of the word 'plastic,' that when a person hands a bouquet of plastic flowers to someone as a 'gift', the receiver of this gift might well wonder if the giver's pronouncement of caring or affection is also "plastic" or phony, in other words, that the gift giver's gesture of appreciation or affection may not be 'real' (i.e., sincere), either.

It is my clinical experience that Atypical Theft Offenders have often given 'gifts' to significant others that they had, in fact, stolen. Even birthday or anniversary cards have been stolen by some sufficiently well-to-do A.T.O.s. The 'plastic' or phony implications of such supposed 'gift-giving' are rather obvious. Often the 'giver' has been harboring considerable resentment towards the gift's recipient. It is as if, at an unconscious level, the 'giver' is saying, "Okay, I know you expect to get something as a gift from me. But I am so angry, or frustrated with you, that I don't really want to spend any money on your gift. So I'll 'give' you something all right, but it isn't a real gift -- it's actually stolen merchandise. So there!"

Note that it has seldom happened, in my clinical experience with Atypical Theft Offenders, that they have recalled that this sort of thinking went on at a conscious level. Rather they are usually at a loss to explain why they stole the items they could easily have afforded to purchase to give as gifts. Not surprisingly, clinical treatment in such cases involves assisting the offenders to more directly and effectively confront and deal with their resentments towards the intended receivers of these gifts.

II--Displacement is the shift of emphasis or interest from one idea or image to another (usually less important in terms of relevance). Dreams of having homosexual experiences with strangers may be somewhat less suggestive compared to dreams of heterosexual liaisons, if the dreamer is a married, heterosexual female who is unwilling to acknowledge to herself that she is unhappy with her marriage.

Displacement may also operate in the realm of thefts carried out by Atypical Theft Offenders. Children sometimes steal money from their parents' pant pockets, wallets or purses. This act of displacement is a sort of compensatory behavior. What these children want is their parents' attention and affection; in the absence of getting same, they may compensate themselves for this lack by surreptitiously taking money from their parents with which they can then buy themselves comforting 'presents.'

Likewise, some Atypical Theft Offenders shoplift when they are angry with their spouses. It is not the store from which the items were taken, that the offender really wants 'the good (material) stuff'. They usually really want attention, support, and love (that is, good *emotional* things) from their spouses. Instead, they may displace their feelings of anger and deprivation onto the retail establishment. Obviously these individuals need to deal with *what* it is they really want, and from *whom*, if they are to stop these self-destructive acts of displacement.

III--Symbolization is the replacement of one idea or image by another that may have various formal features in common with what is being symbolized but which disguises the latter's dynamic significance. Thus, a man who is going into the hospital for a vasectomy may dream of the Tower of Pisa collapsing. Extensive analysis would probably be unnecessary to suggest the essence of this dream's symbolization, specifically that the male in question is fearing becoming impotent. In the realm of acts by Atypical Theft Offenders, however, it is only sometimes true that what has been taken represents in some clearly obvious fashion that which the offender is distressed about.

$$*****$$

Case # 19 Clara; the woman who stole a china figurine that symbolized her relationship with her recently deceased aunt

Two days after her aunt Sally had died Clara went to the department store where she periodically purchased china figurines to add to her already extensive collection. She went to pick up two pieces that she had ordered several weeks earlier. While she was waiting for the clerk to complete the sale she saw another piece with a name similar to her own, and she stole it.

Initially she was totally at a loss to explain why she would have actually stolen, rather than paid for, the piece. She certainly had more than ample funds to buy any china piece she wanted, and had always paid for the other items in her collection, all purchased from the very same store. She valued the store's policy of ordering pieces that she requested even though it evidently took some additional time, paperwork, etc... . The store had appreciated her as a loyal client for over two decades.

After sobbing in my office for several minutes she finally said, "I thought it would be nice to have a piece close to my name that would last. (The piece was called "Clarisa's granny". I picked it up and put it in a bag. Nobody saw me. I felt sick, hot, and dizzy. I couldn't make myself take it back out... It was of an old woman in a rocking chair and a little girl at her feet. I had seen it so many times. It gave me such comfort when I held it. I always wanted my mother to be white-haired and wear glasses and make brownies; aunt Sally was like that."

I don't know why they couldn't hear my heart beating so loudly. I walked around thinking, "Where do I go? What do I do? "Everything was turning around. "Can't they hear my voice?" I thought. I felt I had a smile painted on my face, just like the china pieces."

*****

I would suggest that Clara's theft of the china figurine was due in large part to her regressed state of early mourning and to its symbolic representation of the kind of relationship that she had just lost. All three kinds of symbolic encoding were involved.

1. Symbolization was involved; the figurine reminded her of the kind of relationship that she had had with her now deceased relative.

2. Condensation was likely involved, also, as the figurine represented a permanence (since it was made of china) of a kind and quality of relationship, and that in the face of the loss of the relationship she had with Sally, the china's permanence meant that Clara could have it with her for her full lifetime.

3. Displacement was involved as well. The figurine became the recipient of some of the emotional energy (cathexis) that Clara had about her relationship with Sally, and she could invest this energy in the figurine.

Keeping in mind these three processes through which symbolic encoding may take place, the reader might now want to review some of the other case histories presented so far to reflect upon the kinds of symbolic encoding processes that may have been operating in these cases. (Incidentally, it should be noted that in the literature the terms "symbolism," "symbolic encoding," and "symbolic transformation" are also used to refer to these same processes.)

Would that all cases were so marvelously symbolically transparent! Unfortunately, it is not the case. Often the object taken bears *no apparent symbolic resemblance* to that which has been lost. At least not beyond the simple essential fact that something was unfairly taken (i.e., stolen) after something else was (as perceived by the offender) unfairly lost. As will be

111

discussed below, however, in the momentarily regressed, child-like state in which most A.T.O.s carry out their acts of theft, 'to hold is to have,' and the person in such a state merely wants something to 'replace' the lost object.

Let us now turn to consider more thoroughly the phenomenon of regression in order to better understand the actions of the individuals who sometimes risk so absurdly much (in terms of career, relationships, self-esteem) for so ridiculously little (in monetary terms).

The Issue of Regression

It is noteworthy that psychoanalytic theories refer to *de*pression as a response to loss (perhaps the loss of a loved one, loss of status, etc...). Whatever the nature of the loss, the depressed person may react so intensely because the current situation reactivates the memory of an earlier traumatic loss that may have occurred in childhood -- as for example, the loss of mother's affection, or the death of one's father. Perhaps, for some reason, the then child's needs for affection and loving were not satisfied: then, a loss in later life causes the individual to *re*gress to the relatively more helpless, dependent state he or she was in when the earlier, 'original' loss occurred. **Regression is a reversion to an earlier mode of thinking, feeling, or behavior.**

Reaction to loss is complicated by angry feelings towards the 'deserting' person. Psychoanalytic theories assume that some neurotic people who are prone to depression have learned to repress hostile feelings for fear of alienating those on whom they depend for support. My findings suggest that in some cases, even essentially 'normal' persons may act out their hostility from within a regressed state of mind.

Many, perhaps most, Atypical Theft Offenders are individuals who experienced traumatic losses as children, often involving loss of affection and/or even outright rejection. Losses in later life may precipitate these individuals' inclinations to regress, and to act out via theft behavior from within this regressed state.

Lest the reader consider such behavior so unusual, consider again the matter of overeating, a most common problem in our society. Like affection, obtaining physical nutrients is one of our earliest requirements. Indeed eating, or more accurately being provided with material sustenance, is at least as important as being provided with human affection.

Investigations took place in an orphanage many years ago where these existed a remarkably high mortality rate among the infants, in spite of the fact that all of them had apparently been fed adequately but not handled or played with. It was found that one particular caregiver had not only fed and changed her charges, but talked to, held and played with them; among 'her' infants there was not a single fatality. This finding clearly indicated the importance of significant human contact and touch upon infants. Both food and fondling are required for sustaining life.

Some persons in our society who need to lose weight find themselves doing well at restricting their food intake until they hit a critical time of the day or night, usually those periods of the 24-hour cycle when, in their childhood experiences, household tensions were relatively high. (The evening is frequently the critical time, a time when both parents may have been at home, and perhaps 'at each other's throats' verbally if not physically.)

Later, in adulthood, the individual who experienced such discomfort at home as a child, may seek substitute comfort by nourishing (actually over-nourishing) himself or herself via food. This activity of eating takes place over a very brief period, so that the individual moves from the world of good intentions (regarding how he or she has dieted most of the day while in a more Adult state of being) to a less rational and emotionally driven Child state of being -- during which that person may devour several servings of bread, cake, bowls-full of cereal, or whatever 'the craving' calls for, in a sort of feeding frenzy.

Such indulgent eating behavior usually takes place in a regressed psychological state, perhaps not so different from that experienced by the Atypical Theft Offender, who feels impelled to take things, and then, after the act, like the over-eater, berates himself or herself for once again breaking the promise made to self to cease eating or taking things inappropriately.

The Establishment of Early Response Sets

Most of us, as children, develop particular response tendencies or styles in reaction to positive and negative events and circumstances. Siblings seldom act identically in response to say, father's frequent absence on long business trips, or mother's unpredictability, or a family's move from one home, city, or country, to another. It is our idiosyncratic responses to these events and changes by which our personalities become defined, and vice versa.

Often, within the same family, one child may tend to adapt well and easily to substantial changes and stressors, while another has great difficulty handling the same stimuli, even when the sibs are close in age, or of the same sex. Kindergarten and grade school teachers are only too aware of the broad spectrum of responses which different children from the same household exhibit to the same circumstances.

The A.T.O.'s regressed state while offending

An Atypical Theft Offender is most often functioning in a regressed state of consciousness at the time of offending. At such a time the person may be feeling frightened, insecure, hurt, and/or angry (or is anticipating experiencing those feelings).

To mention a not entirely different (from a psychodynamic point of view) phenomenon, consider the otherwise 'normal' but substantially overweight person with dangerously high cholesterol who knows that eating another piece of cake with whipped cream is verboten. Or the alcoholic who realizes that having another drink is not in his or her best interest. Nevertheless both the overweight and the alcoholic individuals may find themselves moving towards the refrigerator or the bar, respectively, and rather immediately reaching for and taking the 'illegal' object..

Likewise the A.T.O. moves towards an 'illegal' object. In all three cases, at the moment of moving towards, and in the act of committing the deed, the persons involved are in altered states of consciousness, from which the rational, critical faculties have been stymied. They exercise child-like behavioral responses akin to the "I want it and I don't care about the consequences" attitude of children.

Many overweight adults know first-hand the phenomenon of a regressed state of being, approximating that of very young children who "know better, but don't care," This regressed state lasts just long enough to permit an aggressive attack upon the contents of the refrigerator or pantry, and is usually carried out within a matter of a very few minutes, at most -- all in the supposed service of soothing feelings of deprivation or discomfort. Fortunately for many of us, one usually is not likely to be arrested for taking food from one's own household's supplies.

When the individual who took to stealing as a child finds himself or herself under stress as an adult, the earlier response set may become a very powerful psychodynamic, driving force with which the person may need to wrestle, with all his or her might, in order to not act out. The possible legal ramifications are often a resisting force in most cases. However, in the case of Atypical Theft Offenders, if the theft offense was committed, then the deterrent effect of potential arrest, conviction, receiving a fine, or even incarceration, obviously did not have enough of a deterrent effect. This is likely to be true if the stimulus, i.e., the actual or anticipated personal loss or other stressor, is of sufficient magnitude. Indeed many of the referrals I receive are cases where the individual has already been charged and convicted on several prior occasions. Therefore the level of potential damage to self in terms of the likelihood of incarceration, of career destruction, and/or of marital disharmony was already very high indeed, at the time of the commission of the most recent offenses. Nevertheless, those deterrents were insufficient to inhibit the offender's theft behavior.

Shoplifting and theft as regressive acts

As a physician-client told me in our initial interview:

"I didn't walk into the department store with the intention of taking anything. I remember picking up the sweater and looking at it, and then thinking, 'I should be able to have this; I want it, and I shouldn't have to pay for it.' I know it sounds ridiculous and I have never thought such a preposterous thought before, but I did think it then. I really just felt that it was right for me to pick up the sweater and put it in my briefcase. Once the sweater was in my briefcase I felt really excited. I remember thinking to myself that I couldn't believe that I was actually doing this, that I was actually taking this object."

In the remaining chapters the reader will do well to bear in mind that the actions of Atypical Theft Offenders are most often acts that symbolize compensation for a significant actual or anticipated loss, and that these acts are most often carried out in a regressed state.

Chapter 12

ATYPICAL THEFT BEHAVIOR AS CONSCIOUS, SUBCONSCIOUS OR UNCONSCIOUS MANIPULATION

Frequently, the acts of theft by A.T.O.s appear to have been attempts of conscious, subconscious or even unconscious manipulation, rather than mere retribution, although both motivations may be operating in some cases.

A.T.O.s who knew they were being watched and shoplifted anyway

Occasionally, clients will report that immediately prior to their acts of theft, they were certain that they were being observed by store employees. In a few instances, persons I assessed described how they had played bizarre versions of "Hide and Seek" with the suspected 'loss prevention' persons by, for example, moving back and forth among and between racks of clothes, just to make sure that the other persons was indeed following them. And sure enough, the loss prevention persons were, moving in tandem with them an aisle or two away! So even when they were positive that they were being followed and therefore were at serious risk if they took anything, they went ahead and stole anyway! And invariably, of course, they were caught by the very persons they had correctly identified as the store's security personnel.

Some media reports, and even some professionals, have referred to such acts of stealing while aware of being observed by likely loss prevention persons as primarily motivated by thrill-seeking. While this may be the case with some youngsters, and extremely immature and markedly handicapped adults, in most cases that I have assessed, the persons involved have been generally well functioning and of sufficiently ample monetary resources to afford very exciting and adrenaline provoking (but legally benign) activities such as rollerblading, cycling, downhill skiing, skydiving, and so on. However (to use a not entirely erroneous analogy) when a person chooses to play Russian roulette when he or she is sure that all chambers are loaded with live ammunition (by analogy, when the theft offender is virtually certain that a loss

117

prevention person is watching), that individual is surely more self-destructive than 'thrill-seeking.'

It is important to remember that the people we are speaking of are often individuals who are intelligent, hard working, normally well-functioning, generally responsible members of society, who may also be church/temple/synagogue/mosque goers, and who themselves find the ideal of stealing an abhorrence. Nevertheless, here they find themselves playing 'cops and robbers' and knowing that the 'cops' are watching them. To add insult to injury, in many of these cases they are entirely inept as thieves. Their theft behavior is blatant, bumbling and probably deliberately so!

Why would these normally law-abiding persons play such bizarre self-defeating games? What could possibly be gained by playing? And why do some offenders state that they committed the acts in spite of the fact that they were certain they were being watched? And why do some of them feel that, even so or perhaps because they were sure of being apprehended, they just 'cannot stop' themselves!

When getting caught stealing is a desired outcome

The subconscious and unconscious states of mind are wondrous mental phenomena. They enable us to construct night dreams, daytime fantasies and other acts that symbolize some of our deeper thoughts, feelings, and desires. Sometimes people just don't want, or aren't yet ready, to face certain highly disturbing issues such as a failing marriage, an unsuccessful business venture, a now-defunct love, etc..., and so our unconscious minds may choose to present to us, while we are sleeping, powerful images and scenes that may even awaken us. These dreams are attempts by our unconscious minds to draw our conscious minds' attention to deal with those upsetting issues that need to be worked through or resolved.

But what if we still will not deal with these matters, and simply turn over and attempt to go back to sleep, literally and/or figuratively, or at the least, avoid the matters pressing for attention and resolution? Then our unconscious and subconscious minds may be forced to take more drastic actions. Slips of the tongue, finding oneself 'accident-prone,' and/or having psychosomatic or even real physical illnesses may act to bring our conscious minds to address, finally, the previously avoided issues. Other acting out behaviors such as discovered extramarital affairs, may also finally precipitate facing distasteful facts. Being apprehended for theft might serve a similar function.

*****

Case # 20: Valerie: the lab technician who wouldn't leave her disastrous marriage

Valerie was referred to me by a psychiatrist who had seen her on and off for about 8 years. In spite of his best efforts, she continued to be arrested for shoplifting. The fact that she was a professional person who earned substantial wages had not inhibited her stealing activities. She felt unable to stop herself. One or two years would pass between successive 'incidents.' Stealing from her colleagues' purses was part of the scenario. Many of her relatives were aware of her acting out and therefore were hesitant to have her visit; they believed she might take something, and so they were usually vigilant for such possibilities. At major family gatherings, more than once her purse was searched when she was out of the room, and objects were 'recovered' and put back where they belonged. Nothing was said to her; they understood that there was something going on that they did not comprehend. So, because they cared for her, they let her be, but invited her over less and less often.

The referring psychiatrist had noted more than a decade earlier that Valerie's marriage was in serious trouble. Both she and her spouse were from well-to-do upper class families. Her problems seemed, at least in part, to stem from her spouse Albert's drinking, and his lack of affection for, or attention to, her.

Following the tragic death of their youngest child while still an infant (several years earlier) Valerie and Albert had drifted increasingly apart. The psychiatrist had been candid; they would not deal with the death of their child, which Valerie blamed on her husband's drinking (he had fallen asleep, drunk, while at home baby-sitting when Valerie was out for dinner with friends) and the child had drowned while playing in the family's wading pool. Valerie's shoplifting had begun shortly thereafter.

After several months of treatment in both individual and joint sessions there had been some minor progress in the relationship between Valerie and Albert. Valerie reported feeling more optimistic than she had in years. The following Friday evening I received a call from Valerie's lawyer. He reported that he had been working late at his office, and had received a call from Valerie who had just been apprehended for shoplifting at her local shopping mall.

In the emergency session that we arranged for the following day in my office, Valerie told me that her spouse had gotten drunk again two days after our last joint session, and had informed her that he had been having an affair, which he had no intention of stopping. She had shoplifted two hours later.

For Valerie divorce was not a serious option; it was certainly against her family's tradition of 'putting up with.' The fact was, however, that living with her spouse, with whom she had not had sexual relations for over two years (now she understood why), had now become intolerable. But her shoplifting was reprehensible to her. It seemed that her acting out via shoplifting was something that she felt driven to do in response to the problems of her home life. She knew that her husband had no intention of leaving her. However her acts of theft were extremely embarrassing to him, particularly as he was employed as a bank manager.

While she did not consciously deliberately set out to tarnish Albert's reputation, her acts of shoplifting were about the only weapon she had to influence him to pay more attention to her. I was convinced at this point that her acts of shoplifting were most unlikely to stop until and unless she made a viable life for herself. And this was now clearly most unlikely while she was still married to Albert, unless he would cease his extramarital activities and be willing to become involved in therapy.

The psychiatrist she had seen previously had urged her to consider leaving her husband. She had resisted doing so, and was still reluctant to take this action. Yet her theft behavior was now clear to her as a powerful message from her unconscious that she had to attend to this issue sooner than later.

Shortly following this last incident Valerie finally separated from her spouse, with at least some of her family's blessing and support. Her shoplifting stopped, and she last reported that she was no longer depressed and angry all the time.

Three years after separating she divorced Albert and a couple of years later she met, and eventually married a high school teacher. If she continues to learn to deal with (rather than avoid) her personal issues, including the death of her youngest child, then I very much doubt that Valerie will act out in the future via theft behavior.

*****

In many cases A.T.O.s act out in ways that bring them to seek some professional assistance. Unfortunately, since many clinicians are still not aware of the likely connections between theft and loss (or between shoplifting and other underlying motivations uncovered through our researches and presented in this book) and therefore they have frequently not been as able to assist their clients in ways that successfully eliminated the theft behavior.

It is not just the Atypical Theft Offender's avoidance of dealing with issues that can get them into such difficulties. Sometimes the A.T.O. is willing to face the problem and take action but his or her 'significant other' is not. In such circumstances the A.T.O.'s subconscious and unconscious minds may despair of getting action until or unless drastic measures (for example, acts of theft) are carried out that will cry out for such attention.

As noted above some persons described a degree of conscious awareness at the time of their offenses that they would "probably" be caught but "did not care." The following case well represents this phenomenon.

*****

Case # 21: Wanda, who wanted to punish herself for her parents' separation and deaths

Wanda had been separated from her father from the time she was three years old. It was only after her mother's death from a heart attack when Wanda was seven, that she returned to live with her father and his new spouse. After the second spouse left her father, Wanda stayed with him until his death, by which time she was twenty-four years old.

After her father's second heart attack had left him partly paralyzed he had insisted that his daughter never place him in a nursing home, and she had agreed. When he then suffered a third major heart attack while Wanda was at work, and had died by the time she had arrived home, she felt terribly guilty for having agreed to his demand. Her guilt escalated after she overheard one of her uncles saying at the funeral, "If only Max had been in a nursing home the doctors would have probably saved him; they're set up for that. I told Wanda to put him in, but she wouldn't listen." Wanda, who had been informed that she inherited a rather substantial estate immediately upon her father's death, began to shoplift the next day.

Wanda reported that she had felt guilty for her parents' separation when she was three, for her mother's death when she was seven, and then for her father's death. Wanda also felt abandoned and resentful when her father had stopped coming to see her shortly after her parents separated. Then, she felt what she considered perverse pleasure when the second wife left, partly because she and Wanda never hit it off well. Her father's death was the latest and most crushing loss.

Her guilt seemed to drive her shoplifting behavior. She described being aware of wishing that she would be caught and punished. She felt she deserved punishment for all her 'crimes.' However, even after she was caught, found guilty, and fined, she still felt she had not been punished sufficiently. Wanda was clearly a suicide risk.

*****

Wanda had a clear awareness of wanting to punish herself. She even felt guilty because she had used some of her inheritance to hire a lawyer to represent her on the shoplifting charges. She feared losing her job as a public school teacher, and therefore felt obliged to be properly represented in court. Her lawyer referred her for an assessment, since he had known Wanda and her family for years and believed that there was probably a psychological explanation for her nonsensical theft behavior.

Wanda's treatment involved dealing with both early and later losses, and completing the mourning and resolution of her mother's death, father's leaving, etc..., and with her ill-founded guilt about several of these events.

The extent of conscious manipulation among A.T.O.s

Wanda's was an unusual case to the extent that she knew full well that she wanted to punish herself for her 'crimes' vis-à-vis her parents' separation, and their deaths. It seemed to her that every person that mattered to her and whose life she touched, suffered and died. Her work as a teacher of young disadvantaged children only partly mitigated her guilt.

Most, but not all, Atypical Theft Offenders acknowledge their theft behavior and are aware also of some element of conscious intention to hurt themselves and/or others by their actions. Some are even consciously aware of seeking to gain the attention of a spouse or some 'significant other,' especially when other kinds of attempts have failed to achieve that desired goal. For example, my clinical experience is that most married A.T.O.s are angry with their spouses at the time of their offenses, but do not realize the degree to which their resentments may be precipitating their acting out.

It is probably true to say that conscious manipulation is a contributing factor in a minority of cases of Atypical Theft behavior. Only rarely is it a major precipitating feature of the behavior. Again, in a very small minority of cases (perhaps 5% to 10% of Atypical Theft Offender cases I have assessed) the offender has reported conscious, deliberate, premeditation.

Only a fraction of these cases have appeared to involve attempts at conscious manipulation of others or events through engaging in the acts of theft. In one such case a client reported that she wanted to return to her country of origin but her spouse refused to consider such a move. She was aware that her theft behavior was partly intended to influence his opinion in favor of returning back to Europe.

The conscious motivations of *Typical* Theft Offenders (T.T.O.s)

In this book, of course, we are dealing for the most part with usually honest persons whose thefts are, for them, atypical acts. The majority of theft offenders, however, are those we refer to as Typical Theft Offenders. A major difference between Typicals and Atypicals relates to their differing consciously experienced motivations. T.T.O.s usually consciously and deliberately plan and carry out their acts of theft. They know *what* they are doing, *why* they are doing it, and have set about stealing in order to achieve their desired goals of obtaining property and/or money.

By contrast, classic A.T.O.s frequently do not consciously intend to steal before they do it. And they are often unclear as to why they stole the particular items that they did.

Another difference between classical A.T.O.s and T.T.O.s is their differing attitudes towards their behaviors. T.T.O.s are proud of their successes in stealing, whereas classic A.T.O.s are usually embarrassed by their behavior and disgusted with themselves.

T.T.O.s are behaving in egosyntonic ways; A.T.O.s are behaving in such egodystonic ways that in some cases they may choose to punish themselves by committing suicide.

T.T.O.s would virtually never suicide for having stolen or being caught.

'Typicals' may be similar to 'Atypicals' in that they may appear to be upstanding members of society, e.g. successful business persons, tenured college professors, licensed professionals, conscientious and dedicated workers in their chosen fields; 'typicals', however, more often operate out of greed, not need. Also, they are not concerned who they steal from if it serves their ends. They may even choose to steal from friends or relatives; they simply want what they want, and easily rationalize their behaviors in order to justify their actions. They have no remorse or shame associated with their actions, whatsoever.

A first mention of The Theft Offender Spectrum
The differences between Typical and Atypical Theft Offenders will be considered in some qualitative and quantitative detail later, in Chapter 18, when the **Theft Offender Spectrum** is introduced. The Theft Offender Spectrum provides a means of evaluating where the offender most probably belongs along the Atypical-Typical Theft Offender continuum. In any specific case, the person may display both Atypical Theft Offender and Typical Theft Offender elements.

The complexity of the motivations of Atypical Theft Offenders

It is worthwhile reiterating a previous comment, specifically that the underlying motivations behind the acts of theft by persons who may be called Atypical Theft Offenders, which we have considered in detail in the last few chapters, are often *multi-determined*. That is, it is not often that only a single motivation that has precipitated the acting out. Rather, there are frequently two or more major identifiable motivations at work simultaneously.

The essential tasks of the clinician who is assessing a theft offender include the following:

1. determine the underlying motivations in a particular case;

2. decide whether one is dealing with an Atypical Theft Offender or Typical Theft Offender; or the Atypical/Typical ('mixed-type'), and

3. develop a treatment plan to assist the client to deal with his other underlying problems.

It bears repeating that, regardless of the type of stealing involved, it is very important for the purposes of clinical assessment and treatment as well as for the legal disposition of the case, to attempt to make a determination of whether one is dealing with a Typical Theft Offender, a Atypical Theft Offender, or a mixed Atypical/Typical Theft Offender type of theft offender.

The **Cupchik Theft Offender Questionnaire** (Chapter 17) and the **Cupchik Theft Offender Spectrum** (Chapter 18) are original tools developed to assist the clinician in these complex tasks. Professionals who are interested in using either of these tools with their clients are asked to seek same by contacting Dr. Will Cupchik at wcupchik@aol.com, or by telephoning 416-928-2262.

Chapter 13

ATYPICAL THEFT BEHAVIOR AS UNCONSCIOUS RETRIBUTION

In our original investigations we noted that some patients whom we had assessed following their acts of theft appeared to have acted with the unconscious intention of embarrassing close relatives, socially prominent spouses, or, as was the case with two patients, relatives with law enforcement responsibilities.

*****

Case # 22: Jane, a teacher and theft offender whose father and brothers were police officers

Jane, a high school French teacher with twenty-five years teaching experience, who had been given several awards for her teaching excellence, and who also regularly taught graduate students in the education faculty at the university, had grown up in a very chauvinistic household. Her father, a police sergeant of 'the old school,' was a domineering figure who did not have very much time for his oldest -- and female -- child, at least not after his first son was born.

Her own accomplishments, from top marks at high school through to being the only one of the children to have completed university, were not considered by her father as being nearly as worthy of recognition as his sons' successes on the local hockey and baseball teams. Decades of frustration and rejection boiled over two days after her father announced during Christmas dinner that he and her mother (who was still, after nearly fifty years of marriage, very intimidated by her husband) had written Wills leaving the family's city home and the country property to her two brothers. Both brothers, perhaps not coincidentally, had followed in their father's footsteps and had become police officers after completing high school. Jane was informed that as a married female "egghead" in a 'cushy' suburban school, she certainly didn't have any material needs that her parents "should be satisfying by dying".

Jane knew that her father held his family's name as highly as he did his own reputation as 'an honest cop.' Being effectively left out of the bulk of her parents' estate was the final blow. In particular, the loss of the family's cottage -- a place of mixed but deep feelings where she and her mother spent many close and happy times together, while 'the men' were out fishing or All Terrain Vehicling or skidooing-- felt to her like a most cruel, final act of rejection and of loss.

Two days after learning that she was to be cut out of the bulk of her parents' estate, and while on her lunch break from school, Jane walked over to the plaza to get her father a present for his birthday (which was three days hence). She was looking for a record album of marching band favorites (his specified choice for a birthday present), when she noticed an appropriate choice as well as a Grateful Dead CD.

All she could tell me at our first session was that she felt impelled, for the first time in her life to steal something. Needless to say, the rock group's name and music were the last things on earth her father would be interested in. She assured me that the irony of the group's name vis-à-vis the dinner table discussion of her parents' Wills a couple of days previously had never entered her conscious mind. She did remember that when she put the two CDs in her purse she was feeling hot and sweaty and she said that she felt her heart pounding. She had some vague sense at that moment that this was a bad thing to do for many reasons, especially in view of her position as a teacher, but just could not focus her mind on anything but getting out of the store with the Grateful Dead and marching band albums, unpaid for. She was apprehended by security personnel, and was spoken with by the store manager who knew her father personally from their brotherhood gatherings. He spoke rather harshly to Jane about what she had done, "You being a teacher and all, and your father and brothers all being such fine police officers. Shame on you, Jane."

Jane remembered thinking at the time, "Actually, shame on them! Good! So there!".

The department store manager, probably as a courtesy to her father, chose not to lay charges. Jane attended for assessment and continued in treatment for several months in order to deal with long-standing issues of feelings of resentment, rejection and loss re her parents, and with her sibling issues as well. As is frequently the case with A.T.O.s, she needed to work on becoming more appropriately assertive not only with her parents, but with others as well, including her authoritarian school principal, and her husband (a generation-younger version of her father), whose dictates had led to their own home becoming a place of 'two solitudes,' now that their last child had gone off to university.

*****

In this and several other cases over the years, I have noted that most Atypical Theft Offenders have not had a recollection of consciously thinking about the potential embarrassment and humiliation that their stealing would bring upon the significant other with whom they were upset prior to their acts of theft.

Sometimes spouses who find that their husbands/wives have been arrested for theft become more receptive to getting marital therapy, even if it is in part an attempt to protect their own reputations. It is unfortunate that such drastic actions seem to have been the first effective means of bringing the spouse into treatment.

Unconscious retribution appears to play an at least minor part in many A.T.O. cases of theft. Only in a very small minority of cases is it likely to be the principal motivation. In such instances the emotions of the offenders are often so intense and complex that they may be relatively more at risk for suicide, especially if the 'offended party' is not sympathetic to the offender, but is inclined to intensify their rejection of the offender in response to anticipating being embarrassed by the resultant publicity attendant upon a court appearance.

Chapter 14

SHOPLIFTING AND OVER-EATING

Clinical experiences have provided me with an awareness of atypical theft offenses and overeating as coexisting and rather related behavioral problems in some persons. Indeed, on the very day that I typed the first draft of this chapter I received a phone call from an out-of-town lawyer who described to me his shoplifter/client who was also bulimic. This and other cases led me to reflect upon the similarities in the two superficially different inappropriate behaviors.

Similarities between Atypical Theft Offenders and those who abuse themselves via inappropriate eating behavior include:

1. frequently, environmental and/or interpersonal factors or circumstances that appear to stimulate the inclination to act out inappropriately;

2. preceding 'felt experiencing of emptiness';

3. a desire to avoid the underlying psychological issues and physiological sensations that would otherwise be experienced by the individual;

4. an inclination to act out in ways that are inappropriate and self-defeating; and

5. the behavior's effect in further reducing self-esteem and increasing levels of frustration and self-anger.

Of course, there are some important differences as well; in particular, the legal repercussions of the theft offenses as contrasted with the 'mere' possibly serious health repercussions of the eating 'offenses.'

Both Atypical Theft Offenders and eating 'offenders' may also be viewed as having the following problems in common:

1- both commit behaviors that they claim to have difficulty stopping permanently, although both may have 'temporary' successes in stopping to steal or overeat;

2- both are aware that their continued behaviors are inappropriate at best, are definitely unnecessary for their survival and flourishing, and are indeed contraindicated by virtue of the fact that they don't need the goods (or 'goodies') they acquire and/or consume;

3- their inappropriate activities can cause them emotional, physical, economical or social harm;

4- in most cases they have been informed by significant authority figures such as judges or doctors that their continued inappropriate behaviors may have increasingly dire consequences;

5- both groups of offenders may go on 'binges,' where in spite of their best intentions, or even recent successes spanning days, weeks, months or years, they may be inclined, especially when severely stressed, to act out once more in these potentially damaging ways;

6- each acting out experience tends to involve very short-term gain, of material goods, followed almost immediately by self-recriminations; and

7- both groups consist of adults whose difficulties have much earlier antecedents; i.e., these persons, when interviewed in depth, will usually report childhood problems in the same offending domains as those in which now, as adults, they are again engaged.

8 – when the Atypical Theft Offender steals food, both problems (i.e., stealing and overeating) converge.

Any persons who have difficulty keeping their weight down in spite of being warned by their physicians that they are at risk for heart attack, stroke, or diabetes, and who continue their inappropriate behaviors in spite of all the good reasons for them to stop, and in spite of the fact that they do not need to eat as they do for purposes of survival, are reacting to powerful, usually unconsciously driven motivations that appear to overpower their better judgment and best interests. Similar statements can be made about Atypical Theft Offenders.

It is because of the commonalties listed above that dysfunctional eaters (which can include virtually anyone who chronically eats inappropriately, and/or in spite of its clear detriment to the individual's health), are in a position to empathize with and appreciate the kinds of powerful dynamics at play with A.T.O.s.

When Overeaters are also Theft Offenders

Given the above discussion, readers will not be surprised to learn that some individuals have presented themselves at my office with both difficulties.

For persons who suffer from both atypical theft behavior and neurotic eating behavior, major stressors and/or emotional pain may be particularly difficult for them to cope with appropriately. Many of these individuals have had seriously disturbed childhood relationships with other family members. The shoplifting and inappropriate eating appear to function as attempts to fill the emptiness in their emotional lives. Their inappropriate and excessive consumption of material goods (by shoplifting) or of digestible goods (by overeating) appear to very temporarily ease their discomfort.

It is also of interest that while the excessive over-eaters I have assessed were consumers of food, and tended to consume 'things' also (through stealing), an anorexic theft offender I assessed and treated had the neurotic need to also 'purge herself financially' by giving away to relatives both her own inheritance and property she stole for the expressed purpose of giving it away. For her, less was 'more', in both departments!

Treating the theft behavior may, or may not, affect the overeating behavior.

To this point in time I have focused efforts upon the theft, rather than the food, offenses of clients. I have not noted whether the ceasing of the theft behavior has been accompanied by appropriate weight changes or modified food consumption patterns, but I would be very surprised if these did not occur as well. However, it does appear that it is possible to address the one offense successfully while not necessarily modifying the other condition. Likewise, I would doubt that weight loss would invariably modify the extent of the individual's theft offending. It remains for future investigations to consider dealing directly with both these acting out behaviors in treatment, and to measure the extent of the reduction in one type of inappropriate behavior when the other has been successfully dealt with.

The fact that overeating often involves physiological action-evoking, as well as psychological, triggers suggests that special therapeutic interventions may be desirable in order to combat such behaviors.

Appreciating the extent of the problem which the offender must address

By appreciating the difficulty which some of us, and/or our loved ones encounter in managing our weight or fitness, and the degree to which we may be inclined to not stop doing that which is unhealthy or unwise for us, we might better appreciate that simply telling an Atypical Theft Offender to stop offending may be similarly ineffective. It may not be any easier for that person to comply with such a suggestion than for a health-risking over-eater to likewise cease his or her misdeeds. While the analogy probably frays at the edges, nevertheless there is very likely some validity in drawing this analogy.

Chapter 15

OTHER FACTORS THAT MAY MOTIVATE AN ESSENTIALLY HONEST PERSON'S A.T.O.-TYPE BEHAVIOR

Theft offenses and recent economic downturns

In seeking to understand the phenomenon of theft behavior by persons who previously would not think of committing such acts, it is important to take into account all of the individual's major intrapsychic and interpersonal issues, as well as his or her social, working, and financial circumstances. **To carry out such a thorough assessment usually requires a minimum of five to eight clinical sessions.**

Consider, for example, the matter of recent economic downturns and corporate downsizing that has gone on in North America in the 1990s, and again early in the new millennium. Persons who have been working more or less steadily for years, who have considered themselves to be dedicated workers yet who suddenly find themselves unemployed through no direct fault of their own, may turn to theft behavior as one kind of acting out response to their new situation. Why?

Principally, I would suggest that such a person may steal as a loss-substitution response, that is, stealing in response to having had suffered what is experienced by the individual who has been laid off, as an unfair loss of a job, and of income. This person may also be anticipating other losses such as the loss of the family home due to not being able to pay the mortgage, loss of the ability to pay for the children's special education needs, etc... .

This brings up another clinically important issue that should also be taken into account by the justice system.

133

When an A.T.O. steals for T.T.O.-type motivations.

How can we assess the degree to which the theft behavior in such circumstances is 'atypical' as opposed to 'typical'? If a usually honest and hard-working person who has lost his job and has failed to find alternate gainful employment holds up a variety store and steals from the cash register to get the money to pay for his child's needed medical treatment, then we can understand that the motivation to obtain the funds was aimed at their manifest, or face value. In other words, an $800 robbery might go a ways to paying for the required prescription drugs for an ill family member.

On the other hand, if another individual's primary occupation for the past ten years has been robbing variety stores, and he or she commits yet another similar offense and gets away with $800, shall we not consider this individual 'more' of a true criminal in some respects, and deserving of a harsher punishment? Especially if the person is quite content to commit robbery as a way of providing his or her family with needed supplies, and if the offender has no desire, let alone intention, to obtain more orthodox gainful employment?

I would suggest that the qualities of mercy and compassion are *not* strained if the judge in the former circumstance might see fit to take into consideration the fact that the offender has recently lost his job through no fault of his own after, say, a long period of steady employment working for the same company. The Loss-Substitution-by-Stealing Hypothesis, which describes acting out by stealing as behavior having to do with loss would seem likely to have been at work here. This is a very different scenario from the one in which the thief has robbed the store because that is simply his preferred way of acquiring money.

Let us take another kind of example, one where the monetary value of what was taken is truly relatively miniscule. If, say, a married person has just been laid off and needs substantial funds to handle the family's day-to-day expenses then steals a $1 chocolate bar from a variety store, it is surely more probable that the person was acting out to obtain the symbolic satisfaction of having "gotten something for nothing" from somebody else and/or from having caused someone else to lose something -- anything -- just as he had had lost something when he lost the job. The taking of the chocolate bar is probably symbolically compensatory behavior in response to losing the job. In such a case, the theft behavior clearly has an 'atypical' flavor.

The neurotic component in atypical theft behavior

Emotionally mature persons usually act in ways that are purposeful, balanced, socially and interpersonally sensitive, and fitting to the circumstances.

Persons behaving neurotically, on the other hand, often act in ways that may have qualities of inappropriateness and immaturity, and often suffer self-imposed emotional distress. They may also have difficulties with peers and/or superiors at work and in their personal lives.

A person in an emotionally mature state knows that stealing a chocolate bar would not answer the financial needs of his family. Nor is such an action likely to provide a useful and appropriate way to deal with his anger and frustration over losing his job. In fact, thinking rationally the individual may weigh the risk to the possible gain and sensibly conclude that the risk is entirely to great for such small possible gain. In an immature or neurotic state, however, the individual might anticipate 'just feeling better' at having released some frustration and anger in however an inappropriate but symbolic fashion, as if taking the chocolate bar might compensate for losing a job.

More mature ways of reducing stress

There is a strong, well-documented case to be made for the value of physical exercise as a means of reducing the effects of stress on the body/mind. We know that such activities as walking, jogging, swimming and cycling can reduce stress and release some of the frustration, anger, and sadness that the individual has been experiencing. Such strenuous activity is considered beneficial from both a physical and emotional health perspective.

Anyone who exercises regularly can attest to the greater intensity that frequently accompanies a workout carried out when one is in a state of agitation. The workout can help 'get it out of one's system.' Of course, the workout does not get a job back, nor does it do anything to provide additional funds to replace those lost by having been 'de-hired.' However there is a reduction, at least temporarily, in the state of high emotional arousal occasioned by the fact of being laid off.

The therapeutic value of speaking with a friend, or of talking out loud 'at' a person who is not present

In addition to working out, other expressive, action-oriented behaviors such as talking out loud 'at' the employer in absentia, that is, when the employer/'significant other' is not actually present, can provide for some release, as can talking with a friend or having a good cry. Employing a punching bag, gardening, brisk walking and other physical activities can also provide emotional release. Talking with an 'intimate other' or a supportive friend about how one is feeling in regard to the loss one has recently experienced can be extremely important. Prayer and meditation can also provide for some release and a more positive –less stressed- attitude.

Most of us act inappropriately, at some time or other

It is likely that no one is immune to acting out from time to time in less mature ways than usual. In fact, it is precisely those persons who are held by their peers and society generally to the highest standards of behavior, who may have the greatest need to stop being 'so darn good'! The stress of being scrutinized and judged with exceptionally high standards, by others or oneself, carries a heavy price. Those who bear the burden of being held in such high regard (and to such high standards) may devoutly wish to act out in immature ways, given the right --or wrong -- circumstances. (Consider, perhaps, U.S. presidents, the British royal family, some political types and certain television evangelists as a few cases in point.) It is for this reason (among others) that the media occasionally reports unusual, bizarre and/or exceptionally immature or irresponsible acts by our supposed leaders or role models. Those who would attempt to carry society and its burdens on their shoulders may be inclined to stumble or 'trip themselves up' by regressing when emotionally stressed in order to 'release the burden.' (This hypothesis may also help explain the shoplifting behavior of the police officer, Tony, Case # 9.)

When regression, i.e. 'behaving like a child' is socially acceptable behavior for grown-ups

Shouting and screaming in public, baring one's top, gesturing violently and provocatively with one's arms or other body parts, in front of say one's boss or in-laws would usually be frowned on most occasions. Perhaps that is one of the main reasons that societies developed 'spectator' sports. As long as one is in the role of spectator at a football game or soccer match or other sporting events, one may re allowed to 'act out,' whether elegantly (as by what one might wear to the Ascot races in England), or by wearing bizarre headgear and body paint and shouting uncharitable comments while gesturing rudely at the opposition team. Such conduct is not only socially sanctioned, but even applauded by many, and serves to allow for the emotional release of pent-up feelings related to the stresses of daily living. Of course, some of these individuals can get way out of hand, as has happened all too often at English soccer games and post-championship celebrations in North American society.

As a case in point, some of the 1992 World Series games were held in Toronto, a city that, at the time, was experiencing the most severe economical downturn since the great depression. Here was an opportunity for a huge catharsis of negative feelings relating to the recession and a crucial national referendum on the future of Quebec and of the country. The Toronto Blue Jays baseball team offered a 'reason'(i.e., excuse) to shout, scream, cry, rejoice, wear outlandish clothes and generally release a lot of intense feelings that were pervasive throughout Toronto, and indeed much of Canada, in October 1992. Conservative estimates indicated that when the Blue Jays won the World series, at about 1:30 a.m. on Sunday, October 25, 1992, over 500,000 citizens (or about 25% of the population) descended on downtown Toronto streets that early morning to celebrate. Thankfully their joyous exuberance did not extend to many acts of vandalism.

Doing wrong for 'understandable reasons' doesn't make it right

It is important for the reader to understand that the foregoing discussion is in no way an attempt to suggest that theft behavior should be sanctioned as a stress releaser. Rather, it has been meant to point out that such conduct is at least understandable, and, although it is not right, it is explainable, and, from within the perspective of a compassionate justice system, worthy of note. Furthermore, genuine justice requires that all factors relevant to an individual's conduct be taken into account while deliberating over how to deal with a theft offender. Indeed, most persons in modern societies would likely agree that understanding, compassion and wisdom are, or should be, inherent elements of all of our court proceedings. In a relatively large number of Atypical Theft Offender cases, such principles are indeed useful.

In difficult times of economic downturns, especially, with downsizing occurring at all levels within corporations and institutions, it behooves everyone involved with the problem of theft behavior -- whether offender, friend or relative, clinician, loss prevention person, lawyer, judge or jury-- to be aware of the possible relevance of the Loss-Substitution-by-Stealing Hypothesis in relation to stealing that follows the loss of one's job[xv], and to keep such considerations in mind when dealing with these cases.

Part Two:

Assessing The Atypical Theft Offender

Chapter 16

GREAT VARIATIONS AMONG THEFT OFFENDERS

An introduction to the issue of differentiating between Atypical and Typical Theft Offenders

Many persons steal for more than one major reason; individuals are complex and their actions are usually multi-determined. For this reason, relatively few theft offenders can be accurately described as pure or 'classic' examples of either 'typical' or 'atypical' theft offenders. In fact many theft offenders display both atypical and typical features.

> **Understanding theft behavior requires the examination of several possible motivations that represent --at the polarities-- features of classic Typical or Atypical Offenders. By carrying out such an assessment of situational factors and psychological motivations, it is frequently possible to categorize a particular offender as primarily either a Typical Theft Offender or an Atypical Theft Offender. Such a differentiation is not only feasible, but it is highly desirable for purposes of dealing appropriately clinically and legally with the offender.**

The consulting forensic psychiatrist or psychologist would like to be able to fully assess the individual, and to prescribe what therapy approaches should usefully be offered the offender, or whether treatment is even feasible.

Furthermore, judges want to know which type of theft offender (A.T.O., T.T.O. or 'mixed') they are dealing with; likewise for the district and defense attorneys.

Below we shall consider the bases upon which such a differentiation can be made. A number of important questions, articulated in the next chapter, will be employed in seeking the answer to the question of whether, and to what extent, a particular offender should be considered more of an Atypical or

Typical Theft Offender. To illustrate the desirability of such a differentiation more clearly, let us draw upon differing assessment impressions of two theft offenders, James (Case #23) and Geraldine (Case # 24), both of whom committed acts of theft that involved relatively large amounts of money. As will be clear from the descriptions offered of these cases, James is clearly an Atypical Theft Offender while Geraldine epitomizes the Typical Theft Offender syndrome.

*****

Case # 23: James, a major fund-raiser who stole a lot!

James, a 45 year old husband and father had been apprehended after an audit showed that he, as a senior fund raiser for a major hospital, had siphoned off over $500,000 for his own purposes over a two year period. Further investigations uncovered that James had, during that period, treated himself to numerous trips to Los Angeles, where he had splurged on upscale hotel accommodations, limos and the best tables at the most expensive 'in' restaurants. He had been the top fund raiser for his public ally run institution for nine years running and had frequently worked sixty hour weeks. He was a boy's club leader, an active member of his church, the assistant conductor of the church choir, and had been awarded several commendations for his high-profile volunteer work in the community.

Shortly after he was apprehended, a psychiatrist-friend of his had recommended that he seek a professional consultation in advance of his trial, in order to perhaps provide himself with a forensic professional's report that might be used by his lawyer to speak to the possibility of a reduced sentence. He refused to do so however, saying that he did not want to 'cop out' of suffering the full and, in his view completely deserved, punishment for his offensive actions.

Incidentally, when initially confronted with the auditor's report of probable wrongdoing, James had immediately confessed his guilt, and refused to even be defended by a lawyer. He told his friend that while he didn't understand why he had carried out his theft behavior (which was an affront to his ethical code and religious beliefs), he reiterated that he nevertheless believed he deserved to be severely punished, and he did not want to enter a plea that would attempt to either excuse his conduct and perhaps reduce his sentence.

James contacted me only after he had served his full term in penitentiary.

He told me that now that he had served his sentence he believed that he had paid some of his debt to society, and he was now ready to undertake an examination of his conduct. He said that he was actually very confused and frightened by what he had done, as he had always believed himself to be an honest individual, had always prided himself for not being a clock-watcher, and had thought of himself as a person who gave 'more than full and fair value' for his wages. He believed the hospital did marvelous work in his community and it was well regarded by the nation's medical 'who's who.'

What scared him most was that he did not have any idea why he had defrauded his employer of a half-million dollars, and why he had acted out by living such an extravagant and bizarre life-style, which was so out of keeping with his upbringing and usual mode of middle-class living. Furthermore he was afraid that unless he dealt with this matter, he might do a similar thing again at some time in the future.

During our early sessions I learned that James and his mother had been abandoned by his father when James was 12 years old. He had very fond recollections of his father although he admitted that he still at times experienced brief but almost overpowering rages whenever he thought of his father having left him and his mother in such dire straits. They had been forced to live with his grandparents for several years until his mother had remarried when James was 18 years old.

James' father was an accountant who had held a very responsible managerial position with a pharmaceutical company. He was also a very authoritarian individual who had a major drinking problem, and when drunk he would mete out brutal punishment to James for his youthful misdemeanors. James remembered only too well the sounds and sights that accompanied his father's weekend binges, and the beatings he had endured. His recollections included painful images of his mother trying to get his father to stop his drinking, and father's violent responses to her pleadings. Father chose to leave rather than change, and shortly afterwards his mother heard through mutual friends that her spouse had moved to another city with a woman he had met months before he left the family home. James never forgave his father, and he never saw him again, other than once at a relative's funeral a few years later. James did not acknowledge his father's calling out to him on that occasion.

142

James' anger towards his father remained undealt with, although he had prayed for guidance regarding how to handle his feelings of hurt and rage. When he received a promotion at work to the post of chief fund-raiser he also found himself reporting to a vice-president who was a much older man and whom James viewed as unreasonable and authoritarian, a man who was an alcoholic and who seemed to be continually berating James over an unending number of petty matters in spite of his obvious competence and success in fundraising. It was after nearly three years of working under that supervisor that James' stealing began.

During his clinical treatment James had to learn to deal in more appropriate ways with his anger generally and towards authority figures in particular. He also had to confront his unresolved feelings regarding his father. When he had faced these issues and other related matters in the course of several months of intensive therapy, he became much more appropriately assertive with peers as well as authority figures, and learned to get his needs met through means that gave him greater feelings of satisfaction and contentment than he had experienced in a long time. He also requested and received a transfer to another department with a supervisor who was fair and welcoming.

A full assessment of James and his behavior suggested that he was a classic example of Atypical Theft Offender. His theft behavior likely occurred in response to the deep-seated anger that dated all the way back to his father's mistreatment and eventual abandonment of James and his mother. These feelings were aroused by his being mistreated by a supervisor whose conduct towards James and blatant addiction to alcohol so closely paralleled those of his father.

*****

Let's now consider a very different case, that of Gerald, a classic <u>Typical</u> Theft Offender.

*****

Case # 24: Gerald: A psychology professor who stole $1,000,000 from his siblings

Gerald was a psychology and history of art professor at a major university in the Southwest. He was reasonably well regarded in his academic department although his attitude often seemed rather self-centered and rebellious to some of his colleagues. Also, it turned out, he lived a shadow life.

Gerald had begun selling drugs to university and acquaintances while a graduate student and seemed to enjoy the notoriety he had among those who knew of his drug-dealing sideline. He continued to sell drugs to his friends and acquaintances even after he obtained tenure. He also rebelliously acknowledged that he had used marijuana daily for over two decades when he first presented.

When his father was setting up his estate, about five years before he died, Gerald persuaded him that, as the eldest of five siblings, he would be the logical one to be the executor of his father's estate. His father, a successful businessperson but a rather socially isolated individual who ran his own retail clothing store, acceded to Gerald's request.

A year after their father died, and in response to having had distributed to them by Gerald what they considered a surprisingly meager inheritance compared to what they had been led to expect, Gerald's siblings hired their own lawyer to conduct an independent investigation into their late father's financial affairs. After a substantial search certain key documents surfaced which showed that Gerald had hidden the existence of several very substantial investments their father had made during his working life. These documents included a handwritten note written by Gerald _four years before his father's death_ to his old high school friend who was also the lawyer that handled the writing of Gerald's father's will, indicating Gerald's clear intention to acquire most of father's estate for himself. The amount that he kept for himself and refused to even acknowledge the existence of to his siblings, was exposed by the acquisition of a computer printout of the contents of an offshore bank account where he had placed the funds. These documents clearly showed that Gerald had planned for at least four years prior to their father's death to abscond with the bulk of his estate.

Gerald denied to his siblings that his actions constituted any wrongdoing until he was confronted with the written documentation. At that point he changed his story and told his siblings that their father, a month before he died at the age of 88, and when he was very ill indeed, had decreed that Gerald alone should acquire most of the estate. Gerald could not explain away, however, his own handwritten note to the lawyer, written four years earlier, that clearly showed his years earlier intention to abscond with the bulk of their father's estate, nor could he produce any written documentation signed by their father to support his claim. Faced with the option of going to court, Gerald and his siblings reached a financial settlement. In my office Gerald said, "Dr. Cupchik, I am only here to satisfy my lawyer's suggestion that I do so. Be advised, however that I have no remorse whatsoever for my behavior, either about the sale of drugs to my friends or the taking of the bulk of my father's estate. It was simply his dying wish, and I agreed to comply."

*****

A close examination of the cases of James and Gerald reveals many major differences in their motivations, behaviors, and the ways in which the criminal acts were carried out. James represents the classic Atypical Theft Offender; Gerald is an excellent example of a Typical Theft Offender.

While in both cases the amounts stolen were substantial, and both James and Gerald used the funds for their own enjoyment, James had clearly suffered from mental and emotional exhaustion, had acted out from a regressed state of mind, and experienced considerable remorse. Gerald, on the other hand, had coolly planned to steal from his siblings several years before their father died, and neither experienced nor expressed any remorse about his theft behavior.

When apprehended, James not only admitted his guilt immediately, but refused an opportunity to gain a favorable forensic assessment; he did nothing to escape his punishment. Meanwhile, Gerald had, for years, continued to deny any wrongdoing, and when caught red-handed so to speak, he refused to take responsibility for his actions, claiming he was merely serving his father's wishes.

As a way of facilitating clinicians in more formally differentiating between Atypical Theft Offenders and Typical Theft Offenders we shall next

145

present two valuable pen-and-paper devices, the **Cupchik Theft Offender Questionnaire** and the **Cupchik Theft Offender Spectrum**.

The <u>Cupchik Theft Offender Questionnaire</u> and <u>Cupchik Theft Offender Spectrum</u> are the copyrighted intellectual properties of the author.

<u>Disclaimer and Copyright Statement:</u> No claim is either made or intended in regard to the reliability or validity, beyond face validity, of the CTOS and CTOQ, two pen-and-paper devices. Rather, these two tools are intended to be of supplementary and suggestive quantitative and qualitative assistance to a competent and suitably trained mental health professional who will need to arrive at his or her own clinical determination as to whether the theft offender being dealt with should be considered to be an Atypical Theft Offender (A.T.O.), a Typical Theft Offender (T.T.O.), or of the Mixed A.T.O./T.T.O. type.

Offenders who have purchased this book are invited to use these to tools for their own cases.

Professionals who wish to use these devices should contact the author at <u>wcupchik@aol.com</u>.

As described in this book, the idiosyncratic, complex nature of the theft offender phenomenon makes it very unlikely that any pen-and-paper or other clinical device will be able to replace the appropriate use of an appropriate mental health professional in regard to reaching a determination of the degree or extent to which any individual theft offender is to be considered as 'atypical' or 'typical'.

Chapter 17

CUPCHIK THEFT OFFENDER QUESTIONNAIRE
Version 2   [C.T.O.Q.-V2]

I have devised the Cupchik Theft Offender Questionnaire as a practical tool that can be used by a clinician who wishes to carry out a comprehensive assessment of a theft offender/client. The C.T.O.Q. is organized into areas that may uncover salient aspects of the offender's case and that may help determine whether this client should eventually be categorized as an Atypical Theft Offender, a Typical Theft Offender, or of the mixed Atypical/Typical type.

Cautionary notice:
This questionnaire can be used to assist the client at home, in the therapist's office, and in court. Therefore its use should be approached with considerable thought and effort. Theft offenders should utilize the services of a competent professional when completing both the Cupchik Theft Offender Questionnaire and the Cupchik Theft Offender Spectrum (presented in the next chapter).

Instructions for completing the C.T.O.Q.

This questionnaire is meant be filled out either by the interviewer (with the client present) or by the client, either prior to or immediately following the first clinical session. In either case it will be important for the clinician to go over with the client all the answers to all the items; clients often miss or dismiss potentially relevant materials because they simply are not aware of the possible connections between their answers and the matters that are the main focus of this book.[xvi]

The purchaser of this book is hereby given permission by the copyright holder to use the Cupchik Theft Offender Questionnaire in regard to one case only that he or she is involved in assessing

---

CUPCHIK THEFT OFFENDER QUESTIONNAIRE, V-2 (C.T.O.Q.,V-2)
ISBN 1-896342-08-6   Copyright 1996, 2001 Will Cupchik

To the theft offender: Please fill out this questionnaire as fully as you can; then, go over the product with your lawyer and/or clinician.

SECTION A: CURRENT INFORMATION
Current Date:____/____/____
Your Name:_____
Age:_____   D.O.B.___/___/___

1) <u>What have you been accused of stealing</u> in regard to the current charge(s)?

2) What is the <u>total dollar value</u> of what you have been accused of taking?
Total value = $_____

3) <u>From whom</u> have you been accused of taking these moneys/materials? (Name of person, company, institution, etc...)

4) <u>When</u> <u>(and over what period of time)</u> did the alleged activities take place?

5) Have you <u>ever been charged with theft before?</u>
Yes ( )   No ( )

6) If you have been <u>convicted</u> of theft before, <u>how many times?</u> _____ times

7) Please list in the table below ALL the instances you have stolen, <u>whether you were caught, arrested, charged, convicted, or not.</u> If you need additional space ask for supplementary table(s).

C.T.O.Q.-V2 copyright Dr. Will Cupchik 2001 All Rights Reserved.

Be as complete as you can; the purpose of doing so is to support the helping professional in being able to be of maximum assistance to you. Complete disclosure is in your best interest.
(Not to be copied except for use in one case only: all rights reserved. Additional copies may be purchased from the publisher).

Item 7 continued...

Event	Date D/M/Y	What was taken? Describe item(s)	Dollar value	From Where	Were you charged?	If Convicted, what was the sentence?
1						
2						
3						
4						
5						
6						
7						
8						
9						

8) <u>Describe in as much detail as you can the most recent incident(s)</u> that led to your coming for this assessment. (Use the other side of the page, if necessary)

9) **<u>Describe below what was happening in your life at about the time of the most recent offense(s).</u>** Mention any stressors, illnesses, marital or other relationship related problems/issues existing at the time, or <u>events</u> such as the loss or a job, change of city, country etc...that may have just proceeded the actions which you are accused of having carried out, and which led to you being here today.

10) <u>For whom</u> was the item (or money) <u>intended</u>?
1. myself   ( );
2. my spouse   ( );
3. my children   ( );
4. other person(s)   ( ).

11) If the answer to #10 is "other person(s)," <u>what is the relationship</u> of these persons to you?
1. friend   (   )
2. lover   (   )
3. in-laws   (   )
4. other   (   )_____

12) <u>Did you think/know you were being observed</u> while you carried out the offense?

    Yes ( ):   No ( )

13) If the answer to #12 is 'Yes" then in your own words, <u>state why you went ahead with the act?</u>   <u>What did you say to yourself</u> in your head while you carried out the act?

#14) <u>Did anyone among your friends, family or yourself, have a diagnosis of cancer or other serious illness at the time of the offense?</u>

  Yes ( )   No ( )

#15) If the answer to #14 is 'Yes', <u>who</u> is it that had that diagnosis? What is that person's relationship to you?

#16) <u>Would you say that you had experienced, or were anticipating experiencing shortly, any personally meaningful loss(es) at around the time of the offense?</u>

  Yes ( )   No ( )

#17) If the answer to #16 is 'Yes', please <u>describe the actual or anticipated loss(es).</u>

18) Are you <u>married or living common law</u> with someone?
     Yes (   )   No (   )

19) If married or living common law, how would you <u>describe the current state of your relationship with your 'significant other' at the time of the offence?</u>
(<u>circle</u> one of the following)

      Excellent   Very Good   Good   Fair   Poor   Very Poor

****

SECTION B: BACKGROUND

20) <u>your age:</u> _____

21) <u>Gender:</u> male_____   female_____

22) <u>Are you ... (check all that apply)....</u>

- married_____
- living common-law_____
- separated? _____
- divorced? _____
- single? _____

23) In what country were you <u>born</u>?
       (i) United States_____
       (ii) Canada _____
       (iii) Other: _____
       (iv) Which country?_____

The following questions deal with your parents, childhood, etc...

24) Your <u>father's name:</u>_____

25) Where was he <u>born?</u>_____

26) Is he <u>still living?</u>　　Yes (　)　　　No (　)

27) If your father is still alive, what is his <u>current age:</u>_____

28) If still alive, what is the <u>state of his health?</u>

29) Your <u>mother's name:</u>_____

30) Where was she <u>born?</u>_____

31) Is she <u>still living?</u>　Yes (　)　　　No　(　)

32) If your mother is still alive, what is her <u>current age?</u>_____

33) If still alive, what is <u>the state of her health?</u>

****

Regarding early separations, losses:

34) <u>When you were a child, were you separated from either or both of your parents for any substantial length of time?</u>
　　Yes (　)　　　　　　　　No (　)

　　If you have answered "Yes" to this question, <u>please explain:</u>

C.T.O.Q.-V2　copyright Dr. Will Cupchik 2001　All Rights Reserved.

153

35) Please think back carefully: <u>did you experience any (other) personally meaningful losses or traumatic experiences as a child?</u>

       Yes ( )

       No ( )

       <u>**If your answer is 'yes' then please describe**</u> **these losses or trauma below.;**

****

Further information about the offense

36) <u>What was your general feeling state at about the time of the offense?</u>

       (a) positive feeling state _____

        or

       (b) negative feeling state_____

37) <u>Were you depressed just prior to the offense?</u>

       Yes ( )

       No ( )

38) If the answer to #37 was 'Yes', <u>what were you depressed about?</u> In detail please.

39) Were you experiencing <u>anger</u> towards anyone in particular at about the time of the theft?

       Yes ( )

       No ( )

40) If your answer to #39 is 'Yes,' <u>towards whom</u> were you experiencing anger?

_____

41) <u>What</u> were you angry about with this person?

_____

42) <u>What stressors were you experiencing at about the time of the offense?</u>

43) <u>Did you use a weapon in the commission of the offense?</u>
   Yes (   )   No (   )

44) <u>Have you previously been convicted of any other kinds of crimes,</u>
   e.g. crimes against people or property (such as assault, or 'malicious
   destruction of property') or 'driving while impaired', etc..."
   Yes (   )   No (   )

45) <u>If</u> your answer to question 44 is <u>'Yes', please describe the charges,</u> and
   the details regarding these events, below.

46) What else about you, your theft behavior, or your circumstances
   would you like the reader to know, or think the reader probably
   should know in order to be of assistance to you in this matter.

   C.T.O.Q.-V2 copyright Dr. Will Cupchik 2001 All Rights Reserved.

155

The individual's responses to the Cupchik Theft Offender Questionnaire will frequently suggest a pattern that may be very useful in helping understand the theft offender and his or her thinking, feeling, circumstances and actions in relation to the offense. This information may be applied to the charts of the Theft Offender Spectrum that follows in the next chapter, thereby assisting the clinician to determine whether the offender is more appropriately to be viewed as an Atypical Theft Offender, a Typical Theft Offender, or an A.T.O./T.T.O. Mixed type Theft Offender. This determination, of course, has major relevance to the defense and prosecuting attorneys, to the judges that must deal with the case, and the clinician who may wish to offer appropriate treatment.

Chapter 18

CUPCHIK THEFT OFFENDER SPECTRUM, V-4
[C.T.O.S.-V4]

Using the Cupchik Theft Offender Spectrum
The information that has been obtained in the initial interview with a theft offender-client and via the offender's responses to the Cupchik Theft Offender Questionnaire may now be evaluated using the following two-part Cupchik Theft Offender Spectrum, V-4.

Instructions in using the Cupchik Theft Offender Spectrum
All questions should be answered and the 'totals' noted. The responses to the questions, when tallied, will be suggestive of whether the offender is:

- •the Atypical Theft Offender type,
- •the Typical Theft Offender type, or
- •the A.T.O./T.T.O. - mixed type of theft offender.

Caution and Disclaimer:
The results gained by employing the Cupchik Theft Offender Spectrum should be considered *suggestive* and not definitive. Theft offender cases are often so complex and multifaceted that it is *very unlikely* that a reliable and valid pen-and-paper instrument will be available in the future to provide a conclusive categorization as to theft offender type in any particular case. It will likely always remain the task of an informed and suitably trained and experienced clinician to make such a determination. The Cupchik Theft Offender Spectrum provides a resource guide that can assist in making such a determination.

The Cupchik Theft Offender Spectrum (V-4)
Copyright 1996, 2001 by Will Cupchik Ph.D.

Mailing address for questions regarding this tool should be sent to : Will Cupchik PhD, c/o Tagami Communications, P.O. Box 23059, 437 Spadina Rd., Toronto, Ontario, Canada M5P 2W0

Please note: This version of the Theft Offender Spectrum is intended for use by the purchaser of this book for one case only. A request for limited permission to duplicate or adapt this questionnaire for research or other purposes should be sent to Dr. Cupchik at the above address

The following 14 questions, if answered in the affirmative, tend to suggest that '*Atypical* Theft Offender' elements were operating in a particular case:

CUPCHIK THEFT OFFENDER SPECTRUM, V-4 (Part 1) ISBN: 1-896342-08-6 *C.T.O.S., V-4 Copyright 1996, 2001 Will Cupchik. All rights reserved.*		ato-type	tto-type
item #	**QUESTION**	**YES**	**NO**
1	Did you experience any unusual and/or major losses as a child?		
2	Do these early losses remain largely unresolved, as may be evidenced by the severe intensity of the person's emotional state when referring to these matters?		
3	Was cancer, or any other major illness, an issue existing either in regard to the offender or a 'significant other' at about the time of the offense?		
4	Did the offender experience any personally meaningful losses close to the time of the offense?		
5	Was the offender experiencing marked resentment or anger towards his or her 'intimate other' at about the time of the offense?		
6	Did the offender steal in such an obvious fashion as if to purposely get caught?		

7	Was the <u>monetary value of all that was taken</u> <u>virtually insignificant</u> when compared to the offender's readily available financial resources?		
8	Would a claim of "<u>partial dissociation</u>" be justified in this case? That is, would it be accurate to say that the offender <u>was not fully aware of what she</u> <u>or he was doing</u> at the time of the offense?		
9	Does the offender <u>attend church or some other</u> <u>spiritually directed group functions</u> on a regular basis?		
10	Was the individual under an <u>unusual or excessive</u> <u>amount of stress</u> at the time of the offense?		
11	Was the offense, at least in part, a <u>regressive,</u> <u>symbolic act</u>?		
12	Was the offense likely <u>an attempt to embarrass</u> a 'significant other'?		
13	Was the act 'egodystonic', i.e<u>. is the offender</u> <u>uncomfortable</u> with his or her theft behavior?		
14	Does the offender appear to be experiencing <u>profound shame or humiliation or embarrassment</u> <u>in regard to the fact of his/her having committed</u> <u>the act</u> (as differentiated from such feelings existing merely in relation to having been caught)?		
	Number of items answered "<u>YES</u>", thereby suggesting the offender may belong to the <u>Atypical Theft Offender</u> category =================>	*A:*_	X
	Number of items answered "<u>NO</u>" thereby suggesting the offender may belong to the <u>Typical Theft Offender</u> category =================>	X	*B:*_

The following 11 questions, if answered in the affirmative, tend to suggest that '*Typical* Theft Offender' elements were operating in a particular case:

	CUPCHIK THEFT OFFENDER SPECTRUM, V-4 (Part 2) *C.T.O.S., V-4 Copyright 1996, 2001 Will Cupchik . All rights reserved.*	ato-type	tto-type
item #	QUESTION	NO	YES
15	Was what was stolen <u>desirable</u> to the offender?		
16	Was what was stolen <u>needed</u> by the offender?		
17	Was <u>greed</u> a probable factor?		
18	Was there a <u>conscious premeditation</u> in regard to the theft?		
19	Is stealing <u>an accepted or sanctioned mode of behavior</u> for the offender's intimate other, peers, or social group?		
20	Was the item stolen <u>made use of</u> by the offender for his or her own purposes?		
21	Was the item stolen <u>sold</u> by the offender?		
22	Did the offender <u>give the item to a 'significant other'</u>, i.e. a friend, relative or life partner?		
23	Was the offender, while still a child, <u>'initiated' into stealing</u> by a parent of trusted authority figure?		
24	Was a <u>weapon</u> used in the commission of the offense?*		
25	Has the <u>offender previously been convicted of any other kinds of crimes,</u> e.g. crimes against people or property (such as assault, or 'malicious destruction of property') or 'driving while impaired', etc..."		
	Number of items answered "<u>NO</u>", thereby indicating an inclination to perceive the offender as belonging to the <u>Atypical Theft Offender</u> category ================>	*C:*__	**X**

	Number of items answered **"YES"** thereby indicating an inclination to perceive the offender as belonging to the <u>Typical Theft Offender</u> category ==================>	X	*D:*__
	<u>**Total number of items checked off in the 'ato-type' columns**</u> (add together the numbers in boxes **"A"** and **"C"** and put the sum in Box **"E"** ================================>	*E:*__ __	X
	<u>**Total number of items checked off in the 'tto-type' columns**</u> (add together the numbers in boxes **"B"** and **"D"** and put the sum in box **"F"**=========>	X	*FF:* __

* re Question # 24: If a weapon was used in the commission of the offense, this would virtually exclude the possibility of claiming the Atypical Theft Offender category for this offender unless there are truly extraordinary circumstances or factors to be taken into account. (As an example, a psychiatric breakdown in response to having just experienced the loss of a child might precipitate such behavior in some rare cases; the use of a weapon in a theft as a means of causing the police to take lethal action in the case of a suicidal individual might be another.)

===

DISCUSSION: A CONSIDERATION OF THE SCORING OF THE CUPCHIK THEFT OFFENDER SPECTRUM

By comparing the sums located in boxes *"E"* and *"F"* you will likely be able to make a reasonable estimation of which category of theft offender the particular case in question represents. There are essentially only three categories to consider:

- •<u>Atypical Theft Offender</u> type,
- •<u>Typical Theft Offender</u> type, or

•<u>Mixed</u> type (i.e. displaying substantial aspects of both categories of theft offenders).

*****

1. Atypical Theft Offenders: Over 23 years of forensic experience with theft offenders suggests that if *at least 80% (i.e., 20 questions)* of the twenty-five questions above are answered in the ATO-oriented direction, then the individual may be initially classified with some confidence as an Atypical Theft Offender.

The higher the number of answers in the ATO-oriented direction, the greater the confidence with which a provisional diagnosis of Atypical Theft Offender may be justified.

*****

2. Typical Theft Offenders: On the other hand, if *at least 80% (i.e., 20 or more questions)* of the twenty-five questions above are answered in the TTO-oriented direction, the greater the confidence with which a provisional diagnosis of Typical Theft Offender may be justified.

*****

3. Mixed-Type (A.T.O./T.T.O.): If neither the A.T.O. nor T.T.O. categories receive at lest 20 answers in their direction, then the client is more likely to belong to the Mixed-Type of theft offender, possessing *both* Atypical Theft Offender *and* Typical Theft Offender qualities.

*****

Please Note: On occasion, even Typical Theft Offenders may become so disturbed and distressed by their illegal conduct and its often devastating effects on their lives that some of them may genuinely desire to cease their theft behavior. Experience with some such clients has shown that the prognoses in such cases, while necessarily guarded, are nevertheless occasionally quite positive.

*****

Who may benefit from the Theft Offender Intervention Program?

The individuals most likely to benefit (in the order of probability of success) are the following:

1. Primarily or exclusively Atypical Theft Offenders
2. many The Mixed-Types
3. even Typical Theft Offenders

as long as they are *genuinely motivated* to cease their theft behavior.

Who would *not* benefit from the Theft Offender Intervention Program?

Any theft offenders, whether Atypical Theft Offenders, the Mixed-type, or Typical Theft Offenders who primarily are seeking a letter or report for court purposes in order to minimize their sentences, *but who have minimal or no genuine interest to cease their theft behavior*, will find the Intensive Intervention Program of no use to them. Since the personal work is indeed very intense and self-revealing, attempts to fabricate an appearance of wanting to stop their theft behavior will very likely fail.

Chapter 19

CLINICAL ASSESSMENT OF ATYPICAL THEFT OFFENDERS: AN INTRODUCTION

My general approach to assessing A.T.O.s

There are usually two clinical purposes to assessing likely Atypical Theft Offenders. First, a clinician (usually a forensic psychiatrist or psychologist) might be conducting a forensic assessment at the request of the offender's attorney, or for the judge, for purposes of sentencing. Second, the clinician may be conducting an assessment directed at understanding the offender so that a suitable treatment program may be devised to help prevent a recurrence of the theft behavior.

My own assessment efforts are usually directed to both of the above purposes, because it has become abundantly clear to me (and the courts) that unless effective treatment is undertaken, there exists a distinct possibility or recidivism – again and again.

Most often, I will receive a telephone call from a lawyer whose client who has recently been arrested for theft and the attorney has recognized that the actions of the client were rather nonsensical, given the circumstances, the value of the items taken or position of the person involved.

Alternately, I may receive an e-mail (wcupchik@aol.com) or a telephone call (to 416-928-2262) from a theft offender who is in dire straits after having been apprehended for theft yet one more time, where the individual may even have been in psychotherapy for some time and made progress in other areas of his or her life yet continues to have major problems with theft behavior.

The client may be a blue-collar or white-collar worker, or an eminent professional with a salary in excess of $150,000 who has just been arrested for stealing anything from a $2 item to $200,000 or more. The client may simply be a reasonably intelligent, generally honest man or woman, with ordinary social, work or family-related obligations, who has already been convicted of theft on one or more previous occasions, perhaps months, years or even decades earlier.

At the time of the prior charge(s), especially if it was a first court appearance, the judge may have let the person off, possibly with a small fine, and at the time the event may have been viewed as an aberration in the life of this individual. Now, some time later, there has been yet another 'aberration,' and the lawyer is dismayed that his or her client would have been so inappropriate once again!

I usually see a new theft offender/client for an initial series of from three or four to eight or more interviews in order to determine whether, and to what extent, it may be appropriate to consider the individual an Atypical Theft Offender, or at least to assess what sorts of motivations the client may have had in relation to their behavior. The reason for the variation in the number of interviews required is due to the fact that some cases initially present as simple but soon emerge as considerably more complex.

Meeting the ATO client: Dealing with their initial discomfort

A.T.O.s often present as very tense, embarrassed, depressed, and angry with themselves, and may well have anticipated that the clinician will inform them either that (1) they are basically 'bad' persons; and/or (2) they are 'sick' individuals; and/or (3) they are entirely undeserving of respectful treatment since they have behaved so abominably and should be viewed as 'nothing better than thieves'. It is most unfortunate and entirely inappropriate, in my opinion, when clients are initially treated in such ways. It is usually the clinician's lack of understanding of the issues underlying most atypical theft behavior that underlies such ill-treatment.

Sometimes (but relatively infrequently) a new client may initially be quite defensive, and say that he or she didn't commit the act, that the whole thing was a mistake, even though the individual may acknowledge having been previously apprehended on one or more occasions for similar offences, possibly even resulting in convictions. In the case of A.T.O.s, while there may be some degree of conscious intention to deceive the interviewer, more often than not the Atypical Theft Offender-type theft offender who denies responsibility for the act with which he or she has been charged is only partially, or not at all, consciously aware of his or her own behavior at the time of the alleged offense. It is possible that partial dissociation has been at work here.

Partial dissociation is the mental mechanism that allows us to drive our cars successfully from point A to point B without our being fully consciously aware of our having negotiated every turn, stop, acceleration, etc.... This sort of driving can happen while we are carrying on some prolonged inner thought or fantasy sequence. Such activity is well within the realm or normalcy; of course, so are accidents and therefore it behooves most of us to 'keep our minds on our driving' and not elsewhere while we are attempting to get from A to B.

The clinician is advised to take the view, as a starting position, that the client's nonsensical theft behavior may indicate that there are underlying psychological issues to be uncovered, identified and dealt with, rather than that the theft offender is a 'bad' person, or that he or she is being deliberately evasive and just does not want to admit that he or she knows full well (i.e., is consciously well aware) of having carried out the theft.

Clinicians, especially those with many years of forensic experience, will usually be immediately aware of some differences in the manner of the possible A.T.O. client as compared with T.T.O. persons for whom theft has become an accepted (and acceptable) way of living, compatible with both their self-images and conscious desires.

An exception: honest persons with few resources and in genuine need!

Generally speaking, it is true that when essentially honest persons steal, that they do so for psychological reasons, rather than out of greed or need. But, as mentioned previously, it is a fact that some honest individuals have found themselves in dire economical straits and that, if they were to not steal, they and/or their loved ones might not eat, or even survive. Sadly, through time immemorial war-time conditions have provided usually honest persons with such circumstances.

Escapees of prisoner-of-war camps have described stealing food or shoes in order to survive somewhat longer. Most readers would agree that such circumstances may have made theft, or other usually morally 'wrong' actions, not only understandable but, in the circumstances, even morally justified.

How many parents would not agree with the statement that if the only way to stop the indefinite suffering and possibly life-threatening distress of our children would involve what we normally would consider reprehensible actions (such as theft), then many of us parents would, however reluctantly, carry out the required actions to help our offspring. I have over the years assessed a few women who were similarly severely restricted by their abusive and controlling spouses when it came to spending money for food and clothing for their children. This happened, notwithstanding the fact that their spouses readily spent money for their own alcoholic consumption. In these cases the 'typical' theft behaviors of these women had distinct 'atypical' theft behavior undertones, which the courts who have been so informed by my reports have usually been both wise and compassionate in taking these facts into consideration at trial.

The writer's investigations have focused upon the more-important-than-previously-recognized role of earlier (frequently in childhood) losses, to later acts of theft by then-adults. The more recent losses appear to have reverberated deep within the psyches of the offenders, stirring up unresolved and emotionally laden memories. The offenders have usually acted out without recognition of the psychological relationship between the childhood events and the much more recent losses.

Cases of clients have been presented in this book where childhood experiences of wartime trauma have precipitated theft behavior. Lingering confusion may inhabit the deep psyche when previous shoplifting or other theft activities have had a genuine survival element, as is not uncommon during war-time conditions. After the war is over and the person is supposedly 'safe and secure' in a new country, say the USA, then, when severely stressed, the person may revert back to the previous life saving (but now unnecessary and probably inappropriate) behavior.

The classical work, Attachment and Loss, Volume III: Loss, Sadness and Depression[xvii] by John Bowlby, and the more recent book, Necessary Losses, by Judith Viorst make the case that more recent losses may 'stir up,' at an unconscious level, the residue of earlier and still largely unresolved losses.

On occasion, more recent losses in adulthood have been so traumatic that they have precipitated theft events without any childhood precursors having been present. (For example, the case of a man who started shoplifting after his daughter died of leukemia, and of a woman who shoplifted after her close relative died of cancer; in neither case were there any significant childhood loss experiences, nor any theft behavior during childhood.)

If the client re-offends while still undergoing assessment

Before moving on the issue of treatment it is worthwhile pointing out that sometimes, even during the assessment process, a client may report that he or she has offended once again. Such a situation, while of course unfortunate, can simultaneously be an important data-gathering opportunity, especially since as the latest theft event and the circumstances surrounding it are so fresh in the client's mind.

The following questions that deal with the offender's thoughts, feelings, behavior and circumstances prior to, during, and after the commission of the offense, may provide answers relevant to the clinical assessment and treatment process, especially when dealing with *Atypical* Theft Offenders.

1- "BEFORE THE OFFENSE" issues:

The clinician is well advised to inquire of the client in regard to the following matters:

- What had happened in the person's life just prior to the shoplifting act?

- Had he or she had a disagreement with a partner or other significant person (e.g., a relative, or a boss)?

- Had he or she received distressing news?

- Had there been a difficult encounter with an authority figure?

- What had he or she been thinking just prior to entering the store in question? Why that store?

- Was there an awareness of entering the store with a conscious intention to steal?

- If a female, where was she in her menstrual cycle? As indicated elsewhere, some female Atypical Theft Offenders have acted out repeatedly during a particular phase of their cycle.

*****

2- "DURING THE OFFENSE" issues:

- What thoughts, feelings, and bodily sensations did the person have *during* the act of shoplifting?

- Did the offender experience excitement, anger, an adrenaline 'rush', frustration, or high' of some sort during the act?

- Was the offender aware or suspicious that a particular individual in their vicinity may have been a 'loss prevention' employee?

- If yes, what was the offender's self-talk when that observer was spotted?

•Did the offender go ahead and steal even with the clear impression that he or she was being watched by store security, or did he or she put the item(s) back? Why?

*****

3-"AFTER THE OFFENSE" issues:

- What did the person think and feel just after taking the object, perhaps while still in the store?

- What bodily sensations was he or she experiencing? Was there a rapid heart beat, or profuse sweating?

- What was the person aware of thinking, feeling, and doing while he/she was trying to exit the store? Were there feelings of guilt, excitement, anger, resentment, distress, disbelief, or satisfaction?

- Once apprehended, how did the offender react? What did he or she say when confronted by store security? What was the offender's inner self-talk like?

*****

It is very important for the clinician to examine these questions in detail, as the offender's answers may be highly relevant to the determination of whether the offender may be classified as an Atypical Theft Offender or Typical Theft Offender, or of the Mixed-Type.

Chapter 20

ASSESSING TREATMENT POTENTIAL

The treatment potential of possible Atypical Theft Offenders may be determined by consideration of the following factors when assessing these clients:

- their motivations for attending clinical assessment sessions;
- their psychological issues with authority figures;
- the degree of their felt experience of remorse, shame, self-disgust in relation to their behavior;
- the genuineness of their desire to seek treatment;
- the willingness to self-disclose during sessions;
- the willingness to "do homework" that may be assigned by the clinician; and
- the willingness of spouses, or other relevant 'significant others' to become involved in the assessment and treatment process.

The Atypical Theft Offender's motivation to attend for treatment

Not surprisingly, A.T.O.s present themselves for assessment and/or treatment with a variety of motivations, including the following:

- they may desire favorable psychological reports for court purposes

- they may feel pressured to see someone so that the lawyers may at least say that 'professional help is being sought.'

- they are frequently genuinely confused and distressed by their behavior and want help to stop stealing. They are frightened by their behavior, feel out of control, and that they cannot stop it even though they know it may ruin their professional, social, family lives, and/or

- they are curious, if not desperate, to understand their aberrant behavior.

Clearly, success in treatment is likely to be a function of that person's motivation for attending. It is only reasonable to expect that the client should be concerned about getting a report that will be 'helpful' in court. Unfortunately, in perhaps 10%-20% of the cases that come to my attention, this is their sole motivation. In such cases they may not be entirely forthcoming in revealing relevant information.

For example, a few years ago a law student at a prominent university on the west coast initially told me one 'story' of misguided innocence; it only emerged after seven or eight sessions that he had decided, having read my book, to 'feed' me what he thought I would want to hear. This he admitted as I persistently followed up on my questioning to better comprehend answers that he gave that did not appear to be likely to be accurate. He then admitted that, in fact, he been a fully involved participant in a scam that had gone on for several months. It eventually emerged that, while he was in no way an 'innocent party', he had been motivated to act out by virtue of the directions his life had taken ever since he had been greatly mistreated by his parents and others during a complex, dramatic, and tragic set of circumstances that occurred when he was fourteen years old.

Deterrents to clients becoming involved in phony assessment and/or therapy include the financial costs they will bear, as well as the emotional and intellectual commitment whose absence will usually be uncovered early in the work together. Insincere theft offender/clients will frequently not carry out the "homework" required of them *between* sessions and/or will exhibit a demonstrable reluctance to become involved in the therapeutic 'exercises' offered *during* the clinical sessions.

I have found, after having been previously involved for many years in dealing with persons charged with all manner of criminal offenses (ranging from theft to sexual assault to murder), that the mere compliance of a client, as opposed to his or her genuine involvement in the therapeutic process, is often, though by no means always, detectable. At the same time I am also convinced that on any given day, almost any forensic specialist, be he or she an experienced psychologist, psychiatrist or social worker, or criminal lawyer, can be 'taken in' by the presentation of at least some clients.

Let the forensic professional beware when dealing with certain apparently Atypical Theft Offenders, lest their displays of sincerity regarding wanting to deal with the issues underlying their theft behavior evaporate post-sentencing. This phenomenon has a great deal to do with the offender's wish to avoid pain; first, the pain of the court's sentence, and later confronting and coming to terms with the painful issues (of losses, of sadness, of anger, etc...) that have been not been previously resolved.

The 'Authority Figure' issue with A.T.O.s

Although many Atypical Theft Offenders are well functioning, law-abiding, and seemingly mentally healthy individuals, many of them have major issues with 'authority figures.' When stressed, or distressed, they may be inclined to behave in ways that can be construed as rebellious or anti-authority oriented. Many of them feel trapped, depressed, unhappy, afraid and reluctant to deal with the negative feelings they may be experiencing towards authoritarian persons or authority figures such as a manager or employer, or for that matter the "critical parent" part of their spouses. Because they may have difficulty expressing their feelings of resentment in ways that are either effective or sufficient, they may be inclined towards acting out against these (or other) authority figures, via stealing.

Of course, clinicians (psychologists, psychiatrists, social workers, etc...) are also authority figures. Therefore, unfortunately, the prospective A.T.O. client may be inclined to act out against, oppose, or surreptitiously sabotage attempts of the clinician to help them. Or, since, after all, their vehicle of acting out is by taking things they have not paid for, they might be inclined to not pay their clinicians' bills for services already rendered.

One of the major tasks of the clinician is to assist the client to uncover and overcome the latter's attempts to sabotage the assessment and/or treatment process. This behavior is often observable in early assessment sessions. Helping clients to become aware of feelings of resentment towards the clinician early on in the clinical process can be an important step in their learning to better deal with authority issues.

Fortunately for A.T.O. clients, their relationships with experienced clinicians (who are alert to such transference phenomena) may allow them to address their 'unfinished business' with authority figures from their earlier years, as well as those persons (e.g., spouses or bosses) whose authoritarian aspects may have helped trigger the clients' recent acting out responses.

It is unfortunate but true that many A.T.O. clients do have spouses whose personalities have pronounced authoritarian aspects; these clients' assessments have shown time and time again that such features in their spouses have been precipitating factors in relation to their acting out behaviors. This issue must be dealt with for successful therapy to occur.

Spousal involvement as a predictor in treatment outcome

My clinical experience is that the majority of married A.T.O.s have serious problems in their marital relationships, problems that usually have dynamic import for their theft behavior.

Furthermore the readiness and willingness of the spouses to become involved in the treatment process may be a determining factor as regards the time required for successful treatment or, for that matter, even the possibility of treatment success.

I have observed the entire gamut of 'spousal willingness' to become involved in the treatment process, and in their willingness to take some responsibility for the problems which may exist in the relationship, and which may have precipitated the theft behavior in question.

For example, one spouse informed me that, since speaking with me during a previous session, she had realized that the timing of her husband's infrequent shoplifting behavior over the previous decade had corresponded to the times of her extramarital involvements. Successful 'treatment' in this case involved the spouse and the offender dealing with unresolved marital issues that had led to her seeking sexual and emotional nurturance outside the relationship.

Both this spouse and her husband/offender worked on their issues at length, and their improved relating style included his talking to his wife about his response to her periodic emotional and sexual distancing, which included considerable fear of abandonment and much anger, which then impelled him towards theft behavior. Over a period of months their verbal and emotional relating styles improved dramatically and, not surprisingly, so did their sex lives.

When it comes to the matter of treatment with Atypical Theft Offenders, if their intimate others are not prepared to become clinically involved and therefore part of the solution, they will almost assuredly be a major part of a continuing problem.

A large minority of spouses are not interested in seeking treatment, or even, for that matter, in attending for even a single session (which I frequently do request) in order to supply the clinician with potentially helpful information about the spouse/offender. A.T.O. clients in such situations may eventually find themselves dealing with long-postponed decisions about whether to continue in the marital situation.

The prospect for success in treatment definitely improves with enthusiastic and willing spousal involvement. As one client's spouse said to me, "I love my wife dearly. I realize that there is probably something I could do to help her but I don't know what that something is. I am here to find out, and to do it, if I can!"

The clinical importance of the A.T.O.'s remorse

Our initial investigations indicated that some A.T.O.s are inclined to act out without as much remorse as they usually would experience for contravening their own moral and ethical codes of behavior if, at the time of the offense, they had experienced what was, for them, an excessive amount of stress.

Most persons can relate to this phenomenon: if we are late for an important meeting related to our job, we might be more inclined to cut off other drivers, or be more aggressive about taking a parking spot that we are well aware another person also has as legitimate a claim to, and we might not feel as remorseful about our behavior as we would in less trying circumstances. We may justify our behavior to ourselves by thinking, "Well, I needed the spot more than the other driver did. His job probably isn't on the line the way mine might be if I don't get to this important meeting on time."

Many A.T.O.s experience remorse very soon after the commission of the offense. They may feel badly about their behavior and very poorly about themselves. At the same time, and this is the confounding element, they may also get a 'high' from the commission of the theft, much as a child may be quite excited and even triumphant after 'borrowing' an older sibling's CD album or tennis racket.

Occasionally, some Atypical Theft Offenders have returned to the store or employer from whom they stole and have asked for forgiveness. Even if the person offended against is not prepared to forgive, the offenders at least may regain a sense of dignity and self-respect for having owned up to their wrong conduct, and having had the courage to face the person or organization they offended against.

As mentioned earlier, a true Typical Theft Offender who has not undergone a substantial personality restructuring, would be extremely unlikely to ever experience remorse for his or her theft behavior, let alone seek forgiveness from those he or she had wronged.

Willingness to attend for treatment

It is rewarding to witness the large proportion of A.T.O.s who demonstrate initial relief and, eventually, renewed self-respect as they learn in therapy to uncover and to better confront their marital, vocational, interpersonal and intrapersonal issues. Until they came for clinical assessment and treatment they almost invariably had not recognized that these personal issues were related to their theft behavior. Then, as the underlying problems were dealt with, their felt desire to 'act out' by stealing diminished markedly. As one client said recently, "Before, I felt like I was handling the house and the children all alone, and shopping and shoplifting, gave me some kind of emotional outlet. Now that my husband (who chose to attend most of the sessions) and I are working as a team and are so much closer, I have no desire whatever to go 'window-shopping', let alone shopping or shoplifting. I can't believe the time and money I spent trying to feel better. It never worked for very long. I would have to go shopping several times a week just to feel I could handle my life. Now we go shopping together, look after the kids together, and I have never been happier in my life."

A.T.O.s have often been avoiding therapeutic help for a long time. And, not infrequently, A.T.O.s are distinctly 'un'- or even 'anti'- psychological in intellectual and philosophical orientation. Indeed, this is probably part of their problem. In numerous cases, they have been avoiding their feelings, and even whole issues of their lives for years, or even decades. The prospect of facing the unconscious or subconscious aspects of their lives, i.e., components of their psyches they previously may not have even acknowledged or recognized, can be very difficult for them.

Of course, the same can be said for many other kinds of clients who come for clinical assessment and treatment. Atypical Theft Offenders may therefore not be very different in these regards from most clinicians' clientele. Their assessment and treatment, however, do involve specific and in certain respects, special elements, as the reader has already learned and will discover more about throughout the remainder of this book.

Willingness to self-disclose: a serious problem for many A.T.O.s

The willingness to discuss my 'self,' to let another person know 'me,' the 'me' below the surface, is something that for each one of us requires a decision to 'open up'. No one 'opens up' about everything to any other single person, in normal circumstances. Nevertheless, it is important for prospective clients to be open about their current and previous living situations, their personal and theft behavior histories, etc... .

In the case of A.T.O.s, these persons may feel coerced to self-disclose because they have committed an offense and are facing a court appearance. *Unlike* most therapy clients, they have usually not come looking for something called "psychotherapy"; they often merely want 'a report for court.' The fact that effective treatment may require a highly focused psychotherapeutic approach that will, necessarily, have to examine and deal with the client's history and crucial elements of his or her previous and current life circumstances, may not be what the A.T.O. client bargained for. The onus is on the clinician to inform the theft offender/client what will be required of him or her, if the professional is to be optimally helpful.

Like their Atypical Theft Offender clients, some lawyers understandably also may desire, when referring the client, that the clinician would write a 'helpful' report for court purposes, *and nothing more!* It is my clinical opinion, however, that the clinician owes it to the client, but as well, to the latter's lawyer and to the court, to make clear the parameters of the problem, as the clinician sees them, and the directions which may lead to genuine solutions of the theft behavior.

> It is important to indicate to the client, the referring lawyer and the court that, if the psychological and/or situational conditions (of home life, working life, interpersonal and intrapersonal problems) which precipitated the acting out theft behavior remain undealt with in substantial ways, then the likelihood of future theft behavior remains, if not as an immediate likelihood, then one that may reoccur months or years in the future.

Once the client is clear that part of the purpose of the clinical assessment is to determine a direction for obtaining successful treatment, he or she almost invariably experiences a marked sense of relief that a solution to the theft behavior problem may be achievable, and then realizes that it is in his or her best interest to assist the clinician. This attitude strengthens the therapeutic alliance, and greater self-disclosure is more likely to follow.

> I inform clients in the first interview that my purposes are two-fold:
> (1) to help them find out why they offended, and
> (2) to help them uncover ways and means of ensuring that the probability of any repetition of such behavior will be minimized.

Clearly if the client were to decide to not self-disclose, even after such assurances and explanations, the prognosis in that case would have to be extremely guarded.

The A.T.O.'s willingness to 'do homework'

I often invite clients to do some "homework," such as, at the least, reading this book, in order that they become familiar with our findings regarding why some essentially honest persons have stolen. Clients are asked to go over the material, preferably with their spouses, and report back, particularly regarding any stressors, and especially any losses, that they may have had, or were anticipating having, at about the time of the offense. They are asked to complete the Cupchik Theft Offender Questionnaire and Cupchik Theft Offender Spectrum as well. By providing such information, clients can assist greatly the speed and effectiveness of the assessment, and subsequent treatment. Good therapy prospects will usually 'dig deeply,' wanting to uncover the factors that may be significant in their having acted out.

Early on in treatment I also recommend to clients one or more books that may also facilitate the treatment process. James' and Jongeward's **Born to Win** is a book that I recommend to most of my clients -- theft offenders and most others. There is so much material in that book that is helpful to clients generally, and for facilitating the therapeutic process in which we shall become engaged, that I request that clients not only to read the book, but do the exercises as well. Their willingness to do so, or not, often has considerable therapeutic import; in other words, if they comply with these requests they are usually well on their way to moving to resolve their problems.

Appointments and fees

Certain A.T.O. clients, as I indicated above, have been shown to have a need to act out against authority figures. Lawyers and clinicians who work with this population would do well to remember this fact and to protect themselves and the clients themselves from the latter's possible tendencies to cancel appointments, and/or write NSF checks somewhat more frequently than clients who would be their socio-economic peers but who do not share the same manner of acting out.

I usually require 48 hours notice for cancellation of appointments without payment. I also request that clients pay for each session at the time of the session. This minimizes paperwork via sending out bills, and as importantly, the likelihood that A.T.O. clients would not cover the fees owed.

My own policy is one of not chasing clients very far for payments owed. They know they are required to pay for their sessions, and I prefer to appeal to their Adult aspect, rather than chase their rebellious Child state, by simply sending only one reminder.

In the event that non-payment of fees happens, it is usually entirely inappropriate for the clinician to take the matter personally. The client is, in all likelihood, merely acting out in his or her usual fashion against an authority figure.

Obviously the client who does cancels sessions without good reason, or whose checks bounce, would not be viewed as a good prospect for therapy, even if such behaviors suggest that the client may need same.

Chapter 21

AN ABRIDGED TRANSCRIPT OF A FIRST CLINICAL SESSION WITH A SELF-REFERRED SHOPLIFTER *WHO HAD NEVER BEEN CAUGHT*: (Alice, Case # 5)

As I mentioned earlier, several years ago I received a telephone call from a woman who said that she had been carrying around in her purse, for over a year, an article which had appeared in a Toronto newspaper referring to the original investigation we had carried out at the Clarke Institute. She stated that she believed she fitted into our categorization of 'Atypical Theft Offender' and that she wanted to talk with me because she had shoplifted "again" within the previous two weeks. She also told me that she had never been caught for stealing, but that this behavior was very upsetting to her as she was not 'that sort of person'.

Our first clinical session took place one week after our telephone conversation. The session was recorded and transcribed. An edited transcript of that session appears below.

This person was relatively unique in that she had never been apprehended for shoplifting, even though she had been carrying out this activity intermittently for more than 8 years.

(I have occasionally taken into treatment other persons who have stolen but have never been caught. These individuals have been highly distressed by their behavior, and frightened by the possible consequences of their being caught and charged at some time in the future. Not surprisingly, they usually make excellent clients as they are highly motivated and, with no charges pending, have no immediate concern with trying to impress me for purposes of any court-directed report. They want merely to understand and cease this behavior, which they experience as egodystonic and out-of-control.)

As the reader will note from the transcript that follows, this woman's comments simply yet eloquently illustrate many of the major

181

points made in this book. Her shoplifting activities represented, at the least, (a) a reaction to stress, as well as (b) unconscious retribution, (c) a response to both actual and anticipated losses, (d) a response to her anger at her spouse, and (e) a reaction to the occurrence of serious illness (in this instance, cancer, in her husband's body). There was, however, also one brief period when she did exhibit behavior that could be classified as of the A.T.O./T.T.O. mixed type.

Case# 5 revisited: AN ABRIDGED TRANSCRIPT OF A FIRST SESSION WITH ALICE, A CLASSIC EXAMPLE OF AN 'ATYPICAL THEFT OFFENDER'

Alice: I understand that you have been doing investigations on cancer patients and shoplifters.

Will Cupchik: Well, really on shoplifters. Some of them happen to have cancer themselves, or are dealing with a person close to them who has cancer.

A. Right, that's what I thought, because it's my husband who has the cancer, not me.

W. Who does the shoplifting?

A. I do. If you want to look up his hospital records you can see that he first had cancer in 1978. He's been a long-term patient. He goes into remission and then gets hit again. After he took his first bout of cancer they operated on him. He has only been able to work occasionally since that time.

W. What kind of work does he do?

A. Well, the last job he had he was a truck salesman. Anyway, he again has been in the Cancer Hospital several times. He had an operation...he had tumors in his stomach again, two years ago and then had to go back for some more chemotherapy and cobalt and it just goes on and on. What has been happening is that I've been shoplifting, but what I've done after I take things is that I don't want them and then I give them to the Salvation Army or the Goodwill Services.

W. You don't keep any of them?

A. No, never.

W. Do you know why?

A. No, I just don't want them. After I take something I feel really bad about it and then I keep it around for a couple of days and then donate it to the Goodwill Services or the Salvation Army Store.

W. Which newspaper article did you read dealing with our investigations?

A. I read it in the Toronto Star about a year ago. You and another doctor.

W. And what was your reaction to reading the article?

A. Well, I said to myself, "This is what's been happening to me, and it must be happening to other people!" I thought I was really strange because after I would take something from a store I would think, "Why did I do that?" because it was mostly stuff I didn't even want, or something I couldn't even use.

W. Had you any understanding why you might be doing it?

A. No. And this has been very upsetting. My husband had cancer for years and he would go into remission, then it would come back again and he'd have to take some more radiation and chemotherapy, then he'd get better again, and you know, over that long period of time it's been very difficult for me.

W. How does the shoplifting parallel the occurrence of cancer?

A. Well, I'd never shoplifted before. The first time was the year he first got cancer. I had never shoplifted before. Never!

W. Do you remember the first time you shoplifted?

A. Yes!

W. Tell me abut that.

A. Well, I just went into the department store and I was walking around, you know, and I had a large bag with me, and I just walked around the lingerie department and I slipped a couple of things into my bag and I left the store, and nobody caught me or anything.

W. What kind of 'things' did you take?

A. A pair of panties and sort of a little black silky nightie. So then after I got home I started thinking about what I had done and I felt remorse about it but I didn't know what I should do. I was afraid to go back and tell them because I thought they would prosecute me, so I didn't. Instead, I just donated it to the Goodwill Services. And the other problem is that there is a sexual problem too because of all the radiation and chemotherapy he's had. He's impotent, and so we don't exactly have a normal marital life.

W. When was he first impotent?

A. Way back when he first had cancer treatment.[xviii] but then he would go into remission and wasn't taking chemotherapy and he wasn't awfully sick, so we'd have some sort of sexual relations, but then as he...then when he....now he's really impotent because when he had the tumors in his lower stomach and they gave him the treatment down there... well, it has made him totally impotent.

W. As of when?

A. Two years ago, when he had the tumors in his stomach.

W. So, for four years he has been totally impotent?

A. Totally impotent.

W. When was the last time you shoplifted?

A. The last time was about a week and a half ago. I went again into the same department store, to the hardware department, and put a little package of... I'm not even sure what they are..... little wrenches or something. I put them into my shopping bag and just walked out. I didn't get caught. I have never got caught!

W. This was two weeks ago?

A. Yeah. And then after I got home I kept thinking, "Why am I doing this?" And then after, I didn't even want them and I don't even know what they are for, and...but they were useless things I couldn't use.

W. Do you remember what day of the week it was? You say it was two weeks ago.

A. I think it was on a Wednesday.

W. Can you connect that to anything that happened with your husband, around that time? Or between the two of you?

A. Yes, I was quite upset with him because he wanted to go to the ball game, and I get concerned because I don't want him to go to the ball game or where I don't go; perhaps he will drink beer when he is there and it always has a very bad effect on him. When he drinks, I don't know whether it's because of the chemotherapy, but alcohol has a very, very bad effect on him.

W. What does it do to him?

A. It's a physical effect. It makes him very ill, physically, and his face gets all red. He has high blood pressure now. His face gets beet red, and he looks like he is going to have some sort of an attack, or pass out.

W. So it's very frightening to you?

A. It frightens me to death because....I don't know...normally he's quite a pale man, his skin is quite pale because his white count is up or down, or something, but normally his skin is not red. But whenever he drinks alcohol, his face gets this beet red look and it goes right down to this part of his chest, and he gets very sick afterwards. He gets very nauseated.

W. Then what happens?

A. Well, he wakes up feeling terrible and scared and sometimes insists that I take him to the emergency department at the hospital. The doctor told him not to drink anyway.

W. Why?

A. Because of the treatment he's had. They tell him alcohol just doesn't ...you know, it's not good for him.

W. So when he goes to the ball game what's happening with you?

A. Well, I stay home but I worry because I think he'll be drinking and then he'll come home and I'll perhaps have to sit up with him all night, because I'm afraid he might pass out or something might happen.

W. And when did you shoplift, relative to when he was going to the ball game?

A. The next day.

W. And how was he when he came home from the game that day?

A. Well, he had been drinking.

W. What happened?

A. He had the same reaction he always gets! His face got beet red and flushed, and he stayed like that and then got very nauseated.

W. After he came home did you have to stay up with him?

A. Sure! I have to stay up all night with him every time because what if something happened?

W. Now that we're talking about it, what's your thinking about your shoplifting?

A. Well, there's some connection there with his cancer and his treatment and what I'm going through with him....there's got to be some connection! I didn't think there was until I read the article in the paper, and I said, "Well, that sounds just like me."

W. You read that a year ago?. What did you do with the article?

A. I cut it out and saved it and said "I'm going to get in touch with these doctors" but it was a very hard thing for me to come here this morning. I made myself, I forced myself to come.

W. Why was it so hard to come?

A. Because I realized that I have a problem and I don't know why it was so hard; I'm ashamed of what I've done. I guess it's hard to face up to.

W. Do you think it's hard for your husband to face up to his drinking problem, like it is for you to face up to your shoplifting?

A. Yeah.

W. Have you ever been caught shoplifting?

A. No, I haven't.

W. Have you been caught for something else?

A. I was caught for writing bad checks.

W. When did that start?

A. That started just after he was diagnosed with cancer for the first time. He was in hospital for 6 months and we didn't have enough money to pay our rent, and I wrote a rent check. Anyway, I was charged with writing two bad checks.... There was no money in the bank to cover them, and I wrote a rent check and a check for something else. We didn't have any source of income at the time and I didn't even know about welfare.

> *W. How do you feel right now, as you are talking about it?*
> *A. Well, as I said, I had to force myself to come here this morning.*
> *W. What's it like to actually talk about this business?*
> *A. It's a little embarrassing, but I really do feel that I have to do something about this because I just can't go on like this. And I think there has to be a connection between my husband's cancer and my shoplifting because I've never, never in my life ever shoplifted or anything before he got cancer, not once, ever in my whole life. And I wasn't brought up that way. I was taught right from wrong and I was never, ever in that position before.*
> *W. I very much appreciate that you did work up your courage to call and come in today and I think it's very worthwhile talking about some more.*

*****

Some comments about this case.

I think that most readers will agree that this person's shoplifting was probably related to her husband's becoming ill, and that according to the definitions and parameters established in this book, that here surely is an almost classic case of an A.T.O.. Interestingly, there was at one time a mixture of A.T.O./T.T.O.-type behavior, when she passed some bad checks after her husband was first diagnosed with cancer and he was off work for so long that they ran out of funds.

To summarize, the data that support the conclusion that Alice was primarily a classic Atypical Theft Offender include the following major points:

- Alice voluntarily contacted a clinician in spite of the fact that she had never been apprehended for theft;

- she had never shoplifted prior to when she started shoplifting shortly after her husband first had cancer;

- she stole what she didn't need;

186

- sometimes she didn't even know what the items she stole were used for;

- she would only shoplift when her husband had another bout of cancer;

- she did not shoplift when her husband was in remission;

- she experienced great remorse and embarrassment after she stole;

- she never kept most of the items she stole. She would give the stolen items away anonymously (to charities);

- she was aware that her theft behavior was bizarre and felt strange and out of control whenever she did it;

- she sometimes stole when she was angry with her spouse;

- some of her thefts were blatantly symbolic, as when she stole lingerie after her husband's treatments had left him impotent;

- She was brought up in a home that taught morals and she had been a sincerely honest person up to the point that she   had   stolen following her husband's first bout with cancer.

It is noteworthy, that Alice did commit another kind of theft after her husband first was diagnosed with cancer and when he was off work for so long that there was no money to pay the rent. This theft behavior involved passing some bad checks to pay the rent. It is probably appropriate to consider this particular acts indicative of the A.T.O./T.T.O.- mixed type of theft behavior, yet this categorization would be mitigated by her other theft behavior and the underlying psychodynamics operating in her case.

Chapter 22

The Case For Inclusion Of The <u>Atypical Theft Offender Syndrome</u> & The <u>Theft Offender Continuum</u> In A Future Version Of The American Psychiatric Association's Diagnostic And Statistical Manual For Mental Disorders (DSM)

The current possibility of a *mis*diagnosis of kleptomania in cases of Atypical Theft Offenders

The Diagnostic and Statistical Manual is a major resource for many clinicians and managed care providers pertaining to the diagnosis, assessment and treatment of mental and emotional disorders. However, over two decades of clinical findings by this author as well as other researchers (including Fugere, R, D'Elia, A, and Philippe) have strongly indicated that DSM-IV does not reflect some important clinical findings in regard to the matter of theft offenses. In particular, acts of theft carried out by persons who can be considered Atypical Theft Offenders but who are not suffering from kleptomania, are not currently recognized in this important diagnostic manual. Indeed, the conceptualization of the Theft Offender Continuum, with Atypical Theft Offenders at one end and Typical Theft Offenders at the other, are unknown to this manual. This is so even though our original article entitled *Shoplifting: An Occasional Crime of the Moral Majority* was published in the prestigious <u>Bulletin of the American Academy of Psychiatry and the Law,</u> in 1983!

For example, DSM-IV considers "the essential feature" of kleptomania to be the recurrent failure to resist impulses to steal items even when the items are not needed for personal use or for their monetary value (Criterion A). DSM further indicates that in cases of kleptomania, the theft offender experiences an increasing subjective awareness of tension before the theft (Criterion B) and may feel pleasure, satisfaction or relief when committing the theft (Criterion C). In my clinical experience, these criteria are sometimes, though not always, experienced by Atypical Theft Offenders.

However, in addition to the above criteria, DSM explicitly states that in cases of kleptomania, "the stealing is not committed to express anger or vengeance..."

It is entirely clear from the findings of our clinical investigations of those theft offenders whom Dr. Atcheson and I assessed while at the Clarke Institute of Psychiatry (and of the cases I have dealt with in the fifteen years since leaving the Clarke) that the vast majority of these individuals most definitely appear to have committed their acts of theft as an expression of their anger (that they are most often aware of being) and, as well, not infrequently, with a clear desire for vengeance.

It is the opinion of both Dr. Atcheson and myself that, of the hundreds of theft offenders we had seen between 1979 through 1986, there were only two or three who could possibly be said to be suffering from true kleptomania. In other words, less than 3% of the atypical theft offender cases we assessed may have warranted the label of 'kleptomania.'

It bears repeating that the vast majority of Atypical Theft Offenders whom we have seen over the past 23 years were very angry at the time of their offenses, and in most cases the offenders were consciously aware of their anger, although they have seldom recognized the link between their anger and their acting out by stealing. Their theft behaviors were an acting out in response to their anger, whether the anger was towards a negligent, abusive or authoritarian spouse, or was a response to the offender having experienced, or anticipating that he or she would soon be experiencing, a perceived unfair personally meaningful loss.

Fugere, D'Elia and Philippe[xix] have pointed out that "researchers agree that kleptomania is present in only a small percentage of offenders (three percent to five percent)."

Fortunately, the DSM represents an evolving clinical database and clinical decision-making process, and in a sense must therefore always be playing 'catch-up' since it takes its cues from the growing body of clinical findings. It is the hope of this writer that, with the additional findings of my own and those of other clinical investigators, that some alteration in the listings pertaining to theft behavior will be forthcoming in a near future edition of DSM.

I sincerely hope that this book will serve to promote the inclusion of the Atypical Theft Offender syndrome in a future version of DSM. I would propose that the general heading that would be suitable to employ would be that of Theft Offenders. Under that umbrella term would then be three broad categories of offenders:

- Atypical Theft Offenders,
- Typical Theft Offenders, and
- ATO/TTO-mixed type Theft Offenders.

A *subcategory* of Atypical Theft Offender might then be labeled 'kleptomania', in keeping with it's current definition in DSM.

Part Three:

Treating The Atypical Theft Offender

Chapter 23

CLINICAL TREATMENT OF ATYPICAL THEFT OFFENDERS: AN OVERVIEW

There are several essential, and in some cases unique, elements of treatment to be considered when dealing with possible Atypical Theft Offenders. These elements have emerged from my 21 years of involvement with such cases and have certainly been influenced by my training and experiences in individual and group psychotherapy, as well as m doctoral work pertaining to assessment and treatment using mental imagery approaches.

Several of these elements are described below and in succeeding chapters.

One of the most unique elements of treatment I have developed for dealing with Atypical Theft Offenders is the unusual three-part, 'fall-back' type of contracting which I have instituted to deal with their possibility of future acts of theft behavior during their course of assessment and/or treatment.

A Three-Part Contract with A.T.O. clients regarding any future theft events that may occur during the course of treatment.

It is obvious that if an A.T.O. client steals while in treatment, then the client has given ample proof that he or she is not yet cured. My experience with these individuals is that a large minority of them may carry out further acts of theft, especially shoplifting, during the assessment or treatment process. Although there are no accurate statistics in this regard, I would estimate that somewhere between 20% and 45% of A.T.O.s may re-offend while still in treatment.

Ideally of course, the client will not steal while in treatment. Indeed, I urge them not to do so. However, unless and until all the precipitating factors have been identified and resolved, and different coping mechanisms have been put in place and made operational so that clients may more appropriately deal with stressors in the future, there is always a possibility that their old issues and inappropriate coping mechanisms will lead to further atypical theft behavior.

****

The 3-part contract I propose to clients regarding the possibility of further theft behavior during treatment
****

Part I: Don't steal again

> **Part I:** My ATO client contracts with himself or herself, *in my presence,* with me as 'witness,' to not steal again while undergoing assessment or treatment.

This contract is sometimes sufficient to assist the client in avoiding acting out through theft behavior. Since the prior theft behavior may have been related to still-outstanding issues with authority figures, and since, by virtue of the mechanism of transference, the therapist is necessarily viewed as such, it is important to *not* ask the client *to contract with the therapist.* A contract with the therapist/authority figure could itself become another precipitating factor in some future acting out.

By making clear to that the contract the client is making *is with himself or herself* , the therapist gets 'out of the way' of the dynamics relating to the contract.

While a client may be consciously willing to stop stealing, (and indeed that is hopefully one of the main reasons for being present in the clinician's office), the fact is that he or she often did not consciously want to shoplift in the first place! How can the clinician then help the client to successfully counter the deeper inner (subconscious or unconscious) press that may be moving the client to steal? Part II of the three-part contract comes into play here.

*****

Part II: Return anything stolen during clinical involvement; at the very least, do not keep it and do not give it away to anyone or any organization that may make good use of it.

Part II: The client contracts with himself or herself that, in the event that he or she does steal, the client will get return the item it back to it's rightful owner or, at the very least, do not keep it and do not give it away to anyone or any organization that may make good use of it.

On occasion clients consider giving away the items they stole by placing then in some charity's large containers (such as exist in many cities), so that the theft offenders could consider themselves as having 'given' something of use to those who may be in greater need and who may have lesser means.

There are, however, ethical and psychodynamic difficulties with this alternate behavior, since the theft offender would then able to gain some satisfaction and/or lessened guilt from having committed a Robin Hood-type 'good deed'. I have learned that it is very important that the client's conscious, subconscious and unconscious minds not be able to draw any satisfaction from the act of stealing, and therefore giving away the stolen goods or money is definitely contraindicated.

Very often, my client is astounded when first learning of this condition of the contract. Clearly, the message to the client is that nothing whatsoever will be gained by committing this act of theft – so, why bother? Well, that is, of course, the point. By twinning any act of gain through theft with a loss by the client's own hand (through having to not keep the item, nor give it away) acts as in internal braking mechanism to the underlying motivation to take something in the first place. By checkmating the motivation to steal (i.e., to gain and keep or give away something of value) the inner game of stealing is itself often arrested.

*****

Part III: In the event of having committed a theft while undergoing treatment, the client is to provide the clinician with relevant data pertaining to the offense, as soon as possible after the act of stealing.

Part III: In the event that my client does re-offend while participating in treatment, he or she contracts to call and leave a message on my answering machine describing any upsetting events or circumstances that may have preceded the theft by a day, a few hours, even a few minutes (e.g., an argument with the spouse, a problem at work, etc...).

This part of the client's contract with self often gives the client even greater cause to pause and reflect before carrying out another act of theft, since the client knows that if he or she does re-offend, there is an agreement in place to report upon the data and situational happenings related to such activity. (This reporting could help to determine what the precipitating trigger(s) may have been.)

Remarkably, many clients have reported that they have thought of stealing but had reminded themselves of their agreed-upon contract, and that they would have to call and relate to me that which would be very embarrassing or shameful, if they indeed have acted out. This awareness of the 'required reporting stipulation' seems to act, in many cases, as a successful deterrent to their acting out. As one client put it, "The idea that I would have to call and report what was happening around the time I would be stealing, made it seem not worth while taking anything in the first place."

These last two parts of the contract function as 'adverse conditioning' stipulations.

*****

Dealing with the matter of other merchandise that the client still has in his or her possession (or has previously given to friends) which were not part of what was recovered by the authorities: do not keep them nor give them away to anybody or any organization.

Clients are asked to give up merchandise that they stole prior to contacting me but which has not been repossessed by the authorities. They are encouraged to return the items to the original owners. If they had 'given' the stolen items to friends or relatives, they are encouraged to ask for the items back and to then return them to their rightful owners.

It is important to assist the client to teach his or her unconscious, subconscious as well as conscious minds that any acts of stealing --past, current and future- will result in no positive payoff whatsoever, and indeed, will yield a negative payoff - the loss of the item, and the pain and embarrassment of asking for the item back, and of letting it go.

Frequently clients will report that they have many (sometimes dozens) of items that they have stolen over the years, and that these items are in their homes or cars, or in the possession of relatives or friends. I attempt to teach clients that it is vitally important, if indeed they wish to stop stealing, to get rid of any and all stolen merchandise that is in their possession, or that of their relatives and friends. Not infrequently, this has involved them asking their spouses to give back the sweaters, briefcases, ties, etc... that they had 'given' to them. It is striking that these other persons are usually very amenable to giving back the items, especially when they are told that by doing so they may be facilitating the cessation of their loved ones' or friends' theft behavior.

A measure of the progress of treatment, I have found, is the willingness of clients in carry out the above directives regarding previously stolen materials. Often, they will report the difficulties they have had in carrying out this part of treatment. The stolen merchandise clearly has a symbolic meaningfulness that is often much greater than its utilitarian value; some clients will report that they were able to rid themselves of most but not all items. Those that have been retained usually have particular symbolic meaning to them.

Atypical Theft Offenders will do well to consider that they will remain A.T.O.s indefinitely (just as alcoholics who no longer drink don't stop being alcoholics). If, however, they have completed a full term of treatment, then they will be much less prone to act out by stealing so long as they enlist their new coping mechanisms when dealing with difficult issues, and that they carry out more psychotherapeutic work whenever desirable.

More about the issue of returning items that have been stolen

In an ideal world it would be wonderful if all Atypical Theft Offender clients returned to their rightful owners the items that they had stolen over the years, or at least reimbursed the legal owners for their losses. That, however, usually had not happened up to the time that the Atypical Theft Offenders have sought clinical help. The role of the clinician is to be of assistance to the client; however, it obviously is optimal if society was served at the same time. In fact, by helping an Atypical Theft Offender to stop the act of stealing both goals can be advanced.

Atypical Theft Offenders almost invariably have serious psychological issues to be addressed. If they do not get the help that they require, then the probability is very high that they will re-offend. Even previous convictions, heavy fines and incarceration have been of limited value with many of these offenders in the past. Most of my theft offender clients have previously been apprehended and charged – several times! The vast majority of them have also previously been found guilty; many have been fined; some have had jail terms; a few have had numerous periods of incarceration. Obviously, the punitive route has not shown itself to be very effective with Atypical Theft Offenders although it may help stop, or at least slow down some Typical Theft Offenders

To help Atypical Theft Offenders stop re-offending they have to deal with their personal psychological issues, and they have to re-program themselves in regard to what stealing means at a deeper level of their psyches.

197

Some Atypical Theft Offenders even prefer stealing items that are on sale!

It has only become clear within the past few years of my clinical investigations that some A.T.O. clients primarily have stolen items that were, at the time, on sale! This finding in relation to some A.T.O. clients seems to be related to their desire to take things that may be rationalized as items that the stores wanted to get rid of anyway and had therefore marked down in price. Shoplifting these items is, in a bizarre way, then rationalized as firstly, *less* of a crime since the value of the item to the store had already been re-labeled as less than previously, and secondly, that an "even better deal" was thus obtained through the act of shoplifting since they managed, by stealing to the item, to get an item at 100% off its full retail price, rather than merely 40% or 60% off it's full price.

(In case the reader finds the above thought process, that has been articulated to me by more than a few clients, rather bizarre, do remember that these thoughts of justification for stealing are, in fact, rationalizations. In other words, they are not actually entirely logical, but instead are convenient cognitive constructs of pseudo-logical statements.)

As indicated earlier, the monetary value of the item often appears to not be a critical issue to many A.T.O.s. In fact, the selling price of the item taken is often merely a few dollars. To an individual who is middle class or above socio-economically, not paying at all for an item that costs only a few dollars anyway, would hardly appear to be a matter of significance. But it is not the 'Adult' part of the Atypical Theft Offender shoplifter that instigates the theft; rather, it is the 'Child' component. (See the chapter on Redecision Therapy for a further exposition of the use of the terms 'Adult' and 'Child.')

(Incidentally, how many of us might be attracted to little "gifts" that may accompany a full-tank purchase of gasoline during some gas company promotions. They (the company's promotions group) know that we all like getting "something for nothing," even if we rationally realize that the concept is an illusion, since we are paying something for the gasoline, and the company is in all likelihood making a reasonable profit, even if the item is a so-called "loss-leader.")

The reader may even recall an occasion when you found that an extra item had been put into your grocery bag, or the cashier had not punched in the correct price, by mistake. There may have been a slight feeling of excitement, guilt and/or pleasure that a little "something" had been acquired (through no wrong doing of one's own, of course) "for nothing." This circumstance might perhaps be considered a 'kissing cousin' to the shoplifting of an item that was on sale. One might correctly think that the gain in the case of the cashier's mistake had nothing to do with what one did. On the other hand, if one did not give back the incorrect change, or point out the cashier's mistake, then the 'extra' something is acquired through an 'inaction' rather than through an 'action' of one's own. An ethics class in high school or university might find such a scenario could be strongly argued from both sides.

Another 'kissing cousin' of 'little larceny' scenarios might be the act of successfully passing through customs without declaring the complete, accurate, and over-the-allowed-duty-free-limit cost of items being brought back into the country from a business trip or holiday elsewhere. (In such an instance, incidentally, it would be interesting to ponder whether one should be categorized as a 'typical' or 'atypical' type of 'smuggler'?) Could it be said that such an act was socially sanctioned by a substantial portion of the North American traveling public? And even it this is the case, does that make it any less of an offense? Why?) The similarly of cutting corners on one's income tax might also be included as another kissing cousin of outright theft.

(The reader might find it illuminating to reflect upon your own feelings and thoughts when you read the above section. Could you relate? If so, did you find yourself wanting to defend your actions? Read the next paragraph closely, then.)

The fact is that the non-shoplifting events just mentioned have a socially (though not legally) sanctioned acceptance among many usually upright citizens. Such persons do not think of themselves as being 'real thieves'-- do they? After all, 'everybody' does it- don't they? And deliberately breaking the speed limit on a deserted stretch of freeway is 'okay' and not really breaking the law, isn't it? Or even if it is considered breaking the law, it is still not really a 'bad' or 'wrong' thing to do -- or is it. Alas, a continuation of these musings is beyond the scope of this book.

Suffice it to say there may be a thin, fragile and rather indistinct line between Atypical Theft Offenders and many other usually upright citizens in our modern societies.

The menstrual cycle and shoplifting

Several of my female clients have provided fascinating evidence of a possible link between their menstrual cycles and shoplifting. E.g., Case #25.

*****

Case #25: Penelope, who usually shoplifted on the first day of her menstruation

In over a year of treatment sessions this client and I were able to determine that her shoplifting behavior invariably occurred on the first day of her menstruation, and most likely when her husband and she had had an argument. Having tremendous difficulty being assertive with her demanding spouse, she found that she frequently felt like going shopping some time during this 'first day', and would be more inclined to shoplift when they had argued.

As have many other of my clients, Penelope reported that knowing that she would have to call me if she did shoplift acted as a major deterrent on several occasions; she now avoids shopping or even visiting stores on these critical days, and especially when agitated with her husband. Not surprisingly, a substantial portion of our clinical work has been directed to helping this woman to become more appropriately assertive with her spouse.

*****

Some female clients have reported feeling 'empty' when menstruating. Obviously there is an actual loss of blood and major biological changes that occur during the menstrual cycle. As well, there is a powerful literal (as opposed to symbolic) meaning to menstruating -- the menstruating woman is definitely not pregnant. Some or all of the above can have a powerful impact upon certain individuals.

Some Atypical Theft Offenders have stolen in response to feeling that they have 'lost' the opportunity to have a child. Other women have stolen in response to wanting to 'fill the empty void' created by the loss of blood.

For some menopausal women it seems to have been the loss of the capability of having children that has impacted upon their self-image as a female, and the theft offense has been a loss-substitution motivated behavior.

It should be understood that the above formulations are not the result of any preconceptions on the writer's part about the possible association of the phenomenon of menstruation with the act of shoplifting. Rather it has been in the course of discussing with many female theft offenders their own articulated awareness that has introduced me to these possible connections. Clinicians who choose to work with many Atypical Theft Offenders will undoubtedly learn additional insights into the psyches of those involved in these activities.

Chapter 24

SPECIALIZED TREATMENT FOR ATYPICAL THEFT OFFENDERS:

S.T.A.T.O. THERAPY

S.T.A.T.O. Therapy is a specific course of treatment I began developing in 1982. This comprehensive treatment program has emerged from my understanding of the underlying conscious, subconscious and unconscious psychodynamics at work in cases of perhaps most Atypical Theft Offenders.

Over the years I have had numerous theft offenders referred to me by experienced clinicians who recognized that their usual treatment modalities were not having the desired effect of eliminating their clients' theft behaviors. Sometimes clients they had had in treatment for years, had repeatedly re-offended.

1.Some therapists have referred their theft offender-clients for consultation purposes;

2.Other therapists have asked me to work with their clients on the theft-offending aspects of their problems while the referring therapist continued to help them deal with other issues; and

3.Still other clinicians have simply requested that I take on the entire treatment program, if I thought that I could be of assistance.

This last arrangement has usually been invoked when the referring clinician is opposed to having more than one therapist involved in a particular case at any one time. At one time I also belonged to this 'one-therapist-at-a-time' school. However, I have long been persuaded that, assuming that both therapists are experienced and skilled, *and* as long as the therapists are not using approaches that are themselves in very major conflict , *and* as long as the client does not get away with playing such games as "Lets You and The Other

Therapist Fight," then the dual-therapist approach can be highly successful. Professional vigilance and occasional therapist-therapist communications can minimize any major problems, in most instances. And there is very much to be gained in such a 'team' approach.

The analogy of a family physician & medical specialist 'combo' is not entirely inappropriate here.

It is the author's intention that clinicians will be able to use the material in this book to improve their ways of assessing and treating Atypical Theft Offenders. Some clinicians may also wish to learn more about working with this population by receiving training that offered in the assessment and treatment of Atypical Theft Offenders.

Inquiries about taking or coordinating workshops can be made by contacting Tagami Communications at 416-928-2262. Also, the reader can check out my comprehensive website, www.whyhonestpeoplesteal.com.

S.T.A.T.O. Therapy may be described as a two-leveled approach, in that both assessment and treatment are aimed at uncovering and dealing with [1] the more recent events (usually loss-related) that have precipitated the acting out behavior, and [2] the chronologically much earlier events (if any) which usually occurred in childhood and which had not been adequately dealt with by the A.T.O. client at the time, or since. These earlier unresolved events can continue to make the client peculiarly vulnerable to loss-related or highly stressed experiences in their current life.

S.T.A.T.O. therapy helps the theft offender come to terms with both earlier and more recent troublesome experiences, and to develop new and more effective coping strategies for the future.

203

S.T.A.T.O. Therapy makes substantial use of:

- **Redecision Therapy**, as developed by Dr. Robert and Mary Goulding, and
- **Reintrojection Therapy**, a therapeutic technique that I developed in the early 1980s.
- As well, several other original therapeutic techniques are employed as required with Atypical Theft Offenders.

Both Redecision and Reintrojection Therapies will be described briefly in the following two chapters.

Follow-up 'Maintenance' Sessions

Some of the more difficult A.T.O. cases are encouraged to arrange semi-annual or annual follow-up sessions so that their progress in dealing with their new, current issues may be monitored and facilitated. By analogy, just as the client with serious *physical* medical problems might be encouraged to 'see the doctor' every six or twelve months for a few years, with the assumption that such visits might preempt the recurrence of the medical condition, so it is that periodic visits to a clinician who is familiar with the Atypical Theft Offender's issues may serve as a proactive measure that can help prevent a recurrence of theft behavior. And, given that a single charge for shoplifting, for example, might cost many thousands of dollars in lawyers fees and fines (to say nothing of the consequences of a criminal conviction upon one's personal and/or working life), the precaution of an occasional follow-up clinical session can be realistically viewed as a very prudent and economical preventive measure.

Revisiting Assessment and Treatment Phases

Treatment begins with a suitable assessment. The assessment, already described in earlier chapters, is aimed at uncovering the extent to which the individual has been acting out in response to underlying factors, and/or out of greed or genuine need. In some cases, the matter is not very cut-and-dried, and a variety of underlying motivations, including all those just mentioned, may have been operating.

In order that the actual motivations be uncovered it is necessary to take a detailed personal history and 'current life' situation assessment. The clinician must be very attentive to the possibility of actual or anticipated losses being part of the dynamic field out of which the client may have been acting out.

In my experience usually between five and ten clinical sessions will usually suffice to provide much of the necessary information, and will also yield a good estimate of treatment potential.

The course of treatment will be formulated on the basis of the data gathered during the assessment. Generally speaking, I have found that treatment usually requires between ten and sixty sessions, with the majority of clients I have seen in the past few years completing most of their therapeutic work in fifteen to forty treatment sessions.

There is a minority of cases where the atypical theft behavior has been virtually entirely due to recent events in the offender's life, where the matter is 'cut and dried', and therefore many fewer sessions are needed to complete the assessment and any required treatment. There is also another minority of cases where many more sessions than usual are desirable; these cases include those where the individual's acting out theft behavior is due to long-time and deeply ingrained inappropriate cognitive and/or behavioral processes.

Spouses: Informing the spouse and the latter's role in assessment and treatment of the Atypical Theft Offender.

Very often clients have not informed their spouses of their (most recent or earlier) theft behavior, even by the time of our first session. The offender may be anticipating rejection, ridicule, or even outright acts of hostility from the spouse, and does not wish to risk the threat of further emotional or physical abuse, or even abandonment.

In all fairness to the spouses of A.T.O.s it should be said that it is very difficult for many of them to learn that, in spite of their knowing their intimate others for years, or even decades, their partners have (once again) stolen. The spouses may consequently feel frustrated, embarrassed, angry, and/or impotent when it comes to assisting their partners to stop their theft behavior.

Indeed, one of the purposes of writing this book has been to provide the information that A.T.O.s and their partners may need in order to begin to deal more effectively with the theft behavior. This is more likely to come about if the spouses gain useful insight and practical information that will facilitate assisting the offenders to finally stop the stealing. Reading this book together can be very helpful, as they can review the ideas presented here and decide which may pertain to their own situation. However...

My usual recommendation regarding informing the spouse

I usually recommend, although I do not usually make it a condition of treatment, that the spouse be informed of my client's theft behavior. The exception is in case I am of the clinical opinion that the client or a significant other may be in physical jeopardy otherwise.

> Safety is of paramount importance here; it is not possible for the writer to know whether it is safe for any particular theft offender to inform a spouse or 'significant other.' That decision should be reached by the offender with the assistance of an experienced and suitable clinician.

It may not be realistic, in a particular instance, for a client to inform his or her spouse, at least not initially. Where the marital relationship may be effectively over, it may again not be very desirable for the spouse to be informed. This issue should always be explored in depth within the therapy sessions. Where there is hesitation to inform the spouse, there is usually fear and apprehension -- possibly, though not necessarily well founded. (Indeed, my experience is that most spouses are prepared to be *very supportive* and involved in the therapeutic process, if they believe that there is some genuine help available.) Regardless of the client's initial reluctance, the exploration of their concerns will almost always be of much clinical value.

The therapist-A.T.O. client relationship

By treating the new client with courtesy, respect, caring, acceptance, and interest, the therapist is committing a very important therapeutic act, especially with Atypical Theft Offenders.

The degree of shame, embarrassment and self-loathing with which A.T.O. clients may come into therapy initially must not be underestimated.

Some of these individuals may have been, or could still be, suicidal. They often anticipate rejection and humiliation from the clinician (and may have already experienced these reactions from uninformed and wary clinicians), even as they may anticipate similar reactions from other significant persons in their lives. Not infrequently they have previously received negative treatment not only from their spouses, but from the loss prevention or human resources personnel involved, as well as their lawyers, the police and/or others who may have heard about their behavior through the media.

Some Atypical Theft Offender clients have reported to me the deep sense of shame and humiliation that they have felt when some professionals, including clinicians, have upon hearing of their theft behaviors, treated them as if they were simply 'common thieves' Some have been told that they were 'kleptomaniacs' early on in their clinical encounters, and have felt both frightened and humiliated when presented with such a diagnosis.

As the competent and suitably informed and trained therapist first welcomes the new theft offender-client in a manner indistinguishable from that with which other clients are greeted, the effect upon an Atypical Theft Offender may well be immediate and most important for the clinical process to proceed well. That they have been greeted with courtesy, even knowing what they have done, can mean a great deal to the shamed Atypical Theft Offender. Also, the client, who usually is at a loss to understand his or her own theft behavior, and who has probably been feeling very helpless and hopeless, almost invariably responds positively to this professional yet caring reception, and may even begin to feel renewed self-respect as a result.

A positive therapist-client relationship is frequently the foundation of personal healing. While such experiences are commonplace for most psychotherapy clients (or should be), they can be particularly important in the cases we are discussing. By the same token, a distinctly negative and harsh reception by a professional might serve to push them over the edge of despair.

Although therapists differ widely in personality and methodology, I believe that a firm but warm, kind yet professional approach to A.T.O. clients can infuse the therapy process with the safe foundation which the client needs in order to confront the issues that pertain to his or her problems. The client needs to be able to trust in -- and feel reasonably comfortable with -- the therapist.

To this end I nearly always invite all clients to use my first name, and I usually address them by their first names as well, regardless of the age differences which may exist between us. Therapy with A.T.O.s can be relatively short-to-medium term, contractually based therapy even as it may be in-depth and emotionally arousing. Due to the kinds of issues to be dealt with and the sort of interventions which may be required, it is highly preferable that the therapists engaged in this work be experienced, and as well, have received training in approaches at least similar to or compatible with the approaches described in the next two chapters -- Redecision and Reintrojection Therapies.

Chapter 25

REDECISION THERAPY

Redecision Therapy is a therapeutic approach developed by Dr. Robert and Mary Goulding, who were the co-directors of the Western Institute for Group and Family Therapy (WIGFT), headquartered in Watsonville, California.

Essentially a transactional analysis & gestalt therapy model and, as defined and refined by the Gouldings, the client is encouraged to deal with current unsatisfactory situations, behaviors, thoughts and/or feelings in part by considering an earlier time (frequently from childhood) when the client may have made a decision about how to think, feel or behave when faced with similar or analogous conditions. Through a repertoire of effective clinical interventions the client is assisted to redecide how to think, feel and behave now and in the future in order to maximize their more mature and joyful living.

Not infrequently in childhood, persons made decisions that may have had, at the time, utilitarian value, in that these decisions may have kept them safe, or allowed them to survive disturbing or traumatic circumstances. Numbing oneself, or distracting oneself from the conscious experience of certain bodily sensations, emotions or thoughts, often by moving towards other sensations (through the use of drugs, or overeating, etc...to avoid feeling tense or physical pain, for example), other emotions (such as becoming chronically angry or sad or depressed to avoid feeling hurt, for example), or engaging in distracting thoughts (such as counting to avoid thinking about issues that are really of concern), may be carried forward into adulthood and become an obstruction to creating more mature relationships and a happier, healthier, and more fulfilling lifestyle.

Often the decisions made in childhood were in response to unspoken and/or spoken messages from one's primary caregivers. Some of these messages received by children may take the form of "don't" messages, or what the Gouldings termed "injunctions." Among the injunctions they found that their clients had received were the following: "don't"; "don't be"; "don't be you"; "don't be a child"; "don't be important"; "don't be close"; "don't succeed"; "don't belong"; "don't feel", "don't feel (sad, happy, etc...).

I received my initial training in this model of personality and psychotherapy from Bob and Mary Goulding at a month-long workshop at WIGFT nearly three decades ago, in 1972, and returned several times for additional training. It was also my privilege to work as guest faculty for them on a few occasions as well.

Using Redecision Therapy with Atypical Theft Offenders

Atypical Theft Offenders have often made certain early decisions in order to cope with their childhood losses or other trauma; these decisions continue to directly influence their now-adult lives. In order for these offenders to stop reacting inappropriately to events and people, they must revisit some of these early scenes in therapy, and make redecisions that will allow them to, at least in part, heal themselves in relation to these early situations. They can then use these redecisions to deal with current (and future) life circumstances and issues differently.

As an example, an Atypical Theft Offender who suffered the loss of her mother when she was very young and who received the injunction "don't belong" from her stepmother, may have started stealing small sums from stepmother's purse as (albeit symbolic) compensation.

In her adulthood she may often feel as if she does not belong. When confronted by new social situations, she may find herself inclined to steal cutlery or other objects from her host's home. In order to stop her theft behavior in the future this individual will likely have to identify and deal with the origins of her feelings in regard to the loss of her mother, and the perceived rejection by her stepmother. As well, her long-standing feelings of anger, inadequacy and not belonging will need to be confronted and resolved. Then she will be much more likely to stop her theft behavior.

Redecision Therapy is well suited to assist clients to deal with such issues. As a Redecision therapist I have found that this approach allows in-depth therapeutic work to be done in a relatively short period of time. This methodology utilizes both cognitive (thinking) and affective (feeling) approaches to assist the client to make a healthier redecision. The client is then encouraged to develop and carry out new behaviors in the future that are compatible with the redecisions that have been made.

I teach clients some of the basics of Redecision therapy in their first or second sessions, so that they can begin thinking about and recognizing their own psychological inner functioning, and also can start to gain insight into their interpersonal transactions. I also use the gestalt therapy empty-chair technique in early sessions so that clients can start to address their unresolved issues quickly.

Learning more about Redecision Therapy

There are excellent books for the practitioner to read and thereby learn about Redecision Therapy. Changing Lives through Redecision Therapy, The Power is in the Patient, and Not to Worry, written by Robert and/or Mary Goulding, illustrate various aspects of Redecision Therapy with wisdom and humor.

Born to Win[xx], by Muriel James and Dorothy Jongeword, is a book that has deservedly sold many millions of copies through numerous printings, and offers a genuine educational experience in the transactional-gestalt approach for both laypersons and professionals, and is my preference still as the primary reading and working-with text for virtually all my clients.

It would be beyond the scope of this book to provide much more detail about Redecision Therapy. Suffice to say that I believe strongly in the value of the theory and practice of this therapy model; I employ it with my psychotherapy clients, and have taught it to graduate students in counseling psychology at the University of Toronto. It has been my preferred primary approach to working with Atypical Theft Offenders as well.

Chapter 26

REINTROJECTION THERAPY

I described the essential procedures involved in Reintrojection Therapy, a method that I developed in the 1970s, in an article entitled Reintrojection Therapy: A Procedure of Altering Parental Introjects[xxi], published in the professional journal, Psychotherapy: Theory, Research and Practice, in 1984. For purposes of this book I shall describe the main features of the approach, and its relevance to Atypical Theft Offenders.

> **Parental introjects are the stored information, however accurate or erroneous, that individuals have about the qualities of their parents, and in particular the early responses and attitudes that their parents had toward them, and vice versa.**

The essential elements of Reintrojection Therapy

Basically, the use of Reintrojection Therapy provides an opportunity for the client to re-evaluate, and subsequently to live differently in the future, in relation to his or her early (or even later or current) significant relationships.

Each of us holds certain perceptions of our relationships with the significant others in our lives, past and present. These views are often based on material gathered at a much earlier time. In the case of our parents, who were usually with us from birth, the information-gathering abilities that we had at the time we obtained the initial data about them and our relationships with them, were quite different from those we have currently at our disposal, now that we are adults, and with a wealth of life experiences -- and hopefully greater intellectual, emotional and perceptual capabilities.

When we were children or even younger yet, as infants, our abilities to gather and interpret the information coming at us was, in some respects, quite limited. To quote from my original article, *"Each of us grows up with impressions of our parents or caretakers that include some inaccurate, misleading, or no longer accurate data because the young organisms that gathered the material had --at the time- limited judgmental facilities. For example, the parent of the two-year-old child is perceived as many times taller, stronger, wiser, more knowledgeable, etc... than the latter -- realities that are usually of a temporal nature."*

"It may be postulated (however) that the infant's first memories are neither eliminated nor even necessarily altered by the older child's or adolescent's updating. For the infant that still resides within the now 35 or 55 year old, 6-ft tall adult, a 5-foot 4-inches tall and now frail parent may still be a giant to be feared. This conceptualization helps to explain why some adults continue to be overwhelmingly frightened at the thought of asserting themselves with their now elderly and weakened parents: ancient memories of a huge parent figure looming over a tiny infant may still be at work."

The function of Reintrojection Therapy, then, is to assist the client to re-examine, in a profound (and often deeply moving) fashion, the "introjects" of their parents that they have been carrying around inside their heads all these years, even after the parent or parents are dead! The impact of these earlier experiences, indeed the parent-child relationship itself, has not died even if the other person has departed life. Robert Anderson, the author of I Never Sang For My Father[xxii], that marvelous play (later turned into a powerful movie starring Gene Hackman), stated that **"Death ends a life, but it does not end a relationship, which struggles on in the survivor's mind towards some resolution that it never finds."** Reintrojection Therapy is used to assist the client to move much closer to that resolution, and sometimes succeeds quite well indeed.

Most clients, and in particular A.T.O.s, often have much to confront in regard to their earliest relationships, and using Reintrojection Therapy provides them with a unique method and opportunity for so doing.

Reintrojection Therapy procedure involves four major, sequenced steps:

Step 1: Selecting and staging the early scene
Step 2: The inquiry of the client
Step 3: The inquiry of the introject
Step 4: The cognitive reappraisal of the parental introject by the client.

Together, these four steps provide a means of thoroughly re-examining the early impressions, memories, emotional responses of (and towards) the parental figure, and a means of altering these at a deep level.

Consider the definition provided by Fagan and Shepherd and stated in Gestalt Therapy Now[xxiii], that *"introjections are complex, integrated ways of behaving or being, adopted wholesale by the developing organism from significant others.... Introjects are one of the main transmitters of pathology across the generations." (1970, p.113)*

Parental introjects are the stored information, however accurate or erroneous, that we have about the qualities of our parents in general and the early responses and attitudes that they had towards us, and vice versa, in particular.

When these introjects contain elements that are inherently unfavorable or rejecting of us, we may have been living with these internalized self-deprecating 'downers' for a long time. Introjects provide us, for better or for worse, and however accurately or inaccurately, with some of the most basic answers to what is, undoubtedly, one of the most crucial questions that individuals have to answer for themselves, namely: "Who am I?".

If our parents brought us up, through their actions as well as their words, to think of ourselves as intelligent, attractive, sensitive, worthwhile, loved and lovable children, then now, decades later, as adults, this is very likely how we currently and usually think of ourselves. It is my clinical opinion that it is relatively unlikely (compared with those who have been brought up otherwise and barring the presence of psychotic processes in the individuals) that people who have been so well and fortunately brought up will ever engage in theft behavior.

On the other hand, if we were brought up by parents, or other primary caretakers, who offered us, at best, only conditional positive regard, or worse, if we were exposed to marked disrespect, disapproval, and other discouraging or disparaging attitudes, then our self-images may have been grossly damaged. Excellent books, such as Toxic Parents[xxiv], by Dr. Susan Forward (Bantam, 1989), and Soul Survivors[xxv], by Dr. Patrick Gannon (Prentice Hall, 1989), have chronicled the potentially devastating effects of early negative child-rearing environments. For many persons who have been so emotionally, intellectually, physically, sexually, or otherwise damaged, the use of Reintrojection Therapy, especially in conjunction with certain therapeutic models such as Redecision Therapy, may be helpful in finally ridding the individual, for the future, of many of the major effects of these negative circumstances and events.

In the more detailed outline of this procedure provided below I shall describe the corresponding aspects of the case of Paula at each stage, for illustrative purposes.

*****

THE FOUR STEPS OF REINTROJECTION THERAPY

Step One: Selecting and staging the early scene

Redecision and some other therapies have made abundantly clear the critically important impact of early life experiences upon an individual.

It is essential to assist the client who has long-standing issues with one or both parents, to deal with the emotional and other material that she may be still carrying about and which may have had a long-time (and still ongoing) impact on her self-image and her intrapsychic and interpersonal functioning.

For the purposes of the Reintrojection Therapy procedure, the client is asked to recall an early scene, one which for that person exemplifies her parent's attitude, behavior and/or feelings towards her. The earliest of such scenes that come to the client's mind is often the best scene to use in this clinical procedure.

Step # 1: The client is asked to recall an early scene, one which for that person exemplifies her parent's attitude, behavior and/or feelings towards her. The earliest of such scenes that come to the client's mind is often the best scene to use in this clinical procedure. The client is then asked to describe the scene in the present tense, as if it were happening now for the first time, providing herself and the therapist with a rich and detailed visual impression of the scene.

*****

Case #26: Paul: who as a child was punished for being happy

Paul presented as an elegantly dressed and attractive man in his mid-forties who was easily able to recall (that when he was four years old) his mother's standard punishment for such misdeeds as laughing, running or singing in the house was being locked in the unlit, non-windowed basement, at whatever time of night or day. At this early age he could not reach the push-button light switch on the wall at the top of the stairs. He recalled his almost nonstop terrified crying and the blessing of finally crying himself to sleep, exhausted.

Paul remembered spending hours at a time in the basement, several days a week. Eventually he discovered that the adjoining townhouse, which shared a common basement wall, had a hole in it the width of a small marble, and the next door neighbor, a retired elderly lady heard Paul's sobbing, and managed to make verbal contact with him. He recalled to me with considerable gratitude the reassuring sounds that came to his in the voice of this kind old woman, who, hearing his cries, would talk and sing to him, soothing his frightened feelings. This experience went on for years, until the neighbor moved away. Paul's basement punishments of 'solitary confinement' went on until just two years before he left home at thirteen.

This scene was one that he remembered still, almost daily, even if only for a few moments at a time, and always with great sadness, terror and rage.

*****

Step Two: The 'inquiry' of the client

Step #2: The therapist elicits more information pertaining to the scene and what it represents by asking the client to speak with the therapist as if the client were at the age at which the scene took place but with the knowledge, understanding and verbal capabilities that has been gained in the intervening years.

Thus begins the increasingly affective (emotional) phase of Reintrojection Therapy. It is frequently a very powerful, raw experience for the client, who often will remember additional information as she describes the scene in the present tense, and the life circumstances then existing in the household when she was that age.

*****

Paula remembered and described with much emotion the feelings of fear, rejection and abandonment that she had experienced when banished to the basement. Her anger was slower in coming but as it did she reported feeling fury and disgust at her mother for treating her so. This was in marked contrast to the self-anger and self-disgust that she had exhibited in previous therapy sessions.

*****

Step Three: Inquiry of the Introject

Step # 3: In this part of the Reintrojection Therapy experience, the client is invited to change chairs (as in Gestalt Therapy) and assume the role of the parent. <u>However, in an approach that is unique to this therapeutic approach, the client is instructed to *speak, as the parent, with the therapist, but as the parent might if only...*</u>

<u>(1) the 'parent' were "completely honest" with 'himself or herself,'</u> and

<u>(2) the 'parent' were "completely honest" with the therapist.</u>

The client is reassured that it is the therapist's belief that no one is ever 100% honest with him or her self, let alone with another person. Therefore, the client is invited to role play the parent as well as possible, and trust to intuition to provide the most suitable and honest responses to the therapist's upcoming questions.

A crucial element during this step in the procedure: the therapist's mental set and manner

It must be noted that the therapist's manner while interviewing the 'parent' is crucial for the successful outcome of the entire Reintrojection procedure. **The therapist views the 'parent' being interviewed as if the 'parent' were actually a client during this step. The therapist aligns with the 'parent' in a way that is simultaneously gentle, nourishing, protective and potent.** Moving somewhat physically closer to the parent, when appropriate, (but not nearly touching) during this part of the procedure, may enhance the sense of empathy and cooperativeness that the therapist wishes to engender.

218

Readers (especially therapists), take note!

Many clients initially present their parent as defensive, intolerant, or even insufferable. It is essential that the therapist arrest these tendencies by gently reminding the client of the two stipulations referred to above. The client may also be told that *"probably no one is ever totally honest and non-defensive with another person, let alone with his or her own self"* and that, therefore, the client will have to rely upon intuition and guess how the parental figure might have responded under these stipulated conditions. Although the factual answers to many of the questions that the therapist will pose may not be known, the client is encouraged to trust to intuition in "making up" responses, and is told that any of the statements made as the 'parent' can later be withdrawn or altered.

Elaborating further on this step is beyond the intent of this chapter; it is sufficient to make the point that this part of the procedure is intended to allow the client 'to enter the world of the parent figure' and to do so from a relatively undefended position so that the underlying aspects of the parent and his or her life, both at the time of the scene under consideration, and in his or her own earlier life, can be examined. The theoretical view underlying this part of the procedure is that in giving the client permission to use his or her intuition, the therapist is also giving implicit permission for the client to draw upon sources of data other than conscious memories.

By stipulating that the client respond the way the parent might if the latter were being entirely honest with himself/herself and with the therapist, we are also asking the client to explore a part of the parent that almost certainly has not been encountered previously. This act of 'role-playing the parent' in what may be an approximation of the latter's more open, honest state, gives implicit recognition to the client to consider the possibility of the existence of this state within the parent. Therefore, for example, instead of seeing mother as essentially mean, cruel, and dominating, a client such as Paula may encounter and become more intimately acquainted with the scared, lonely, brutalized, insulated aspects of her mother.

*****

Indeed, Paul, in role-playing his mother in this part of the procedure, uncovered memories of his mother hiding for days in her room, and connected mother's isolation of Paul in the basement to mother's own fears and early modes of behavior, and to her own experiences of sexual and physical abuse at the hands of her own father.

Also, it emerged in this part of the procedure that mother may well have been afraid that her son's loud and quite natural childhood exuberance might bring him to the attention of this grandfather who still lived with them as Paul was growing up! Grandfather had also abused his other children, including two sons in their childhood and Paul's mother may well have feared a repetition with her own child being the victim this time, especially when she was out working... and Paul's grandfather was still at home, baby-sitting.

*****

Step Four: Cognitive reappraisal of the parental introject by the client

---

Step # 4: the therapist invites the client to again take the client's chair and to state what has been learned from this experience.

It is important for the client to stand back from the previous, usually very emotionally laden step, and now assume a more objective, rational state, and articulate her experience of the process to this point. This relatively less emotionally intense, more cognitive, component of the Reintrojection procedure moderates the emotional experiences of the previous steps and allows for a reappraisal of the introject and the attendant self-regard that the client may have been carrying ever since the scene under consideration actually transpired.

*****

When Paula reviewed her experience during this step, especially her comments "as mother" in the preceding step# 3, she was astounded to realize that although she had heard in later years that mother's own father had evidently sexually molested his daughter, she had never consciously considered that mother's putting her in the basement may have also served to protect her from grandfather, whose emphysema and heart condition would not allow him to go up or down the basement steps of the house in which they lived together.

*****

Please Note: I always invite clients to make inquiries among their siblings or other relatives, or even, if they consider it to be safe at this point, to speak to the parents themselves about the incident that has been recalled and been dealt with using this approach.

On the basis of a great many instances of such inquiries on the part of clients following Reintrojection sessions, the 'newly acquired information' most often is eventually supported by external, and occasionally even consensual, validation by other family members of these 'newly acquired' insights.

The fact that the Reintrojection experience takes place at an emotional Child ego state (in Transactional Analysis terms) allows for tapping into early memories, impressions, and emotions of many kinds and, as well, by using the Adult ego state in step#4, facilitates cognitive and emotional changes on the part of the client.

In this regard, I am reminded of the parable by Fritz Perls, when he referred to the loud argument that Memory and Pride had;
Memory said "It was like this."
Pride said, "No, it was like that!"
Pride won!

In other words, our conscious memories of early (to say nothing of later events) may be markedly influenced by our unconscious and/or subconscious minds' vested interests in holding onto certain perceptions and interpretations of particular events, so that then may be used to justify our positions regarding people and events – disregarding the fact that the truth may lay hidden somewhere else.

Incidentally, nothing in the foregoing should be construed as suggesting that young persons' memories are necessarily wrong, let alone invalid. On the other hand, few of us are privy to absolute true and undistorted memories. Indeed, I was gratified to find that Christine Courtois, in her important book, <u>Healing the Incest Wound: Adult Survivors in Therapy</u>[xxvi] understood this point and referred to Reintrojection Therapy as a potentially suitable and helpful therapeutic device for use with incest survivors who have sufficiently worked through parental issues to be able to see their parents differently now, "As people with their own problems, hurts and disappointments, and to forgive them." (p.208).

In the over 20 years since I first developed the procedure, a great many clients who have experienced Reintrojection Therapy have reported long-lasting changes in their perceptions of their parents, the latter's reactions to them and their relationships with one another, as well as in their own self-percept and self-definition. Many who had considered themselves unloved have reevaluated their early experiences, and have come to different interpretations of some of the salient events in their young lives.

*****

As Paul, the man we have been considering in this chapter determined, his mother's mistreatment of him did not necessarily indicate a lack of caring or concern, but indeed may have involved both, albeit as inappropriately handled by a mother whose own issues with her biological parent, were probably still unresolved.

In time, Paul learned to accept that he was indeed lovable, and worthy of better treatment than his mother, or he himself had thus far provided for him. He also learned to intercede with inclinations to shoplift, which were misguided and inadequate ways of giving things to himself to compensate for the perceived lack of love and lovable-ness. Instead, he learned to function in a much healthier and more mature manner whenever he experienced what felt like deprivation or abandonment. He learned, for example, to give himself good food, good self-loving and good times, instead.

*****

More about the power and influence of parental introjects: The search for one's biological parents by those who were given up for adoption at birth.

As children we are all faced with acquiring an 'identity.' When we are asked, throughout our lives, "Who are you?", most of us respond with our name; first, last and possibly middle. Our last name is our word-connection to our parents. For example, I might respond to this question with "I am Will Cupchik; David and Chana Cupchik were my parents."

When we are really small, and if we are lost, for example, the finder may ask, "Whose little boy (girl) are you?" and will certainly want our last name so that our parents can be summoned. Interestingly, in Israel, some adults change their names to indicate more directly their lineage. For instance, if I was to follow this tradition (think of the way people are first identified in the Bible) I would call myself "Will Ben David" which literally means "Will, son of David".

Adopted children's' drive to find out 'who they are'

Many adopted persons find themselves powerfully driven to locate their biological parents. This strong motivation is, I believe, a normal and fundamental part of being human and socialized. We want and need to know 'who we are', 'where we come from', 'who our parents and siblings are', all in order that we may fill in the volume entitled "This is who I am!". And by obtaining the answers to these questions, or by filling in the blanks ourselves with fantasies and wishes --or delusions, even--, we come to 'know who we are.' This provides us with our identity.

But what happens to persons who do not know who their fathers and/or mothers are? I would suggest that the notion that "nature abhors a vacuum" has some analogous relevance here. If we don't have the information that tells us who our biological parents are, and therefore, in some important sense, *who we are*, we may be inclined towards either, (1) making up the answers in order to satisfy this inner need for data, or (2) at the very least, be excessively susceptible to accepting answers that are provided by others, including the adoptive parents, relatives, etc...or others who might claim, "Oh, I heard that your (father/mother) was a ....".

A remarkable example of this phenomenon was made known to me while I was working at the Clarke Institute. Here was an instance of a middle-aged woman, Laura, who had devoted much of her adolescent and adult life to carrying out her own version of what she was told was characteristic of her own father's personality -- acts of irresponsibility whenever faced with impending greater work or social obligations. Laura's avenue for these acts of irresponsibility was through theft behavior.

*****

Case # 27: Laura, the Theft Offender who modeled her criminal activity on the basis of what she was told about her "irresponsible father," whom she had never met

Laura was a very bright, articulate and attractive person who was also a repeat theft offender. Without having realized it, she had actually modeled her life of criminal activity according to what she had been told about her father, who left the family home on the very night she was born was born. Laura had never even met her father.

When Laura first came to my attention, she was 45 years old, and had spent over one-third of her life in jail, as a result of more than 15 charges of theft. A rather sophisticated looking, well educated and, and soft-spoken woman, Laura had a history of gaining employment with a variety of businesses, and being rewarded for her highly effective work in her middle management positions, usually by a series of rapid promotions through the ranks until she would eventually achieve a highly responsible position. At that point she would find himself very inclined to begin defrauding her employer of rather substantial funds. The last time she had been charged, she was found in a suite in a major hotel in Taos, New Mexico, having absconded with over $140,000 of company funds.

As she reported to us, she never felt the inclination to defraud until she was handed major responsibilities by her employer. She was not able to explain her self-defeating behavior, for which she had always been caught. She voluntarily approached our clinic because she had recently remarried and was afraid that she would once again "screw things up." She was also facing the fact that she was getting along in years (being at the time, 45 years old) and would likely repeat again unless she got some effective professional assistance.

At the time we met she was highly successful in her job at a major marketing firm. Consciously Laura seemed a determined, work-oriented family person who wanted very much to live a normal life. However, she pointed out to me that in the past, invariably, after accomplishing a great deal in monetary and career terms, she had sabotaged her situation by stealing substantial funds from her employer and leaving town. That had been her MO throughout her life, ever since she was a teenager. And she didn't know why.

It was only when we examined her childhood experiences that we located what was probably the essential underlying psychodynamic motivation for her inappropriate acting out. In a remarkable therapy session (which happened, by pure coincidence, to be videotaped), Laura described for me for the first time, one of her earliest recollections. On the very night that she was born her father had left the family home. Laura, who was told that she looked very much like her father (pictures she brought in bore out the remarkable resemblance), had also been told, whenever she misbehaved, that she was an irresponsible person, "just like your father". She was repeatedly reminded how he had not been able to handle the responsibility of having a child, and that that was why he had left the family home the night she was born.

When Laura was 14 years old she learned from a relative where her father was living with his common-law spouse. Laura decided that she wanted to meet him. She recalled for me, with considerable emotion, going to the door of the house where she had been told that her father resided, and knocking on the front door. A young boy about 9 years of age came to the door, and brusquely asked Laura who she was and what she wanted. When she gave her name and said that she wanted to see her father, the boy replied curtly, "You wait out here!", and then slammed the door shut. A few minutes later the boy returned, and with a smirk, told Laura that her father did not want to see her. Two weeks later Laura began stealing, and was soon placed in a detention home for so-called juvenile delinquents.

In our therapeutic work together Laura dealt with many issues, including several painful early scenes, using both Redecision and Reintrojection Therapies. She had never realized she later told me, that she had been very likely acting out a life (script) that emulated the irresponsible one she had been told her father had led. She realized, in retrospect, that as long as she had little responsibility at her place of work, she did not experience any desire to steal. It was being put in a position of major responsibility that seemed to be the sole identifiable trigger of her acting out (which had always followed very shortly upon her having assumed the new position).

*****

225

I employ Reintrojection Therapy in both individual and group sessions, as appropriate. It is important to keep in mind that it is best employed as a 'finishing' technique, one that assists clients to achieve closure after they have dealt with all manner of resentments towards the introjected person. As it usually evokes some of the strongest and deepest-felt emotions that clients get into during therapy sessions that I conduct, I am convinced that clinicians who would use this approach should be experienced professionals who, ideally, also have had some personal training and experience with Reintrojection Therapy.

Some other therapeutic techniques

I-- The 'Imaginary One-way Mirror and Soundproofed Room' technique

There is a technique that I developed years ago that I want to mention briefly here because it tends to be effective not only with many of my regular psychotherapy clients, but in particular with Atypical Theft Offenders. I employ this technique with clients who find the gestalt therapy 'empty chair' exercise too foreboding. This can occur when they are dealing with parents and other persons who are, to them, still too frightening to confront, even in absentia.

In fact, evidence of the potency of the gestalt therapy 'empty chair' technique is this reluctance on the part of some clients to carry out the exercise. This occurs, even though the 'other person' is only to be *imagined* sitting in front of the client, and is not actually present. This reluctance to confront a particular 'other person,' in my clinical experience, is not necessarily an indication of the client's 'resistance' to therapy, but more often is an indication of the intense fear or anxiety aroused at the prospect of confronting the other person.

Essentially the technique I developed emerged from my doctoral work in the clinical uses of mental imagery.

> **It is very important to greet each new theft offender-client, as we would hopefully treat any other clients we are meeting for the first time-- i.e., with courtesy and respect.**

Rest assured that the client will probably get your spoken, and unspoken messages-- whatever they are! I frequently have theft offender-clients spontaneously verbally express at the end of their first session their appreciation at having been greeted and treated like decent persons and not as 'criminals.'

The point I have stressed repeatedly in this book is that classic A.T.O.s are very uncommon perpetrators of criminal acts. Indeed, they generally do not possess criminal-oriented personalities at all, but are (or at least were, up to the point they offended) in most ways indistinguishable from other hard-working, generally honest and law-abiding citizens. The value of the clinical work that will follow will be dependent upon laying a solid foundation of respect and compassionate treatment of the offender.

Modifying transference

As also mentioned before, I give explicit permission to all my clients (theft offender or not) to refer to me by my first name. Among the many reasons I do so is to make clear that we are dealing at a more person-to-person level, rather than from a heavily doctor-patient dynamic. This model was learned from my trainers and mentors, Bob and Mary Goulding, nearly three decades ago, who emphasized the therapeutic value of reducing transference in the service of a more power-balanced therapeutic alliance. The resultant therapeutic process is more accurately described as cooperative and joint, as opposed to prescriptive and authoritarian. Also, since many of these individuals have had and/or have ongoing, serious issues with authority figures, the use of first names may minimize the initial transference.

Positively stroking the A.T.O. client as a means of facilitating the re-establishment of self-respect

To the extent that one is indeed dealing with an A.T.O.-type client, the clinician can utilize positive (non-physical) stroking in supporting the client for persevering even as he or she struggles with prominent feelings of shame while describing the theft behavior in detail, elaborating as to where, when, what, how and why he/she stole. Because, all too often, A.T.O. clients are extremely self-punitive, they may need the clinician's acceptance to decide to not harm themselves even more after they have divulged their 'dirty little secrets.'

A.T.O.s sometimes present with painful and unusual personal histories. Child abuse and abandonment of various kinds have frequently been their lot. I inform clients who have previously been mistreated by authority figures that our relationship and clinical sessions will be boundaried by clear, professional and safety-enhancing limits.

Because it is usually necessary that we deal with material from childhood, little time should be lost establishing the parameters of our encounters. Clients are reminded that they should not say or do anything that they do not wish to, but that, of course, holding back important or troubling information regarding their past or current circumstances will likely not serve them in the therapeutic process. I also advise them that if there is anything about which they do not wish to talk, that they so inform me directly rather than distort or outright lie about any of the issues and areas that are brought forward.

Client Access to The Therapist

My business card lists my office and phone numbers, as well as my e-mail address, currently *wcupchik@aol.com*. I also inform them that I use call-forwarding so that I can be reached when I am not in my office. Clients are given to understand that they may call me at home between the hours of 8:00a.m. and 9:00 p.m. seven days a week, or e-mail me anytime, if genuine need arises. This access has almost never been abused; rather there has been an appreciation of my willingness to be available, if and as the need arises. As A.T.O. clients are not infrequently dealing with early loss or abandonment issues, such potential access is especially appreciated, and I believe, is inherently therapeutic, even if not acted upon, especially when the clinical material being dealt with is particularly emotionally sensitive.

The therapist's responsibilities

I believe that the clinician who wishes to assess and/or treat Atypical Theft Offenders has a responsibility to these clients that involves not only dealing with their most recent charges, but also their history of theft offenses. Another responsibility of the treating clinician is to assist the theft offender to cease such behavior in the future.

On bringing stolen items into the clinician's office

At some point during their first session clients are asked whether anything they have brought into the clinician's office, on their person (clothes, jewelry, etc...), or in their purses or briefcases, overcoats, etc... is stolen merchandise. Very often the sheepish answer given is an embarrassed "yes." The individual is asked to henceforth not bring into the office anything that has been stolen. This request is made to ensure that the client will be less inclined to be acting out non-verbally in a rebellious state while attending therapy sessions. Bringing stolen items into the clinician's office can be an unspoken way of thumbing one's nose at an authority figure who is asking all those distressing and personal questions.

> **In all of the above matters, and in general, the clinician attempts to form a therapeutic partnership with the client in the service of assisting him or her to become more honest and forthcoming, and to minimize acting out 'games' within, and hopefully outside of, the therapist-client relationship.**

The A.T.O. client's multi-determined desire for treatment

Initial contact with clients usually comes about after they have been apprehended and charged with theft. Clients almost always claim to want help, which is certainly true. However, one of the main things they may seek from a clinician is a way out of facing the consequences of their actions, rather than determining and eradicating the underlying reasons for their acting out behavior. This is understandable, of course; at the same time such a motivation is not conducive to promoting 'treatment' past the court date, by which time the client hopes that, with a 'good' psychological report. there may be either a dismissal of the charge or at least a more lenient fine or sentence.

I have even, on at least two occasions, had persons entirely unknown to me call from the courthouse hallway while awaiting a hearing of their cases, to request appointments. I now understand full well that, in most of these instances, their lawyers have suggested that they quickly get an appointment date with me so that the lawyer might inform the judge that his or her client "has an appointment to see an expert in this area, your Honor! In the next few weeks or so." Of course, it is much more likely that a genuine interest in having an assessment will be signaled by a much earlier phone call.

I attempt to avoid taking part in this charade by informing the person on the other end of the telephone line that if he or she genuinely wishes to get help to stop the theft behavior, then a call can certainly be made to me *after* the current court appearance is over and the case has been postponed or the outstanding charge has been dealt with, at which time I will be pleased to see the individual. In the jurisdiction in which I practice, a person who has been charged with almost any crime always has many months during which to seek help between the time that the charge of theft was laid and the date of the court appearance. If the desire to get professional assistance and to stop stealing is genuine, it is most likely that an appointment will have been made, and the client seen, many weeks, if not months, prior to the court date.

Even in cases where the client has been in apparently authentic clinical involvement for some time, it is not very unusual that, once the case has been dealt with, a client may suddenly become reluctant to continue in treatment. This is due in large part to the wish to avoid fully confronting and dealing with disturbing material pertaining to the individual's current difficulties, and still unresolved earlier issues.

> Incidentally, I usually request of my clients' lawyers that they ask the court for enough time prior to trial (at least three to six months) to permit a thorough assessment to be carried out and for some psychological treatment to have been initiated.

It is hoped that in the interim, the clinician-client relationship will have become sufficiently strong, safe, and productive that the client will become genuinely therapeutically engaged in the clinical process and will *want* to continue in treatment even after the court situation has been resolved. Failure to become so engaged will usually mean that the client will be inclined to cease coming for treatment once the trial is over.

> I reiterate here that if the client is at least in part of the A.T.O. type, then premature termination of the therapeutic process will likely leave their self-sabotaging psychodynamics in place. The probability of an eventual recurrence of theft behavior, from my clinical experience, is high.

Involvement of 'significant others' in the clinical process

I inform the A.T.O. (usually within the first few sessions) of the desirability of having at least one significant other (S.O.) involved in my client's assessment and/or treatment. I explain some of the reasons for this proposed involvement (which has been mentioned previously and is outlined in detail in the next chapter). The client's responses to this information is usually indicative of many aspects of his or her life's circumstances. An affirmative response is usually a good predictor of a positive outcome for treatment. An even better predictor of positive treatment outcome is the ready and genuine compliance with this request by the significant other, especially when that significant person is the client's spouse.

In other words, when the client indicates that the spouse does know of the theft behavior, and is willing to become involved in the process, and if the client is comfortable with the anticipated involvement, then the likelihood is that considerable good will emerge from this collective clinical involvement.

On the other hand, where no one close to my client knows of the problem, and/or the S.O. is not willing to come in for at least one session, and/or my client is afraid or otherwise hesitant to even divulge the problem to, let alone invite, the S.O., then the prognosis is correspondingly poor. We shall elaborate upon these findings in the next chapter.

Summary

In this chapter the aim has been to outline some issues and procedures that will facilitate the clinician and client coming together to form a therapeutic alliance to help eliminate the client's self-defeating behavior. Greeting the client with respect and treating him or her as one deserving of support and kindness helps to renew the client's self-respect and self-confidence. The client is ensured of the safety of the relationship by delineating its boundaries and parameters. Procedures such as the "Stopping Future Theft Behavior" three-step program (discussed earlier in this book) assist in helping the client uncover and deal with the psychodynamics underlying the theft behavior.

Chapter 28

WORKING WITH 'SIGNIFICANT OTHERS':
JOINT SESSIONS WITH A.T.O.s

My clinical investigations into atypical theft behavior have shown that, very frequently, seriously dysfunctional aspects of the relationship between the offender and a 'significant other' (usually but not always the offender's spouse) have been a major psychodynamic component of the A.T.O.'s theft behavior. Therefore, dealing with this central relationship so as to resolve it's issues must be considered an essential part of effective treatment with the Atypical Theft Offender.

A CAUTION!
Sometimes it is neither psychologically nor perhaps even physically safe for the A.T.O.s to involve significant others in the intervention treatment process, especially in the early stages. The A.T.O. may be unwilling to even inform the S.O. that he or she has been apprehended or charged by the police. The A.T.O. may be justified in not telling an abusive S.O. about the theft behavior.

Each case must be considered on its own merits, and the timing of informing and involving the S.O. is always a judgment call to be made jointly by the client and clinician. If the client remains firm that the S.O. not be informed then the clinician will have to make a decision as to whether further treatment is likely to be effective, especially if the Atypical Theft Offender is involved in a seriously abusive relationship and is not willing to change either the relationship or his or her living situation.

The material in this book provides general clinical investigation findings, assessment and treatment guidelines, exercises and approaches. Such information may or may not fit or be relevant to any specific case.

I do offer telephone consultations to clinicians who are dealing with theft offender cases. The responsibility for successful assessment and treatment must lie with the client and the clinician involved in the case.

The A.T.O. and 'Significant Others'

In my clinical experience, time and again it has transpired that the offender, at the time of the offense, was having major interpersonal problems with a 'significant other.' While in some cases it was an employer or friend with whom the offender was having difficulties, in the vast majority of these cases, the problem pertained to his or her spousal relationship.

Let me hasten to add that this does not mean that the difficulty in the spousal relationship was the A.T.O.'s only problem, but rather that these marital difficulties may have also been 'pushing buttons' connected to the psyche of the offender. Most often these 'buttons' are also attached to much older material, especially unresolved issues from childhood. The current issues in the spousal relationship may have had psychodynamic elements in common with the earlier (and still resolved) material.

Successful treatment with A.T.O.s must deal with earlier unresolved matters as well as with current issues.

For successful treatment with A.T.O.s it is essential that the earlier, unresolved issues from childhood be dealt with in therapy, in addition to matters of current concern. Not dealing with these earlier issues will leave them in place and 'psychoactive', i.e., free again, on some future occasion, to precipitate further acting out behavior.

At the same time, not confronting and resolving current life problems such as serious marital disharmony can leave the offender with ongoing stressors that may 'go critical' again at some point in the future, thereby leading to more theft behavior.

What I have termed Specialized Treatment for Atypical Theft Offenders (S.T.A.T.O. Therapy) is virtually always a two-pronged approach, one that deals with the unresolved earlier *(there-and-then)* plus the current *(here-and-now)* issues in the client's life.

Individual interviews with Significant Others

At the first interview with each A.T.O. I inquire as to whether the offender's spouse knows about the theft behavior and charge. Sometimes, at the first meeting, and without my having requested or required it, the spouse will be sitting with my client in the waiting room outside my office. Experience has shown me that this is usually a very good sign; it usually means that the spouse knows why their partner is seeing me, and that he or she cared enough to take the time from other activities to be with, and supportive of, my client.

Leaving the spouse in the waiting room, I will invite the client into my office, and shortly thereafter inquire directly what awareness the spouse has as to why my client has made the initial appointment. Depending on the amount of material to be covered and the particular details presented to me I may, with the client's permission, either invite the spouse to join us for the latter part of the first session, see the spouse separately for a session, or invite the spouse to join us for part of an upcoming session.

This policy of meeting and interviewing a 'significant other' is one that I have employed for over 20 years with virtually all clients who have sought treatment with me. It is a matter of much debated opinion, usually begun in the clinician's professional training and theoretical orientation, which determines whether clinicians are willing to ever meet, let alone interview, their clients' significant others. My own view is that when the 'significant other' gets to at least meet who it is that their partner is talking with, they have a sense of not being entirely excluded from the process.

> There are, particularly with theft offender cases, several advantages in interviewing a 'significant other'. Indeed, such involvement is sometimes essential to fully uncover and deal with the underlying problems that led to the behavior that has brought the A.T.O. to the clinician's office in the first place.

Advantages of seeing a 'significant other' of the A.T.O. client

• The first advantage is that I could conceivably listen to my client talking for months or years about his or her 'significant other', and still have only one-sided and second hand, albeit potentially valuable information about the spouse. Without employing the spousal interview, such data would be skewed by my interpretations of my client's verbal descriptions of his or her perceptions. First hand data can be as important as, or even more important than, second hand information. Meeting the significant other provides more comparative data that frequently turns out to be of considerable clinical value.

•Second, it is important to gather as much information as possible about the client and the client's situation and relationships. A husband or wife is likely to have information and insights about the client that supplement and support or contradict the client's perceptions and presentation. While this would be the case with most if not all clients, of course with A.T.O.s the existence of so much embarrassment, defensiveness, and/or high anxiety regarding their charges may act to inhibit their providing what could turn out to be very crucial data about themselves and their lives.

As an example, I am reminded of the A.T.O. who answered in the negative when I inquired whether she had experienced any personal losses in the time period prior to her offense. She had replied that she had not. However, when I spoke with her spouse the following week, he informed me that in the three months prior to his wife's shoplifting she had lost her mother, her oldest brother, and her grandfather. Furthermore, he himself had been laid off from work, and his wife (my client) had had an operation to remove a malignant growth on her breast. His wife stated when I saw her next that she had "simply forgotten" these events. I suggested that she may have temporarily suppressed the memories of these events in response to the psychological immensity of this multitude of losses, and that she was still largely blocking on their meaningfulness to her. As clinical investigation has shown, denial is a common early phase of many persons' grieving processes. With Atypical Theft Offenders such denial can have very unfortunate legal consequences.

•A third reason for interviewing 'significant others' is that they often provide information about their partners' emotional state and overt behavior just prior to and/or just after the theft event that may be crucial for a valid assessment.

One client's spouse had become aware that his wife had been very uncommunicative, depressed and emotionally abusive for a couple of days just prior to each theft offense. My client had not conveyed this important information.

When queried by me following the spousal interview, my client altered certain of her previous statements. Whereas she had initially claimed that there had been little change in her pre-theft emotional state or interactions with significant others, after being confronted with the information provided by her spouse she now offered that an increased use of alcohol had occurred, and that she had emotionally and on occasion even physically abused her spouse. Although she had not thought of it previously, she now recalled that such behavior had indeed preceded many of his previous shoplifting offenses.

(In the future, any such experiences (drinking, feeling depressed, abuse of her spouse, etc...) could now be considered signals for her to exercise greater vigilance, seek professional help, and take other constructive measures to curtail these behaviors and to prevent stealing in the future.

•A fourth advantage of interviewing the spouse is that a useful therapeutic alliance can be struck, whereby if any further similar behavior such as that referred to in the previous paragraphs were to be observed by the S.O., he or she could communicate with me in this regard. My client would then be confronted in the next interview with the spouse's observations, and would hopefully address these issues, thereby perhaps preventing a recurrence of theft behavior. By thus working cooperatively, with the full approval of the A.T.O., the three of us can form a treatment team in the best sense. Incidentally, the A.T.O.'s inappropriate behavior is often related to the spouse's own actions or attitudes and therefore a joint session may involve each of them looking at their respective conduct and the effects of such upon the other's state of well-being and behavior.

   • A fifth advantage of meeting the spouse is to inform him or her directly about the general findings of my investigations into atypical theft behavior. At the initial stages of assessment and treatment this can be important as the spouse may well have been feeling confused, frustrated, or downright angry about the offender's behavior, and may not understand why the partner would ever have stolen.

   Not infrequently the spouse initially presents as angry at my client for "being so stupid," and may have berated the offender, perhaps saying that "if you really wanted to stop stealing, then you could just do so".

   It should be understood that spouses are usually no less shocked by the offenders' behavior than are the offenders themselves, and frequently, neither has any appreciation of the psychodynamic factors that may have precipitated the offensive behavior. In addition, the spouse often feels impotent because he or she has not been able to influence the offender to stop stealing.

I, of course, do not reveal anything to the 'significant other' without the express permission of the offender, and vice versa.

Continued Involvement of The Spouse

   As mentioned earlier, very frequently the spouses are asked back, following their initial individual interview, either for a second individual interview to complete the information gathering, or to accompany their partner to one or more future sessions. Usually a 'significant other' will readily accept the invitation to accompany the client. It is my experience that most spouses care about the welfare of their partners, regardless of the fact that there may be serious problems in their relationship. Furthermore, they often welcome an opportunity to learn more about what is really going on in their partners' minds, thereby lessening their own confusion.

Treatment, prognosis / spousal involvement: 'The Good & Bad News'

The 'good news' is that cooperative, supportive, and willing involvement by the spouse can be a major factor in successful treatment outcome. The client feels supported and loved; long-standing marital issues can be resolved; the couple becomes a team with a common goal of preventing any acting out theft behavior in the future.

The 'bad news' is that in cases where the spouse takes the tack that this matter has nothing to do with him/her, that it is the offender's problem and the offender's problem alone, then the prognosis for successful treatment may be significantly diminished, so long as their relationship remains unchanged. After all, if the precipitating preconditions for acting out (e.g., major marital disharmony) remain, then the offender may well re-offend.

If the marital relationship is not to become an active ingredient in the seeking of a lasting solution to the client's theft behavior, it will likely remain a part of the underlying problem.

*****

Case #29: Rodney: A lawyer at the marital breaking point

Rodney sought help after being referred for a consultation by a forensic psychiatrist. My colleague had sought my clinical opinion in an attempt to better understand what could be only be described as extremely self-defeating, entirely nonsensical theft behavior by a prominent lawyer whose income exceeded $500,000 per year.

In our first interview this offender readily admitted that he had entered a department store and walked through the video department picking up and stuffing into his briefcase a few audio and video tapes, including a video cassette of the film, Gulliver's Travels. The cost of the items stolen was less than $135. At the time he was apprehended he had over $900 cash on his person, plus three valid credit cards.

247

Interviews with this client brought out the fact that his had been an exceptionally restricted childhood. Severe punishment had been meted out for the kinds of spontaneous behaviors that healthy children ordinarily exhibit in abundance-- namely laughter, enthusiasm, and boisterousness. In his home, supposedly in order to not disturb a severely ill parent, he was instructed to whisper at all times, or better yet, remain virtually mute unless directly addressed. Studying exhaustively and gaining top marks in school became his means of stimulating himself and receiving whatever positive stroking came his way.

In his early twenties this man married a person who soon thereafter developed migraine headaches, irritable bowel syndrome and chronic back pain. A multitude of medical tests showed no demonstrative sources of her problems. Psychiatric consultation was recommended and vehemently refused. She became seriously depressed, sometimes bedridden, and in the throes of her severe headaches, claimed not to be able to tolerate in the house or the family car, either from her husband or their children, sounds above the loudness level of a whisper. An accomplished pianist, he was repeatedly berated by his spouse whenever he played the instrument while she was at home. Both he and the children were repeatedly screamed at to "Stop playing so loudly!",..."Turn the stereo lower!", or "Use a walkman while you are in the house!". His wife also refused to go out to visit friends, go to the movies, etc... . She said that all kinds of social activities bothered her and she really only wanted to be left alone in her study. The marital relationship deteriorated gradually over the years, and my client recalled that he had become increasingly depressed, as his marital life became the uneasy coexistence of two silent solitudes.

In retrospect, one can imagine the frustration and fury building within this man! The conclusion that I arrived at was that his theft behavior, twenty-five years into the marriage, was his unconscious mind's way of signaling him that he was living an intolerable life and that things could simply not go on in this fashion any longer. **He was Gulliver** *in a marriage that was extremely restrictive, unsatisfying and destructive.*

In the spousal interview his spouse stated that she viewed her husband to be "sick in the mind" as evidenced by his shoplifting behavior, while her various physical problems were real and not of her own making. She stated that she had no need nor intention of attending any further sessions, with me or any therapist, with or without her husband. She acknowledged being very angry with her husband for a myriad of reasons, saw him as a "weakling" and "boring," and declared that she was "not in the least interested 'in working on' the relationship" although she said that she had absolutely no intention of ending the marriage.

Rodney was faced with the potentially professionally devastating consequences of disbarment for such an "unfathomable and stupid" act of shoplifting; nevertheless he, initially resisted looking at the major question of why he would have risked so much for so little gain.

Eventually the enormity of the potential consequences of his actions began to dissolve his resistance. Slowly, he began to acknowledge that such a high-risk, low-gain act might actually have been an attempt by his unconscious to force him to look at his life, and the "lack of living" in it. He also eventually confronted his feelings regarding his own mother's illness, her unavailability to him through much of his childhood, her agonizingly slow deterioration and death while he was still a teenager, and the unresolved childhood guilt that he still carried with him that perhaps she would have regained her health 'if only' he had been even quieter and less enthusiastic about his activities.

His long-standing guilt had been 'tying him down,' like Gulliver, with newer strands being continually added through his being aware of his lack of 'Christian compassion' for his wife.

Ten months later, after very intensive psychotherapy and numerous sessions with his minister, and after several failed attempts to get his wife to see a marital or individual therapist, Rodney and his wife separated. Within weeks his feelings of guilt and depression lifted, as if, as he described it, "Gulliver had finally decided to sit up, only to find that the ropes that had been supposedly been tying him down had merely been laying over his prone body and were not attached to the ground at all." With such marked changes in thinking, feeling, and behavior, and by carrying out the work of mourning his losses of childhood and of his failed marriage, the prognosis in this case became excellent.

*****

Spousal involvement in treatment sessions

Spousal attendance in treatment sessions does not necessarily imply that 'marital therapy' will or should take place. For successful treatment with some A.T.O.s it is sufficient to have their spouses attend only once, or at most, occasionally. As many A.T.O.s have considerable difficulty with being either verbally or emotionally open, a spousal presence can provide a means whereby the spouse may gain greater awareness of the content and processes of the A.T.O.'s thoughts and feelings. As one spouse put it, "She never talks to me very much at home; I never knew what was bothering her. Now, at least I can be more sensitive about bringing up certain matters. Maybe eventually she will be more open with me outside of this office. I'm going to stick with her anyway. Partly because I now understand that she needs me, and that she does care for me."

Some moments during sessions in which the partner is in attendance do become, in effect, marital sessions. For the rest of the session, the 'significant other' may simply be a 'silent witness.' Spouses are advised that they may choose to attend sessions or not, and to participate if and only to the extent that they wish, with, of course, the client's permission and my agreement. In the majority of instances, spouses are very willing, and indeed grateful for the opportunity to help their partners, and their relationships as well.

Spouses are cautioned not to unfairly use information learned during their attendance at their partners' sessions. And, experience has shown, they *are* generally sensitive and supportive in this regard. Of course, if the significant other does not appear to be ready to be present in a helpful and safe way for the client, then such participation is either minimized, or cut out altogether, at the therapist's discretion.

Sometimes outright marital therapy does play a major part in the treatment process. I have no hesitation whatever in offering clients and their partners opportunities to deal with relationship issues. Any progress made towards improving their relationship cannot help but promote the A.T.O.'s treatment. It is primarily up to the client and the partner to bring up relevant issues, although I may also introduce topics that need exploration.

Keeping Secrets: Dealing with 'significant others' when the client does not wish their theft behavior to be known by the S.O.

I do not believe that it is always necessary for the family member to be informed of the theft behavior. On the other hand, I strongly recommend, in most cases, that my A.T.O. clients <u>do</u> tell their S.O.'s, sooner or later! Avoidance of providing this information may unnecessarily prolong the self-disgust feelings that the A.T.O. has towards himself or herself.

On the other hand, there are times when telling the S.O. is contraindicated. For example, if the relationship has deteriorated significantly, and/or separation is contemplated, then informing the spouse may not be psychologically safe or helpful.

Summary

In this chapter we have seen that a 'significant other' can play an important and even crucial role in the treatment of the Atypical Theft Offender. In individual as well as joint sessions, as full participant or as caring, silent observer, the S.O. can assist at many stages during treatment. When marital issues are relevant to the acting out behavior of the Atypical Theft Offender then resolving these problems is critical for successful outcome.

Chapter 29

GROUP TREATMENT WITH ATYPICAL THEFT OFFENDERS

In 1984 I developed and ran a group for Atypical Theft Offenders at the Clarke Institute of Psychiatry. The relief that the participants experienced when coming into this group of sensitive, caring people was immediate and usually profound. A serious initial problem with Atypical Theft Offenders is that they frequently view themselves as 'rotten, bad, and awful' people, and often present with very low self-esteem. Finding themselves in a group of theft offenders who usually are readily recognized as the basically 'good' people they are, reinstates some of their own former positive feelings towards themselves.

For several years while on staff at the Clarke Institute I only dealt with Atypical Theft Offenders in individual sessions. In spite of my own attempts, within these sessions, to have them consider themselves to be "essentially okay persons with problems that needed to be dealt with," rather than as bad or immoral persons, they tended to tenaciously hold on longer than desirable to the disapproving views of themselves that they had when they originally entered my office. Group therapy provides an instant micro-society that can almost immediately stop the social isolation that the Atypical Theft Offender may be feeling in relation to the problem behavior. As Yalom[xxvii] has pointed out, the sharing of a common difficulty with others, which he has termed 'universality,' can be inherently curative for the participants of a therapy group.

By having them meet in a group with others who had the 'same problem' but who they readily see and accept as basically "OK" persons, almost all the participants find it easier to accept themselves as essentially honest persons who have stolen, rather than continuing to see themselves as dishonest hypocrites whose previous and general law-abiding nature was a sham.

Hence, with greater ease and rapidity than was possible in one-to-one therapy, they are able to alter their self-percepts in the positive direction, and learn about the numerous ways (as outlined in previous chapters) that 'good' people could have committed such 'bad' actions.

The 'Imaginary One-way Mirror and Soundproofed Room' technique

I ask the client who is reluctant to express his or her true feelings and thoughts to a spouse, parent, boss, or whoever, to imagine that there is a one-way mirror between himself or herself and the imagined person, and also, that the imagined person is in a soundproofed room as well so that he or she would not be able to hear what is being said, nor see the client speaking, even if he or she were actually present. It is important for the client to imagine that the 'other person' can be seen through the one-way mirror, sitting in the soundproofed room.

I may reinforce these conditions with the client by adding, "<u>your (imagined person), who, of course, isn't actually in my office or the imaginary room anyway, cannot either see you or hear you, and so you can say whatever is true for you without having any concern about how the imagined person might respond.</u>"

The use of these imaginary devices of the 'one-way mirror' and the 'sound-proofed room' usually results in markedly greater openness and assertiveness on the part of the client, which is particularly noticeable when the client has just previously balked at talking to the 'other person' in the usual 'empty chair' approach.

II-- Using an actual mirror to assist the client to 'see' himself/herself

Many persons are not really aware of the ways in which they present themselves physically. They may not consciously realize how frightening, or sad, or depressed they may appear, either to their partners, children, colleagues at work, or friends at a social gathering, let alone to strangers. When many of us look at ourselves in the mirror in the morning, our purposes are usually functional, i.e., having to do with getting makeup or hair right, or shaving, or straightening a blouse, or putting on a tie, etc... . It is remarkable how many persons look at themselves, but without really 'seeing' their facial expressions, body postures, etc.... I have found that the judicious use of a hand-held mirror, or full body-length mirror, or the use of a videotape freeze-frame, can be very useful feedback devices in helping clients see themselves anew.

In two recent group therapy sessions, for example, I employed a movable full-length mirror to assist two clients to gain new and updated perspectives of themselves.

In the first case, a relatively new member of the group, a woman whose stated goal was to learn to be more open with people, was readily able, with the mirror positioned just outside the group circle, to see her almost constant and most inappropriate smirk. She acknowledged that people had frequently asked her what she was finding so funny, when she was not consciously experiencing anything humorous at those times, at all. Her use of this facial expression was a defense against letting her true feelings of discomfort, unhappiness, anger, sadness, etc... be known. The smirk also was very successful at keeping at bay even those persons she consciously wished to approach.

Given that this person was a trial lawyer who often was required to appear in court, her expression had likely put off both judges and jury alike. With the use of the mirror she was able to better recognize the tendency to put on this 'mask,' and learned that it was in fact more helpful to allow herself to express, when she consciously wanted to, the full range of emotions on her face, and in her verbal expression as well.

The following week I used the mirror with a client whose problem was, in a sense, quite the opposite of the woman above. This second client was a married 42-year old man whose visage was an almost constantly excruciatingly pained expression, one that seemed to exemplify a combination of sadness, depression, helplessness and inadequacy. His was the classic 'victim' expression, one that may have invited others to take advantage of him when it suited their purposes, and to ignore and avoid him when they wanted the 'pleasure' of someone's company. This expression turned out to be one that was learned from a highly depressed mother, and a very sad, defeatist father. Interestingly this man occasionally would tell a joke at the beginning of sessions, and at those times his expression changed entirely. At those fun moments, the pinched, knitted eyebrows-tight and down-at-the-mouth expression he usually wore, gave way to a wonderfully delightful smile and relaxed, easy-going facial expression. The transformation was shocking, inasmuch as the two expressions were so totally opposite.

In this case, I positioned the mirror so that the client could look at his reflection throughout the rest of the meeting and to alter his expression as he saw fit.

Using the mirror as a continual feedback device this client, whose face was one that could definitely be termed 'very highly expressive,' learned to drop the pained, sad mask and allow himself to look --and feel-- more comfortable and relaxed. Over the next few months he reported that he became more appropriately assertive at work and in social situations, and in the process had improved several relationships, including those with his spouse and children. The latter, it turned out, had been deliberately avoiding "Mr. Grouch" for a long time. They reveled at being greeted by a much warmer and more approachable looking dad.

Perhaps it is not necessary to state, but just so that the reader not misunderstand, the point of the use of the mirror was not to program these clients to have "a more socially acceptable 'mask'"; rather it was to help them encounter the masks they were already wearing and give them an opportunity to learn to let go of them. When the individual's true self is revealed, that self's visual representation is usually beautiful, even in the case of persons who might otherwise be considered, according to our society's current standards, as not bearing the optimally 'beautiful look.' When we truly are our open, honest and non-defensive selves, the inner beauty and humanity that resides within virtually all of us usually emerges, and is both lovely to behold and a pleasure to encounter.

For Atypical Theft Offender clients, as with the rest of us, dropping their masks and becoming more authentic may be a vital step in improving their relationships.

Chapter 27

THE CLIENT-THERAPIST RELATIONSHIP: KEY ISSUES FOR EFFECTIVE A.T.O. TREATMENT

The quality of the relationship that the therapist establishes with the client is usually a major facilitating element of the therapeutic process. The therapeutic relationship may be even more important when working with authentic Atypical Theft Offenders.

A.T.O.s are often so ashamed of their theft behavior and so self-punitive, that their self-esteem is almost invariably very low at the time that they are first seen by a clinician. When the clinician treats these persons with genuine courtesy and respect the therapeutic effect can literally be life-saving, since, as already mentioned, some Atypical Theft Offenders may be suicidal, especially as they contemplate the imagined forthcoming public humiliation of facing court.

The forensic portion of my practice is currently restricted to probable atypical, or atypical-typical 'mixed'-type theft offenders. I generally do not assess likely Typical Theft Offenders. The latter's defense lawyers, if they have contacted me and I have seen their clients for one or two sessions, are told directly if I conclude that a court-bound psychological report would be of little use to their clients and therefore a waste of both time and money.

At this point I usually receive referrals from defense lawyers whose clients' theft behaviors seem clearly nonsensical given the clients' requirements, reputations, or resources. I point this out because I shall continue to address in this chapter, as I have in others, the matter of the likely Atypical Theft Offender or A.T.O.-T.T.O. (mixed) type of individual, rather than the Typical Theft Offender.

This is not to say that Typical Theft Offenders are not in need of professional help if they are to stop their behavior. But I maintain that their that you were traveling substantially over the speed limit, and from a legal perspective had no excuse, recall your feelings at the time that the flashing red light appeared in your rear-view mirror, accompanied perhaps by an attention-getting siren.

Or recall another situation where you were knowingly speeding and how you felt when a uniformed police officer quickly emerged from an unmarked cruiser and signaled in no uncertain finger-pointing 'sign language' for you to pull over. Were you delighted to be picked out for a speeding citation? Did you feel pleased and happy, or instead, did you feel frustrated, angry, disgusted -- either at yourself, the police officer, and/or the fate that picked you, of all people, to be the one pulled over?

And how did you behave to the officer when asked: "May I see your driver's license?" Did you smile a genuine smile and say, "Thanks for pulling me over, officer."?   And even if you did smile, were you actually happy at that moment? How did you really feel? Often, even the nicest, most gentle and honest individual can feel embarrassed, frustrated, resentful and/or anxious upon being apprehended by the police. This same generally levelheaded, honest and law-abiding person could even become somewhat belligerent, especially if the officer is rude or speaks to him or her in a tone we would associate as being more appropriate to use with a 'common criminal': *"Let me see your driver's license, buddy!"* This same good citizen might even fib about having to rush home because her menstruation has just begun, or his child had been hurt at school, or that he/she was rushing to a seriously ill patient, or relative.

Many of us are *not* at our best when caught doing something wrong, or (worse) illegal -- even if it is 'merely' speeding.

It will be useful for the reader to keep in mind your reactions, including the images and feelings that were aroused in you when reading the above vignettes regarding speeding, when you contemplate the behavior of the theft offender who has just been apprehended and is facing something a great deal more serious than a speeding ticket!

*****

233

Case # 28: Ramon: The speeding shoplifter

Actually, one of my clients, Ramon, the owner of a medium sized manufacturing company, was stopped for speeding the week following our third session. He had shoplifted months earlier following the loss of his spouse to cancer. He was doing grieving work in our therapy sessions, plus dealing with a childhood loss he had never fully dealt with previously -- specifically the death of his mother when he was six years old.

When the police officer returned from his cruiser where he had used his on-board computer terminal to pull up data about the driver he had just stopped, and as he was handing back Ramon's license, the officer said to him in what seemed to Ramon to have been a most demeaning tone; "Hey, you're a thief! You steal things from stores!"

When Ramon described this incident at our next session he said that, responding to the police officer's tone of voice and his words, he had felt as if he had been called a wife beater or child molester. He got angry and flustered and began to stutter, something he had not done for years. The officer interrupted Ramon's halting response saying, "Just get going, Mac. And don't speed any more! And stop your stealing!!!"

Feeling terribly humiliated and embarrassed, Ramon continued on his journey home, experiencing more and more embarrassment and more and more anger. He also reported that what he felt like doing was going to his favorite shopping center to 'just look around'. He did not, however, because he had an inkling that what he really would have done was shoplift something -- anything -- yet again!

*****

Like Ramon, most theft offenders, particularly if they are at least partially of the A.T.O. type, will come to their first session in a state of marked embarrassment. Many of those I assess and/or treat have seen other clinicians previously and some of these clients have reported being treated by these professionals as if they were 'common' thieves.

underlying issues and dynamics are often qualitatively different from A.T.O.s and their motivations in seeing a clinician are usually very different as well. They tend to only want a report to mitigate against their anticipated sentences; they are seldom interested in understanding, let alone ceasing, their theft behavior.

Working with Typical Theft Offenders: A difficult but not impossible task

Within the past few years I have seen a few heretofore Typical Theft Offenders who have been so fed up with their lives of stealing and jail, stealing and jail, etc... that they have truly wanted to stop their theft behavior. In a couple of these cases, their 'organismic disgust' and therefore their motivations were sufficiently strong to enable them to deal with ceasing their decades-long lifestyle. Not surprisingly they had had troublesome childhoods and complex earlier motivations to steal that needed to be confronted. The tasks involved were neither easy nor brief to get to the point that they stopped stealing.

Greeting the new Theft Offender-Client

Most of my theft offender clients are of the classic A.T.O. or mixed A.T.O./T.T.O. types. They are usually very embarrassed, frightened and/or confused as to the reasons for their theft behavior. And too often, unfortunately, they have been treated as 'common criminals' by the persons involved in their apprehension and the laying of charges (usually store owners, loss prevention persons, and/or human resources personnel with strict zero-tolerance rules to follow when dealing with cases of employee theft). In actual fact, of course, many of them are the most uncommon of criminals. The police officers who are called to the scene may also have been less than tactful or sensitive to the offenders' state of upset, particularly if they present as belligerent or aggressive (usually due to feeling humiliated and frightened.

It is understandable that the individuals involved in the apprehension and laying of charges of theft offenders might not treat them with much sensitivity or kindness, let alone compassion. After all, the offender may have tried to get away from the apprehending individual, and may have even denied having done anything wrong, or having any knowledge of how the items, or moneys in question came to be on his/her person, etc.... How many times on the past has the individual who has just caught this offender heard similar stories, denials, and outright lies? Far too often! One's patience can wear thin. The moment of apprehension can be anxiety-provoking and adrenaline-producing for both parties.

To give credit where it is certainly due, however, I have been privy to some few stories of remarkably gentle, kind, insightful storeowners, loss prevention personnel and police officers. Recently, for example, a very long-term theft offender, probably of the mixed A.T.O./T.T.O. type told me that the final straw that broke his resistance to get help was his having been followed out of a variety store by the very large and powerful owner, who gently tapped him on the shoulder and said in a quiet and compassionate voice to my client, "Please! No more stealing! Please!". My client had gone back to his office and burst into tears that flowed for over an hour. He told me that he remembered looking up at the gentle giant of a store owner's face, and seeing only compassion and concern. In his office, after he had stopped crying, he remembered the words screaming inside his head, over and over; "Enough! Enough! This must stop!!!"

The dynamics involved when accused of something 'bad' or 'wrong'

Most individuals react negatively to being accused of something that is "not a nice thing to have done," whether, and regardless of why they did the thing.

Has the reader ever been reprimanded in the working situation or in interpersonal relationships? Even where the criticism is justified, the person on the 'receiving end' seldom likes having such an experience, and not infrequently will attempt to justify, explain away, or even outright deny the validity of the accusation directed his or her way. Many of us can identify with Winston Churchill who once said that while he was always willing to learn, he didn't always like being taught. Or caught, perhaps!

There is value in recognizing the nature of 'accusation-reply' dynamics. Therefore, let us take a different sort of issue as an example, one that is nevertheless relevant to the one we are examining in this book.

Recall the last time you (or a friend) were knowingly speeding in your car, and were caught and stopped by a police officer. Even though you knew

Most A.T.O.s share several, if not all, of the same major
psychodynamic issues, including the following:
(i) unusually brutal, or in other ways, traumatic childhoods;
(ii) unresolved early issues, especially regarding losses;
(iii) inadequate coping mechanisms under stress;
(iv) early inclinations towards theft as a way of seeking affection,
acceptance, compensation and/or revenge;
(v) recent losses in adulthood;
(vi) a lack of appropriate assertiveness with peers and more
particularly, partners.
(vii) consciously experienced anger towards significant others at
the time of their offenses.

The importance of placing people into suitable groups for treatment

One of my recent activities was to teach graduate courses in group
therapy to students in counseling psychology in the University of Toronto's
graduate education faculty (OISE/UT). One of the issues I stressed with
students is the importance of matching particular clients with suitable groups. In
the last two decades there has been a plethora of therapeutic groups. Atypical
Theft Offenders certainly need to be placed in groups with others who have
similar issues, if their stealing is to become known by the other group members.
On the other hand, A.T.O.s can work in non-A.T.O. groups on many relevant
issues, without divulging their theft problem directly. To divulge that problem in
a group that has no other A.T.O.-members, given North American society's
attitudes towards theft behavior, could lead to major ostracism and hostility that
may be more than the A.T.O. can handle, and may cause the A.T.O. to withdraw
within the group, or for that matter, *from* the group in short order.

Clinicians familiar with conducting therapy groups will appreciate the
advantages, both in terms of psychodynamic efficacy and economics, of
conducting groups with A.T.O.s rather than see them always in individual
therapy. For obvious reasons it is especially important with A.T.O. groups to

remind the members of the very serious responsibility they have to observe the usual group rule regarding confidentiality.

The supplemental individual session for group members

I always offer group therapy clients the opportunity to request individual sessions to either deal in even more detail with material that has come up in group sessions, or to discuss matters that they are not yet comfortable mentioning 'in group.' In these individual sessions I often learn things about my client that he or she had not divulged previously. Trust in a group of people can build slowly, and clients sometimes need the protection provided in individual sessions to discuss issues that they are still reluctant to mention in the group.

I used to be rather rigid about whether to allow individual sessions for group members. I now recognize the value of greater flexibility in these matters, notwithstanding the fact that I will frequently counsel clients to consider bringing up the issues they have discussed in individual sessions, at a later time, in the group situation.

Out-of-group contact among members

My clinical experience with A.T.O.s indicates that there may be some value in permitting group members to have some social contact outside of the group. Frequently some of the members of the group I ran at the Clarke Institute would meet before group for coffee, or after group for lunch. In so doing, their own OK-ness was reinforced, and they learned to be more open within a social context in addition to operating more openly as members within the more formal structure and setting of the group session. While it is theoretically possible, of course, no inappropriate extra-curricular activity (including theft behavior) appears to have occurred in over five years of conducting this Atypical Theft Offender group at the Clarke. It goes without saying that it might well be inappropriate to permit outside-of-group contact when Typical Theft Offenders are members.

*****

Case # 30: <u>Naomi:</u> An educated, cultured A.T.O. who had kept herself virtually housebound for years
&
Case # 31: Sybil: A workaholic executive A.T.O. who wouldn't relax

Naomi was a member of an Atypical Theft Offender therapy group. She was a highly educated intellectual who, within a few years after she married her very successful but chauvinistic car dealership owner/husband, had ceased virtually all outside-of-the-home activities. For the ten years prior to joining the group she never allowed herself to take part in virtually any social or cultural activity without her husband -- and he was not interested in the arts, music or higher learning. She became a near caricature of the housebound, dutiful homemaker -- she pressed clothes until 1 a.m. and was up at 5:30 a.m. to begin preparing everyone's lunch. Not surprisingly, she was filled with both suppressed and repressed anger that expressed itself in her acting out via shoplifting.

Within a few weeks after she joined the group she clearly felt most comfortable with another female group member, Sybil, and with my agreement, they began to meet for coffee before group. Sybil was a workaholic/writer whose interests somewhat paralleled Naomi's own. Sybil also was inclined to be socially isolated, even though she too enjoyed cultural events, plays, concerts, etc....

After months of individual therapy had failed to effect changes in their leisure activities, I took note of these two women's' mutual interests and comfortability with one another to suggest, since they clearly enjoyed each other's company, that they consider meeting downtown for lunch and visit the galleries and museums that they were so reluctant to take in on their own. They both reacted immediately and positively to my suggestion, even though my previous similar suggestions, made when they were each in individual therapy, were resisted mightily.

Over a period of about three months their weekly sojourns took on a considerable importance to them, and they each were better able to address the underlying issues that had kept them as prisoners-of-guilty-consciences who had not permitted themselves pleasures that their husbands basically disapproved of their doing. Naomi, particularly, became much more assertive at home, and to her surprise, her spouse, after some initial resistance, also began to change his chauvinistic behavior. In fact, one day Naomi came to group with a Polaroid shot of her husband washing the floor at the entrance near the front door, a photo that one of her adult children had snapped with wonder and glee at seeing dad 'voluntarily' doing a household chore. Other healthy changes followed, and the shoplifting behavior of these two women ceased as they reclaimed their own interests and pleasures.

*****

The appropriate "mix" for an ATO group

Compatibility and complimentarity of the underlying psychodynamics of group members is important to aim at achieving for most therapy groups, and the same is true for a group of Atypical Theft Offenders. As an example, at one point I had in the same group a female banker who had absconded with $250,000 from her employer and a businessperson who had stolen several items of wearing apparel from a department store.

Both had remarkably similar underlying psychodymanic issues to deal with:
- both had been seriously abused as children;
- both had been abandoned by a parent when very young;
- both functioned as isolates who experienced lack of self-worth;
- both their crimes were precipitated by the loss of major relationships, and
- neither had dealt with their respective losses in a healthy fashion.

I believe that these two group participants were able to complete their therapeutic work faster due to the presence of the other, as both were dealing with similar issues, from a psychodynamic perspective.

It is important to keep in mind when working with Atypical Theft Offenders who have carried out such seemingly dissimilar activities as shoplifting, break, enter and theft, or fraud, that they may have a great deal in common at a psychodynamic level.

256

Part Four:

For The A.T.O., His Or Her Family And Friends

Chapter 30

SOME INTRODUCTORY REMARKS TO A POSSIBLE ATYPICAL THEFT OFFENDER

PLEASE NOTE!

1. THIS BOOK IS INTENDED PRIMARILY FOR THE USE OF PROFESSIONALS IN THE CLINICAL, LEGAL, LOSS PREVENTION AND POLICING FIELDS. THE ISSUES DISCUSSED ARE COMPLEX AND USUALLY REQUIRE EXPERT INTERPRETATION.

2. THIS BOOK DOES NOT PURPORT TO OFFER LEGAL ADVISE, PSYCHOLOGICAL DIAGNOSES, THERAPEUTIC DIRECTIONS OR PROGNOSES REGARDING TREATMENT OR OUTCOME FOR ANY INDIVIDUAL CASE OF WHICH THE READER MAY BE AWARE.

3. THIS BOOK ALSO DOES NOT PURPORT TO DEAL WITH ALL KINDS OF CASES OF THEFT.

4. DO NOT EMPLOY THIS BOOK AS A SUBSTITUTE FOR COMPETENT LEGAL OR CLINICAL HELP.

5. PLEASE ALSO READ THE DISCLAIMER AT THE FRONT OF THE BOOK FOR FURTHER DETAILS.

In this chapter I aim to speak directly to those individuals to possible Atypical Theft Offenders. My clinical approach is to encourage P-A.T.O.s to be compassionate towards themselves, and to assure them that it is very likely that there exist both understandable reasons for their theft behaviors and effective ways of dealing with the issues that precipitated the offensive behaviors, and thereby stopping such acts in the future.

The P-A.T.O. reader is invited to consider seriously several questions that are aimed at helping him or her to begin to uncover possible underlying dynamics related to the thefts involved. This chapter also offers suggestions about how they might approach their spouses about the matter of their theft behaviors, and how to find professionals, including lawyers and clinicians, who may be of assistance to them.

Introductory remarks to the Possible Atypical Theft Offender

This book may be, to some extent at least, relevant to you, and to those laypersons and professionals whose assistance and informed understanding you may need as you make your way through the possibly confusing and conflicting aspects of your theft behavior.

You may be a hard-working, ethical individual who believes in genuine effort and just rewards. At the same time, you may be a person who has stolen, perhaps knowingly (or not), and to some extent consciously and deliberately (or not). This book is directed to helping you deal with this problem.

On the one hand you may believe that thieves are disgusting 'low-lifes.' On the other hand, here you are, someone who has stolen perhaps a small item or on the other hand, some property or money worth a considerable amount. Perhaps you have been charged. You may believe that you deserve to be very harshly punished; as an eminent lawyer told me when he had been apprehended for shoplifting: "Doc, I have always believed in the law. I don't know why I did this thing but don't try to use some fancy theorizing to get me off. I am what I despise -- a thief!"

How to use this book

By all means read all (or most) of this book. If you have started with this chapter, that's fine. After finishing reading this part of the book, however, please go back and start at the beginning. It's important that you gain some understanding of some of the possible reasons for your theft behavior. Such understanding can facilitate your dealing with your lawyer and perhaps the mental health professional (psychologist, psychiatrist, social worker, etc...) who may be involved in your assessment and/or treatment. Understanding is also an important step towards your not committing any other theft behavior in the future.

While you are reading the material do keep an open -- and a gentle -- mind, when it comes to judging your theft behavior. Withhold judgment until you have come to a more thorough understanding of it, and until you have discussed the matter with an appropriate mental health professional.

WARNING: Any attempt to use this book for the purpose of subverting or avoiding justice may backfire because appropriately trained and experienced clinicians, crown and district attorneys and judges, are usually quite skilled at identifying serious flaws in a client's renditions of events and circumstances.

Over the years I have had a few individuals who read my articles and/or this book and then attempted to 'give me what (they) thought (I) wanted'. As the assessment and treatment process outlined in this book has both considerable depth and breadth their efforts to 'mold' their answers to 'fit' what they thought I was looking for backfired quite badly.

Of course, on a given day, even the best experts can be fooled, so undoubtedly more will try to do so in the future. The likelihood is that they will waste a great deal of their money and both our times!

On the other hand, some genuinely Atypical Theft Offenders, because of feelings of guilt and their holding the view that anyone who has done wrong deserves to be punished severely, may be inclined *not* to seek clinical or legal help just so that they can get the courtroom experience 'over with' as soon as possible, and 'take the deserved punishment.' This may be an unwise move, I believe, one that often does not promote either justice nor minimize the likelihood of reoccurrence of the problem behavior.

By considering the material in this book, and by answering truthfully and fully the questions posed to you in Chapter 17 (The Cupchik Theft Offender Questionnaire) and using the Cupchik Theft Offender Spectrum (in Chapter 18) you may come to a beginning of an understanding as to some of the reasons for your theft behavior, and some preliminary conclusion of whether you are, in some respects at least, one of those persons who might be considered an Atypical Theft Offender. If you are, then please do ensure that you get qualified and informed legal and clinical help.

Indeed, regardless of whether you come to believe that you are an Atypical Theft Offender, Typical Theft Offender, or of the A.T.O./T.T.O.-- mixed type of offender, I urge you to seek competent legal and clinical professional help.

Do not attempt to come to any <u>definitive</u> conclusions on your own as to whether you are more appropriately categorized as an Atypical Theft Offender, Typical Theft Offender, or of the A.T.O./T.T.O. mixed type theft offender. Such a determination should be made only with the consultation of a suitable clinician.

By all means *do* bring this book and your notes pertaining to the issues dealt with in this book, to your lawyer and/or your mental health professional. For your personal use, you have the permission of the publisher and writer to copy and fill out one copy each of the Cupchik Theft Offender Questionnaire and the Cupchik Theft Offender Spectrum, and to give a copy of your filled out responses to the professionals whose help you seek.

Consider addressing the issues brought up in this book that pertain to your act(s) of theft with your 'significant other(s)' as well. To feel hesitant to do so is natural, and if you have any doubt of the appropriateness of talking with your spouse, best friend, etc... then discuss this reluctance with the professionals as well. Keep in mind that many A.T.O.s have issues involving their spouses, parents etc...that should be or perhaps, must be, discussed with those involved, but may be best approached at the direction of a suitable clinician.

> Sometimes A.T.O.s steal and get caught in order to force themselves to address the following sorts of issues:
> - marital problems
> - the demise of a relationship
> - the need to change jobs
> - the negative effects of excess stress in their lives
> - their intrapsychic (i.e., inner) issues.

Remember: Atypical Theft Offenders can be found in all walks of life, all occupations, all socioeconomic classes, both sexes, as well as all adult ages and social milieus.

Don't keep facts from the professionals you've hired.

It is essential to be forthcoming with the persons whose help you will be seeking. On occasion A.T.O.s are so embarrassed or frightened that they will not inform their lawyers and/or clinicians of previous offenses. Not usually a wise decision! If your lawyer or clinician is not aware of all the relevant and related facts of your case, aside from giving you inappropriate or inadequate advice or assistance, they can look very naive or even downright ill-prepared or foolish in the courtroom when your record is introduced by the prosecuting attorney. Such a situation will not benefit you!

Do remember that all of our behaviors, including apparently bizarre theft behavior, have reasons that can in most instances be uncovered and can help the individual to cease future acting out.

Chapter 31

AN OPEN LETTER TO THE A.T.O.'s
'SIGNIFICANT OTHER'

Dear Important Person in the Theft Offender's Life:

*In my over two decades of investigating why some honest persons may shoplift or commit other acts of theft, I have come to appreciate the potentially powerful and even crucial part that spouses or other persons may play in the theft offender's life. You may discover that, however unintentionally, you might have played a part in the problem being faced by your loved one; whether or not this is true, **you almost certainly can play a positive part in the achievement of the solution** to the problem.*

My clinical experience suggests strongly that if you have just recently learned about the theft activities of your spouse, child, parent, or friend, you may be having any one or more of the following responses to the news: shock, surprise, anger, frustration, disgust, embarrassment, resentment, compassion, and/or guilt.

If you know that the theft offender has stolen previously, and that it has happened once again, you may be not only be experiencing some of the feelings just mentioned, but you may also be saying to yourself something like: "Oh, No! Not again! I thought that was behind us. What's wrong with you? You promised you wouldn't do that anymore! If you loved me you would stop doing these things."

Or, you may merely have suspected that he or she was involved in theft behavior previously when things 'just appeared' on dresser counters, or in drawers. You might have brought the matter up and were told that the items had been bought with savings from household expenses, but you were never quite sure.

You may also find yourself thinking:
- *"What will the neighbors (children, friends, co-workers) think?!"*

- *"How can I help?"*

- *"How can I get her/him to go for help?*

- *"Should I bring this matter up, or should I wait for (the person who has been charged) to talk about it?*

- *"Does the fact that he or she has been shoplifting mean that this person is not the fine, basically honest and honorable individual whom I had thought?"*

Let me assure you, first of all, that all of the above responses, and many others as well, are normal and natural. They do not indicate betrayal of the other person. Let me also assure you that the person who has stolen may be thinking and feeling comparable thoughts and feelings about himself or herself, and wondering whether to discuss the matter with you and/or how upset or willing to listen you might be!

It may be easier and more productive, for all concerned, if you consider approaching the person who has been stealing and let that person know that:
(i) you know about the problem; and
(ii) while you may not understand why he/she did it, and while you don't condone the behavior, nevertheless you do care about the person, and are willing to help in whatever ways you can.

Let me repeat that it is often very valuable to let the offender know that you will attempt to help that person and to stand by while he or she seeks assistance with the problem.

My experience with the essentially honest and hard-working individual who finds himself or herself stealing and may even be having trouble stopping, is that he or she very often feel confused, embarrassed, and humiliated, and may fear that, if found out, he or she will lose your love and respect, and will be shunned by yourself and possibly other family and friends 'who know'.

> *Especially if this is a repeat offense, and the offender had promised you that "it will never, ever happen again!"*
>
> *What else can you do to help? Let me suggest, first of all, that you read this book carefully, and that you give the person about whom you are concerned this copy to read as well.*
>
> *In order to assist you to better understand the important part you may be able to play, let me mention a couple of different avenues or alternate approaches that two spouses took in cases that I have dealt with in recent years. The path you will follow will be your own choice, of course. Consider the following cases as possible options .*

*****

Case # 32: Rita: whose optometrist- budding politician husband closed his office to attend sessions with his theft-offending wife

Ross drove his distraught spouse into Toronto for our first session, and sat in the waiting room while she and I discussed her problem in general terms. With her permission I then asked her spouse in for a three-way consultation. He immediately made it very clear that he believed that he was, in some way at least, partly responsible for his wife's difficulties. He reasoned that she had been upset with him on both prior occasions that she had recently shoplifted and that her thefts may have been partly a retaliation for the rough time he had been giving her while he was experiencing severe business problems. He acknowledged that he could be expected to be embarrassed by her appearance in court in their city of less than 170,000 population, where he held both business and political positions of prominence. On the previous occasions the charges had been dropped as a favor to him, and they had made full restitution. The materials stolen on this most recent occasion were valued at $35 total.

Ross was both direct and moving when he told me that what mattered most to him in this world was his wife's well-being, and that he would gladly take part in sessions with her if it would be helpful ("It would be," I quickly assured him!), and that he wouldn't hesitate to close his practice early on those days that she needed to come in for her appointments with me. Furthermore, he stated that, if letting go of his political ambitions would be decisively helpful to his spouse, then he would do so -- immediately. I told him that I was not in a position to comment on the latter notion, as of yet. (It turned out to not be necessary for his wife's sake for him to cease his political activities.)

After a few joint sessions, Ross asked to see me alone to work on some personal issues that he thought were getting in the way of his relationship with his wife. His devotion to her, and his genuine interest in coming to terms with his own difficulties, made it that much easier for his wife to develop new patterns of coping with their marital and other issues. Instead of building up major resentments in response to disagreements, which she would then "take on the road" via shoplifting, this couple learned to ' process' issues as they came along.

His wife knew, from not only her husband's words, but from his actions, that he cared for her deeply, and that he understood that her problems were at least partly 'their' problems, and that to the extent that he could, he would be actively involved in promoting their resolution and his wife's feelings of security and comfort. His wife's treatment process was not without its difficulties, but because of his participation, was relatively straightforward. If they continue to deal with issues together as they occur, rather than permitting a buildup of resentment and bitterness, I would be extremely surprised if she were to get into any further difficulties via theft behavior

*****

Now consider a very different (composite) scenario taken from my files.

*****

Case #33: Harriet, whose entrepreneur-husband, Hank, considered his wife's shoplifting behavior to be none of his business.

In contrast to Ross, Hank took virtually the opposite position on all counts. A rather prominent figure in his own community, Hank was much more concerned with the embarrassment that his wife's behavior could cause him, than with the distress she was experiencing. He was extremely disappointed in her, especially since she had assured him that she was not going to every shoplift again. As in the previous case referred to above, this was not her first

266

offense and Hank was not being successful in having the charges dropped this time, as he had been on the past occasions.

(It is important to understand that atypical theft behavior may well reoccur at some time in the future unless the underlying causes are dealt with. Be assured that most of the A.T.O.s who see me are convinced that they have forever stopped the theft behavior. In most of these cases, however, they had this same belief previously, yet re-offended. They did not realize that they would have to deal with the underlying causes of their behavior if they were to not be susceptible to stealing again in the future.)

It took several invitations before Hank would even agree to come in to see me. The individual I interviewed when he finally did make an appearance was an angry, authoritarian man, one who was decidedly psychologically unaware, and who lived a North American rendition of the southern European culture where he was raised. He regularly joined the other husbands from his home country at their local espresso hangout where they stayed until closing hours in the early morning, at which point they made their way home to their wives, who by this time had usually cleaned the house, fed the children, helped them with their homework and put them to bed, and would be waiting up for their husbands to make an appearance and be served their late evening snacks.

Hank's spouse had an accumulation of resentment that clearly related to her dissatisfaction with this way of living. Hank was not willing to discuss the matter however, and made clear to me that he was not willing to come back for another session either; nor was he willing to attend with his wife. My client was far too frightened to deal with this man, and with her intense feelings of anger and frustration, and she dropped out of therapy shortly thereafter.

*****

It might be useful to mention here that both Hank and Ross, and their wives, came from the same European culture, and were raised not far from one another in neighboring villages. (They did not know one another, however.)

In these two cases I believe that the attitudes of the spouses made for the major differences in clinical outcome. I would not be surprised at all if Hank's wife were to contact me again at some time in the future with a virtually identical problem as that which she presented with originally. After all, she never dealt with her feelings of frustration and resentment over the way in which she and her husband were living their separate lives, and unless things changed in their relationship the likelihood of her acting out by shoplifting would remain very high, in my clinical judgment.

On the other hand, I would be most surprised if Rita, having reconciled with her husband, and having learned to be more appropriately assertive generally, was to re-offend.

So, what now?

I would strongly suggest that, as one of the most important persons in the theft offender's life, you can help a great deal by reassuring the person charged that you are willing to do whatever you reasonably can to help solve any underlying problems in your own relationship with each other, and that you will be available to support the offender with regard to whatever other issues may need to be dealt with.

You might also assist the person who has been charged with theft, in finding suitable professional legal and clinical help. Often the theft offender is so embarrassed or upset that he or she is not thinking very realistically. For example, on occasion Atypical Theft Offenders may be inclined to go to court without the benefit of a lawyer, just because they feel guilty and think they deserve to be punished.

Guilt and punishment aside, the most crucial matter is that the underlying reasons for the offending behavior need to be uncovered and dealt with. Otherwise, the unresolved issues will likely lie dormant and may well provoke another instance of acting out behavior by stealing in the future.

So, please remember:

(i) You certainly do have an important role to play in assisting your loved one to come to terms with and resolve the problems underlying the theft behavior.

(ii) Express your caring, concern and willingness to stand by the offender and even involve yourself in the clinical process, as required.

(iii) Remind yourself, and the offender, that he or she is a worthwhile, essentially honest individual whose theft behavior may well have been an

indication that there are some underlying issues that need to be identified and dealt with.

(iv) By reading this book thoroughly (perhaps together) you will hopefully come to an understanding of the kinds of underlying processes that may be acting upon the offender, and that need addressing. It is not necessary to be a mental health professional to learn to recognize some of the stressors that may be operating to trigger the theft behavior.

(v) During and following the course of clinical treatment it is worthwhile being vigilant regarding the offender's apparent state of mind and manner. If or when you become aware that he or she is withdrawing, holding onto anger or sadness, or experiencing strong mood swings, then you may be able to help ward off further inappropriate acting out by discussing the matter and together attempting to locate the triggering problem, such as unresolved current relationship issues, possibly between the two of you, or between the offender and a someone at work, or perhaps a friend or relative. You might also suggest a visit to a mental health professional who is familiar with you and the theft behavior problem, and who is familiar with the material outlined in this book.

(vi) Remember, that awareness and conscious effort are required to improve one's coping style. Patience is also essential.

So, you see, there is probably much that you can in assisting the person you care about to deal with the genuine and serious problem of his or her theft behavior. Be assured that your involvement will likely not only be appreciated but may well be of direct assistance in yielding improvements in the matter of theft behavior, and very likely, in your relationship with each other. Again, be assured, you can indeed make a difference. A BIG DIFFERENCE!

All the best, Dr. Will Cupchik

Chapter 32

FINDING SUITABLE PROFESSIONAL HELP
FOR A.T.O.s

There are many sensitive, intuitive and experienced lawyers to whom it is almost immediately apparent that their clients' illegal activities were likely 'out of character' and that, at the time of their stealing, they may well have been experiencing severe emotional distress or mental disturbance. Some lawyers with whom I have dealt since 1984 have reported to me that they had read our original articles or the first edition of this book and that our published findings had confirmed what they had previously suspected, namely, that there probably had been underlying precipitating factors such as the loss-substitution and stress-reactive phenomena that had likely initiated the bizarre theft behaviors of certain of their clients.

Fortunate is the person who, having been apprehended for theft, and who is shocked by him or her own aberrant behavior, contacts a lawyer who has a good intuitive and educated sense that this new client needs appropriate clinical, as well as legal, help.

Be honest and totally disclosing with your lawyer
A week before writing this chapter, a new client, at the end of his initial interview during which he had divulged a life-long, though intermittent theft behavior, asked me as he was leaving, "Do you think I should tell my lawyer about these earlier thefts?" My answer to such a question is always an unqualified "Yes, absolutely!"

To not be totally self-disclosing with your lawyer may be ultimately self-defeating. Faced with the humiliation, fear and self-recrimination that often accompanies such acting out theft behavior, some A.T.O.s have omitted informing their own lawyers -- and even their own therapists-- of the existence and/or extent of their theft behavior problems. Even more self-destructively, some have told their lawyers that their apprehension was a mistake and that they didn't, wouldn't, couldn't do such a thing as steal, when they knew very well otherwise!

Most self-destructive of all are the offenders who have convinced themselves that they are innocent. (Of course, I am not referring here to persons who are innocent of what they have been accused.) These persons are into denial to such an extent that they refuse to accept that a problem even exists. No professional or layperson can provide much help to someone who has a problem but who claims that the problem does not exist.

Usually the persons who are referred to me have offended previously, and have already been through various degrees of denial about their guilt. Occasionally, however, I do get a new client who is still in major denial about the current charge. This denial may persist even when faced with the fact of a previous, virtually identical stealing scenario, for which he or she had been charged and convicted, which may have occurred only a few weeks or months earlier.

Alas, some clients have admitted lying to me at some earlier points during their assessment. However, as they have come to realize that I truly have their ultimate best interests in mind, they often voluntarily correct their previously offered mis-information.

I inform clients that I have two general functions in conducting an assessment in theft offender cases:
   1. **to ascertain the reasons for the theft behavior, and**
   2. **to minimize the likelihood of their re-offending.**

   Success in both these ventures can only be forthcoming if the client is totally self-disclosing.

It is my clinical experience that attempts on the part of clients to hide, omit or alter information about their recent and past theft behavior, once there has been an opportunity for a positive clinician/client relationship to have been established, are likely indicative of underlying T.T.O. (Typical Theft Offender) aspects in the individual. It is important to note this inappropriate behavior, and to be increasingly conservative in terms of prognosis. In short, such deceptive behavior does not augur well for the client's possibly acting out at some time in the future.

Beware a professional's attempt to achieve short-term gain at the risk of long-term pain

Occasionally some lawyers, in their initial conversations with me, have obliquely or even directly suggested that they are not particularly interested in my including in my court-directed Psychological Reports, mention of their clients' previous theft behaviors. I understand their motivation is to not add information in a court-directed report that might be considered to aid the prosecution, and that in cases of Typical Theft Offenders there may well be validity to such a decision. However, in cases of Atypical Theft Offenders such information is usually an indication of the severity of their clients' psychological problems.

The desirability of including such material is usually recognized by the counsel. After all, if their client gets off without a clear recognition -- by the court and the client -- of the latter's problem in the area of theft, then neither justice nor the accused might be ultimately well served -- as my clinical experience shows that the likelihood of re-offending is markedly increased in such circumstances.

Take a proactive, informed approach with all the professionals associated with your case

Do let your lawyer and any clinician associated with your case know as much about you as you can. *Do not* hold back information about any past theft behavior, and *do* disclose the status of your current major personal relationship, and of your working situation. Indeed, any stressors in any part of your life are potentially important for the professionals with whom you consult to be informed about.

You may be very helpful to these individuals if you have made use of the **Cupchik Theft Offender Questionnaire**, as well as the **Cupchik Theft Offender Spectrum** and bring along the completed form for their consideration.

In summarizing, do be as totally open and self-disclosing as you can with the professionals you consult to assist you in dealing with your theft behavior and its consequences.

Part Five:

Issues For Loss Prevention, Employee Assistance Plan & Human Resources Personnel, The Police And The Judiciary

Chapter 33

ATYPICAL THEFT OFFENDERS AND THE COURTS

Is a period in jail advisable for Atypical Theft Offenders, particularly if this is their nth appearance in court for similar offenses?

To the extent that the person may be correctly classified as an Atypical Theft Offender, then incarceration is usually not likely to be very effective in helping to stop further occasions of stealing.

In fact, many of the A.T.O.s whom I have assessed and treated have already been incarcerated in the past, some several times, with no apparent lasting deterrent effect. Indeed, since the Atypical Theft Offender is often self-sabotaging and self-punishing, the use of punitive sentencing may actually increase the likelihood of further reoccurrences of such behavior.

As bizarre as it may seem, some Atypical Theft Offenders have actually shoplifted again the very day that they had already appeared in court to face a charge for a similar offense and were fined or given a non-jail sentence. Others have shoplifted the day after their term of probation ended, or shortly after they were released from jail. These individuals, at some levels within their psyches, continue to be attracted to stealing (usually for unconscious motivations that still have not been recognized, let alone dealt with). Therefore some will soon again be in that awful situation, charged with theft and awaiting trial and punishment. It is surely more worthwhile for all concerned for the Atypical Theft Offenders to begin to deal with their issues, and stop stealing (which is, in their cases, almost invariably a symptom of –and deflection away from- their real problems).

Punishment is far more likely to be a suitable deterrent for <u>Typical</u> Theft Offenders. For these persons, stealing is an endeavor that seems to have sufficient financially remunerative appeal to justify the risk of being caught. The prospect of a jail term may therefore cause such persons to be less inclined to act out again.

What if the person *who is currently in treatment* for stealing, does it again!?

If the individual was undergoing treatment at the time that he or she committed yet another theft offense, it might be asked by some how one could justify the continuance of treatment! Surely, however, the fact that he or she has re-offended may only mean that the treatment process was not yet effective or completed?

Let me use an analogy from the medical model to consider these issues further. If a person with an infection is treated with a 10-day course of antibiotics, the fact that he or she is found to still have the infection half way through the course of treatment does not mean that the treatment is ineffective! Treatment was not yet completed; it was still in progress.

When an Atypical Theft Offender is in treatment, issues and events that arouse strong emotions may surface during the therapy sessions. When dealing with such matters, the individual may become temporarily psychologically vulnerable and at risk for acting out again.

What to do? Actually a new acting-out-by-stealing event while still in treatment can provide considerable and possibly therapeutic information (albeit at a price for the offender). Now the clinician and client have a fresh, just-transpired act of theft, the circumstances surrounding which they can examine in detail.

The desirability of follow-up sessions

I frequently recommend that the client continue in therapy weekly for at least several months in order to make major progress in the relevant areas of concern and which might precipitate future acting out unless dealt with to a greater extent.

I also suggest that the Atypical Theft Offender be seen at least quarterly or semi-annually for a year or two after the court appearance. Why?

Well, for persons who have had a great deal of difficulty stopping to shoplift, it is usually true that they still have some distance to go in changing the ways in which they deal with frustrations, hurts, losses, etc... in their everyday life. It is only within the context of real problems and situations that we may expect these persons to solidify changes in handling distressing situations differently. My clients are also informed that they may choose to call me to request a supplementary appointment should they feel the need, or if their life circumstances are seriously stressing them.

Semi-annual 'check ups' allow for a highly desirable intermittent review of how the person is getting on in his or her life. New issues usually have emerged just as a function of daily living; and examining how the client has attempted to deal with these issues gives the clinician valuable data about the client's then-current strategies for coping with life events.

STOPPING TO SHOPLIFT -- FINALLY!

What do I think is the state that the Atypical Theft Offender should attempt to achieve so as to not re-offend?

The A.T.O. must change his or her way of living, and of responding to life. Nothing less than changing one's circumstances and/or the ways of responding to these circumstances -- whether at home, at work, intrapsychically, or interpersonally -- will do. And, of course the underlying material that has remained unfinished for years or decades (often from childhood and/or early adulthood), must finally be addressed and resolved, at least on the psychological plane.

The different and sometimes conflicting roles of the defense lawyer and the clinician

There is an inherent and fundamental distinction to be made between the goals of the defense attorney and that of the assessing or treating clinician.

277

Defense attorneys are paid to defend their clients, specifically in relation to the current charge(s). Some of them can be inclined to be quite adamant as to what they may or may not wish to see included in a court-directed report. And it is understandable that they may not wish to see anything in a report that might give a judge cause to consider that the defendant may still have an inclination towards acting out by stealing at sometime in the future.

At the same time, however, criminal lawyer Michael Bury, in his review of the original hardcopy edition of "Why Honest People Shoplift Or Commit Other Acts Of Theft" [that was published in the May 28, 1998 edition of the Criminal Lawyers' Association Newsletter], wisely pointed out that *"... the underlying factors which lead to these crimes are extremely important both in identifying and assisting the atypical offender. It is extremely tempting these days to simply process such clients by way of diversion or a small fine. Such an approach, however, does not necessarily assist the client to prevent repetition of such an offence... . While Defense (lawyers) are not social workers, we are still obligated to ensure that our client's problems are properly identified and responded to by the courts."*

Clinicians are usually concerned with assessing the client in order to determine causative factors and hopeful therapeutic directions. In my experience the courts are often relieved to learn that the client's atypical and sometimes bizarre or non-sensical behavior is explainable and that successful treatment is possible. Too many judges have too often heard from defense attorneys that the offender will never do such a thing again, without such assurance being accompanied by an explanation of why the offender did it in the first place and that necessary remedies to reduce the likelihood of recidivism have been instituted. A satisfactory explanation must be psychodynamic in nature, I believe; such behavior cannot be satisfactorily explained by merely stating that the defendant 'had been depressed.' <u>Why</u> the defendant was depressed, and <u>why, being depressed, he or she had chosen to steal rather than overeat, or over drink, or ... something else</u>, is the crucial information that the judge needs in order to determine the appropriate finding and sentencing (if any).

It is very important for assessment reports to articulate a succinct and understandable explanation of the defendant's behavior, and to make clear the underlying issues that must be dealt with if the person is not to act out again. It is also important to clearly state that as long as the underlying precipitating causes continue to exist, then if/when the person again becomes 'depressed' sometime in the future, he or she may well act out again, unless corrective measures in the offender's thoughts, feelings and behavior are instituted. These measures then become the goals of appropriate psychotherapy interventions.

Chapter 34

PROACTIVE AND PREVENTIVE MEASURES FOR RETAILERS, HUMAN RESOURCES & EMPLOYEE ASSISTANCE PLAN PERSONNEL, AND THE POLICE

Dealing with the *Atypical Theft Offender*-employee

During the past several years I have assessed and treated both blue-collar and white-collar workers who had stolen from their employers. In some of these cases atypical theft behavior had been carried out by essentially honest and valued employees who were then fired and treated as would have been any typical thief.

To his own (and his company's) credit the head of human resources for a multi-national company based in Buffalo, New York, consulted with me after a senior-level administrator, one who had been with the organization for over a decade and whose performance was considered both productive and highly valuable, was apprehended leaving the premises with a 'sample' of the company's products. The total cost of the items taken was under $20. Since the company had a 'zero tolerance' policy in effect, the employee was immediately fired.

In this instance it was obvious to the personnel involved in the decision to fire the employee that the requirement that he be let go was an instance where the punishment far exceeded the crime. The offender's coworkers knew that his spouse had left him the previous week, and had taken their children with her to another city: he was clearly reeling from these events. She also had informed him that she was going to live with one of her coworkers, who had been transferred to another division of her company, located in Philadelphia. Because the offender's company's employee-theft policy was firm, and in spite of the appeal of his superiors and the head of human resources, and because the possible dynamics that might have been at play here were not fully recognized or understood, there had been no recourse but to fire the theft offender.

I described to this head of human resources my findings in the area of atypical theft behavior carried out by customers and employees alike. I pointed out the advances made in corporate culture in North America of offering treatment, rather than termination, for alcohol and drug dependent employees. This treatment approach was often taken even though some of these individuals could have serious, even lethal effects on the limbs if not the lives of the company's customers or fellow employees, such as could happen if their jobs included, as examples, either handling heavy or complex machinery, or carrying out maintenance of cars, truck, trains or aircraft). I also mentioned that providing or recommending treatment was often the preferred path even the troubled employees were in positions of major decision making re company policies, acquisitions, etc... . Surely, then, I suggested, there should be room for considering the beneficial handling of employees whose atypical <u>theft</u> behavior had cost the company a relative pittance.

The head of human resources agreed with many of my observations, and said that he was going to push for some changes in company policy that would allow psychological factors to taken into account in future cases of atypical theft behavior.

In another case, I was called by the co-worker of a research physician who had been caught stealing inexpensive office supplies, including pens, boxes of file folders. After he was interviewed by the head of the hospital and had agreed to pay for some $300 worth of supplies he had stolen over a three month period, this reserved and refined gentleman and doctor went home and fired a shotgun into his open mouth. Again, there were feelings of guilt and regret by many of this man's colleagues that they had not done enough to help their colleague.

Differentiating between Typical and Atypical Theft Offenders customers, for your <u>store's</u> sake!

The previous chapters in this book have clearly described the Atypical Theft Offender as the sort of individual who may well have been, for many years, a loyal, good, and spending customer. This person, under usual circumstances, is virtually exactly the kind of customer that the store's management has worked so hard to attract, often through the expenditure of many, many thousands of dollars in advertising expenses each year!

The following are some of the economically important questions for retailers and their loss prevention personnel to ask themselves when a potential Atypical Theft Offender-type customer has been apprehended.

•How many hundreds of dollars will the store need to spend to bring to trial a previously valued, and paying, customer, thereby perhaps losing tens of thousands of dollars in this customer's future purchases?

•What are the goals, and what are the consequences, of the indiscriminate prosecution of Atypical Theft Offender-type customers?

•Is there another way of dealing with such persons who have been found to be stealing?

A proposal for a <u>Profit Retention</u>™ Department: some suggestions for retailers and businesses

There is no doubt that loss prevention personnel face a very difficult task! One of their problems, I submit, is reflected in their name, which has an inherently negative aspect. I would recommend that stores institute a change in the name of their *'loss prevention'* departments to a designation that is more likely to promote the concept of *Profit Retention*. After all, a proprietor does not merely want to 'lose less,' but actually wants to 'make more'(money)!

I propose the use of staff to perform profit retention as opposed to merely 'loss prevention' functions! (The fact that the initials of profit retention are P.R. is a fortunate coincidence.)

I want to suggest further that the individuals involved in store security need to, and can learn to, reasonably rapidly screen theft offenders, and make more educated judgments regarding the apprehended persons so that these individuals might be dealt with in ways that better benefit the employer, now and in the future.

All too often retail store security personnel may be little more than the company's version of 'municipal street parking violations' officers; their managers may view their jobs as merely involving the apprehending and charging of shoplifters. They may even have quotas of 'apprehended customers' to fill, and/or may be paid 'by the head' like retail 'bounty hunters', earning bonus points for apprehending and charging more and more customers. Interestingly, it is often the small store owners who realize the very considerable losses of time, energy and future revenue from the previously honest but now 'caught customer', if they were to indiscriminately prosecute each and every case of shoplifting to the full extent of the law.

By differentiating between typical and atypical type theft offenders, store management may retain valued and now very grateful customer and thereby obtain even greater profits in the future. Now that's doubly good P.R., good 'public relations' plus 'profit retention'! (The analogy to dealing with employees who are caught stealing is hopefully obvious.)

An example of the problems that can emerge when a company's loss prevention and marketing departments don't communicate well and don't coordinate their philosophies and their practices

After a talk I gave a few years back to the loss prevention section of a large retailers' association, a senior member of a large upscale department store's marketing staff approached and complimented me on my presentation. He then privately complained about the damage being done, in his opinion, to the store's reputation, ambiance and bottom line, by a particularly heavy-handed loss prevention department who had a 'make no exceptions' mission statement vis-à-vis theft offenders, and whose successful apprehension of shoplifters was catching many good (and wealthy) paying customers. He stated that the crude (and in his opinion, rude) signs and security functions set up by the loss prevention department had an increasingly negative, cumulative effect upon the previously cultivated amiable ambiance and relaxed browsing atmosphere that his marketing department had been promoting for years. Of course, he made clear, he had no problem with the loss prevention personnel acting with appropriate and restrained vigor in regard to the apprehension of the professional thieves that also frequented his stores. The 'net' that was being used to catch the latter, was picking up and in his opinion, 'killing off' too many of the good customers.

To illustrate this point, imagine that a good customer visits a car showroom and is caught stealing a cigarette lighter belonging to an expensive floor model vehicle. What should the employee do? Should the person who has been caught be thrown out of the showroom? Should the police be called, and the person arrested and thereby the proceeds of a possible sale be lost in the name of 'loss prevention'? Or is it more desirable, and 'profit retentive', to handle the matter with greater finesse --and informed wisdom -- so that the individual might remain a customer, and perhaps even make a $50,000 purchase of the car that came with the lighter?

One can extend this example to cover all sorts of retail establishments, manufacturing companies and business situations.

Coordinating Profit Retention™ and Marketing departments

So-called Profit Retention™ personnel should work closely with Sales and Marketing staff in order to have a more unified approach to dealing with customers. Currently some stores make their establishments look somewhat like an armed camp (with a security guard located at the entrances and exits, real and phony prominently placed television cameras, threatening signs, etc...) so that it is not only potential thieves that may stay away, but also many good and paying customers who may wish to shop in more pleasant surroundings, one that does not resemble a fortress.

A good example of a bad 'loss prevention' idea

In the context of the subject of this chapter, I am reminded of the loss prevention poster I was privy to seeing aver fifteen years ago while it was still being considered by the large department store chain. The poster showed a *very large* policeman with his hand firmly clutching the arm of a *petite*, frightened looking woman; underneath the photo was the statement that "Shoplifting can bruise you!" Asked to give my opinion of the poster, which was being considered for a nation-wide, in-store theft prevention campaign, I pointed out that the photo seemed to embody every feminist's and other women's worst fantasies, that of being literally man-handled by a very large male authority figure. I strongly suggested that such a poster would offend a great many honest women shoppers who would see an image of a small woman being man-handled by large, looming and physically intrusive male. This was not, I suggested, the way to kick off a campaign aimed at increasing profits. (*I was later informed that the poster in question was not used.*)

At the same time it should be stressed that loss prevention personnel can be sympathized with when they experience frustration, or even anger, when dealing with adults whom they have clearly seen taking an item, and who now stand before them boldly denying that they "never did and never would" would do such a thing as steal! It may be wise to remember that no matter how old, or how well-dressed the shoplifting individual, simultaneously, at the very moment he or she is apprehended, that person may also be inclined to act -- and react -- like a three year old who has just been caught with a hand in the cookie jar, and deny that he or she ever even had the lid off the cookie jar.

When apprehended, atypical type theft offenders often report feeling very guilty, embarrassed, scared, and/or disgusted with themselves. Consequently they are frequently thrown into an exceptionally vulnerable state. At such times, regression to much earlier ways of operating (including childish denial, excuses, etc...) may then be expected.

The importance of deducing if one is dealing with an Atypical Theft Offender

It is very important to determine if there are observable clues that the person who has been apprehended may be an A.T.O., in part because, if the apprehended person is indeed an atypical type of theft offender there may exist <u>a serious suicidal potential</u> which should be taken into account when dealing with the individual.

As we had noted in our original article, in 1981 in England, Lady Barnett committed suicide immediately after being convicted of a minor shoplifting offense. In a major North American city a few years later, the newspapers reported that a police officer killed himself after being charged with shoplifting.

> Therefore, loss prevention and human resources personnel are encouraged to read this book in its entirety in order to become very familiar with the Atypical Theft Offender syndrome.

How *should* theft offenders be treated at the time of being apprehended?

It is probably good policy for loss prevention personnel to treat all apprehended shoplifters with courtesy, and with firm but kind authority. It perhaps bears stressing that rude, caustic or insulting intervention by the persons whose job it is to apprehend people who steal is virtually always inappropriate -- even if provoked. At the time of apprehension the loss prevention person, and shortly afterwards the police officer involved in taking personal information when laying the charge, may not be able to tell whether the apprehended person had been acting out of greed or need, or whether the major motivation is psychological and/or neurotic.

> Atypical and Typical Theft Offenders may initially appear indistinguishable from one another at the time of apprehension of the offender. It is important to learn to differentiate one from the other for both the offender's and the retailer's sake.

Some possible indicators that one may be dealing with an Atypical Theft Offender

Atypical Theft Offenders are usually generally honest individuals for whom such behavior as that for which they have just been apprehended is egodystonic, i.e., they don't see themselves as the kind of person who would normally do such a thing. When apprehended they may 'break down,' i.e., begin to cry, shake, or look and sound rather terrified. Of course, good actors can also produce such responses, as well. However, the professionals involved in apprehension and laying the charge should probably err on the side of caution, noting that if the apprehended person is of the Atypical Theft Offender type, such behavior may be an overt indication of a potential acting-out-against-themselves response, such as a suicide attempt.

The unhelpful or even dangerous type of loss prevention professional

As is true in all professions, some persons may not be suited to the work but are drawn to it for deep psychological reasons, nevertheless. For several reasons, it behooves companies to be particularly cautious when hiring loss prevention personnel.

I had an opportunity to interview a very powerfully built thirty-five-year-old man, who worked as a loss prevention person. This man spoke spontaneously and at length of his tremendous anger towards women. He described the pleasure he got in apprehending women who had shoplifted and in intimidating them with his size and manner. He said that he would enjoy squeezing the apprehended woman's arm "extra tightly" as he led them to the security office, hoping that the person would attempt to pull away or become verbally abusive so that he would then be "forced to give them the treatment they deserved." The fact that, as a child, he had himself been greatly physically and sexually abused by his own very disturbed mother explained, but of course did not excuse, his behavior. This man was encouraged to seek additional professional assistance and to strongly consider changing his line of work.

Theft Offenders whose own professions involved dealing with theft offenders

I have had occasion to deal with policemen, loss prevention personnel, lawyers, a psychiatrist and a psychologist who had themselves been involved in theft behavior. All these individuals held responsible jobs in which they came into contact with theft offenders, and the fact that they were offenders themselves was a matter that added to their distress.

On a positive note I am delighted to be able to report the slowly growing awareness and appreciation of the Atypical Theft Offender phenomenon in some segments of the general population (perhaps, in small part, because I have been favored with many radio, television and newspaper interviews in the U.S., and Europe in the past several years, and especially since the first edition of this book was published in 1997). As a result, I have been very gratified upon hearing of the exceptional loss prevention individual, police officer or criminal lawyer who, upon encountering Atypical Theft Offenders, have been very kind, compassionate and helpful in dealing with these offenders, including by suggesting that their atypical theft behavior probably reflected personal issues that they should seek help in dealing with.

Chapter 35

SOME ADDITIONAL CLINICAL FINDINGS SINCE THE FIRST EDITION OF THIS BOOK APPEARED

The increased use of Mental Health Diversion for shoplifters

In the 20 years or so since our initial clinical finding were published and we have been conducting assessments and treatment of Atypical Theft Offenders the treatment of such cases in the courts has changed profoundly. Increasingly such individuals have been referred for Mental Health Diversion, i.e., for counseling by agencies that deal with such cases on a regular basis, using approaches compatible with those outlined in our clinical work. This has cut down the court's time and expense and provided better disposition of cases that are better dealt with in the counseling office than in the jail system.

High Profile Atypical Theft Offender shoplifting cases

It is almost breathtaking to encounter the apparently nonsensical theft behavior of some wealthy and high-profile Atypical Theft Offenders, who have risked so much in terms of their reputations for so little monetary or material gain. Such cases really do 'make the case' that atypical theft behavior must have some serious underlying psychodynamics, for someone to do something so completely unnecessary and apparently self-destructive.

Atypical Theft Offender Cases where the amounts stolen are in the $100,000 and up range.

Obviously there are numerous cases of middle- and high-echelon employees who have stolen a considerable amount of money from their friends or firms. In some cases, because the amounts taken were large, and were used to acquire items (things, trips) that the offenders wanted, the case could almost never be made that the person was a pure Atypical Theft Offender. Rather, it is sometimes more the case that the offender is of the Mixed-type (A.T.O./T.T.O.) of theft offender. Still, in certain instances the crimes committed by heretofore hard-working, honest employees were so outrageous that the courts and lawyers are left amazed at the audacity of the acts.

In conducting clinical assessments of some such cases it has emerged that the perpetrators were acting out in response to major losses and/or anger towards their bosses and/or partners, where it seems likely that if they were not so upset at those persons then they probably would not have stolen. The stealing may thus represent a hugely inappropriate acting out behavior in reaction to experiencing and not dealing at all well with feelings of anger and resentment.

If the reader finds it hard to believe the above statements it may be worthwhile to remember that some persons, in response to feelings of great anger or hurt, respond by overeating to the point of true obesity, even at the risk of endangering their physical health. And they find it exceedingly hard to stop their gorging themselves, even when their doctors have warned them of imminent dire consequences if they continue to display such nonsensical eating behavior. So it is for some persons who respond by stealing.

One such client was accused of stealing over $350,000 over a period of two years. Given that this man and his wife, both lawyers, together earned in excess of $700,000, and given that they had no children and had no outstanding debts, and owned both their home and cottage outright, there was hardly any need for this man to jeopardize his entire working, family and social life. Nevertheless he risked and lost them all. His shame and humiliation reached such a magnitude that he was a genuine suicide risk.

In contrast, recently the media carried an article of a man who defrauded a great many people in both Canada and the United States, and did so without any feelings of remorse or shame. He plea-bargained and received a sentence of a very few years. When he gets out it is believed that he will make contact with millions of dollars that he is believed to have squirreled away in foreign bank accounts. This individual is very possibly a classical con man and Typical Theft Offender.

Stealing when under the influence of prescribed medication

Over the past few years I have had several clients whose atypical theft behavior seems to have been facilitated by the changes in mood, thinking and behavior brought about through the use of prescribed medications. Some medications are known to produce such side effects as aggressive outbursts, confused thought, paranoid thinking, marked depression and other reactions, some or all of which may be factors in precipitating acting out theft behavior. It behooves all people who have been prescribed medications to inquire about their possible side and interactive effects. Any awareness of unusual feelings, thoughts or actions should elicit caution in the individual.

One woman called me from California. She had been prescribed several medications to help her deal with several major illnesses simultaneously. A prominent lawyer in her city, she was charged with walking out of a Sears store with a so-called jewel case of the type used to house a CD of Adobe Acrobat. She did not need this software; the case was empty; she didn't even know what that particular software product was used for. She was charged and was at risk of losing her license to practice law. I suggested that she have her various physicians hold a conference call and discuss the medications they had prescribed and the possible interactive effects of these medications. They did hold the call and then her family doctor wrote a report outlining for the court what they believed was a plausible case that the simultaneous introduction of certain of this patient's medications might well have triggered acting out theft behavior.

The unfortunate and continuing mis-application of the label of 'kleptomania'

It is most unfortunate that some 18 years after the publication of our first article on the subject of Shoplifting: An Occasional Crime Of The Moral Majority, in which we explained why it is inappropriate to apply the label of 'kleptomania' to most cases where anger and/or vengeance and/or major personally meaningful losses are concerned, that far too often, well-meaning clinicians continue to do so.

A very few years ago two of the major U.S. television networks contacted me, after the trial was over and the offender was found guilty, about the same case in which this appears to have happened. The judge in that case was clearly not persuaded that the theft offender concerned suffered from this exceptionally rare affliction. The judge was probably quite right to be unconvinced. However, it may well be that the individual was an Atypical Theft Offender or perhaps a 'mixed-type' (A.T.O./T.T.O.) of theft offender. This hypothesis was never presented to the court and the accused was given a substantial jail term, and treated as if he were a Typical Theft Offender. The fact that he was a lawyer, his wife a doctor and that together they earned well in excess of $300,000 a year, and that he had been brought up in a household filled with major losses and abandonment, makes his long-time stealing at least possibly an example of the Loss-Substitution-By-Stealing Hypothesis in action.

Too often, even in this new millennium, the term 'kleptomania' is used in court in the same way that in that old story, the boy cried wolf -- much too often, erroneously, and with most unfortunate effects. Hopefully this book will help to educate and inform more of those involved in the legal system, and more lay persons involved in such cases, so that these cases will be more correctly assessed and more appropriately treated in the future.

A FINAL COMMENT

Clinical investigations into the phenomenon of the Atypical Theft Offender can provide us all, professionals and laypersons alike, with a unique view of the unconscious as it helps precipitate bizarre or unusual behavior in otherwise relatively 'normal' and even successful or wealthy persons.

Perhaps the key notion to remember is that Atypical Theft Offenders are usually good and essentially honest people who have done 'bad' things by stealing; these actions, however, do not negate their goodness nor their worthwhile lives.

I am always interested in hearing from readers about their own personal and/or professional experiences with the Atypical Theft Offender phenomenon. While I may not respond directly to all persons who provide such materials, I will be pleased to add those that are appropriate to my files, to further deepen my own understanding of this fascinating area of human behavior.

APPENDIX A

Contacting Dr. Will Cupchik and
Checking out *www.WhyHonestPeopleSteal.com*

The reader is invited to visit Dr. Cupchik's comprehensive website, *www.whyhonestpeoplesteal.com* at any time, to obtain the latest information regarding articles and findings of Dr. Cupchik's clinical efforts. Detailed information about the **Atypical Theft Offender Intensive Intervention Program** as well as the availability of a **Brief Free Consultation** is also available on this web site.

Readers wishing to consult with Dr. Cupchik may do so either via e-mail at *wcupchik@aol.com,* or by telephoning 416-928-2262.

SUGGESTED SUPPLEMENTAL READING

- Anderson, Robert, I never Sang for My Father, Signet Books, 1970

- Bowlby, John, Attachment and Loss: Volume 3, Loss, Sadness and Depression, Penguin Books, copyright 1980

- Courtois, Christine, Healing the Incest Wound: Adult Survivors in Therapy, W.W.Norton, 1988

- Cupchik, Will. Clinical Imaginative Imagery, Unpublished Doctoral Dissertation, University of Toronto, 1979

- Cupchik, Will. Reintrojection Therapy: A Procedure for Altering Parental Introjects, Psychotherapy: Theory, Research and Practice, Vol. 21, Summer, 1984, #2

- Cupchik, W and Atcheson, D J Shoplifting: An occasional Crime of the Moral Majority, Bulletin of the American Academy of Psychiatry and the Law, Vol.11:343-354, 1983

- Fugere, R, D'Elia, A, and Philippe, Considerations on the Dynamics of Fraud and Shoplifting in Adult Female Offenders, Can J Psychiatry, Vol. 40, April 1995

- Goulding, Mary and Bob, Changing Lives Through Redecision Therapy, Brunner/Mazel, N.Y., 1979

- James, Muriel and Jongeward, Dorothy, Born to Win, Addison Wesley, Reading, MA, 1971

- Viorst, Judith Necessary Losses, Ballantyne Books, 1987

---

[i] Cupchik, W, Atcheson, D.J. *Shoplifting: An Occasional Crime of the Moral Majority,* Bulletin of the American Academy of Psychiatry and the Law, Vol.11: 4-343, 1983

[ii] *Clinical Criminology: The Assessment and Treatment of Criminal Behavior,* Edited by Ben-Aron, M.H., Hucker,S.J., and Webster,C.D., Clarke Institute of Psychiatry/University of Toronto, 1985, Chapter 18. Cupchik, W, Atcheson, D.J. *Shoplifting: An Occasional Crime of the Moral Majority.*

[iii] From a news release, dated February 7, 1996, by the Republican National Committee.

[iv] Egosyntonic refers to thoughts, feelings or actions which the person is comfortable with, likes and accepts as part of his or her self.

[v] The 'tools' referred to here are the following:
The Cupchik Theft Offender Questionnaire,   Chapter 17
The Typical-Atypical Theft Offender Spectrum,   Chapter 18

[vi] Cupchik W *Clinical Imaginative Imagery*, unpublished doctoral dissertation, University of Toronto, 1979

[vii] The reader should note that usually the only cases that are referred to me for assessment and/or treatment are those in which the defense attorney thinks that there may be some grounds for appealing to the court that might mitigate against a finding of guilt, or at least result in a lesser sentence.

As lawyers who have requested my services would attest, I am sure, I am quite conservative when it comes to considering a theft offender's position along the ATO-TTO continuum. Some lawyers are inclined to refer their clients for assessment in the hope that by doing so they might obtain a psychological report that would be helpful, regardless of the fact that there was little to suggest that their clients were not other than very *Typical* Theft Offenders.

[viii] Viorst, Judith *Necessary Losses, Ballantyne Books, 1987*

[ix] Copies of the Cupchik Theft Offender Questionnaire may be purchased from the writer by using the order form at the back of the book

[x] Figurer, D'Elia, A and Philippe *Considerations on the Dynamics of Fraud and Shoplifting in Adult Female Offenders*, Can J Psychiatry, Vol. 40, April 1995

[xi] "The Rope Trick" is an original imagery exercise that I developed about 1975, that is arguably the optimal fantasy exercise with which to assess and deal therapeutically with a significant interpersonal relationship. This exercise was shown to be both reliable and valid through an experimental investigation that was the subject of my doctoral dissertation.

[xii] The title of my doctoral dissertation was *Clinical Imaginative Imagery*, and it describes the experimental investigation of the reliability and validity of The Rope Trick as an exercise that assesses the statics and dynamics of an interpersonal relationship. This research showed that The Rope Trick is indeed a reliable and valid assessment tool for relationships. I have presented numerous workshops on this device, including a workshop at the 2nd Annual World Conference on Imagery: Ninth Annual Conference of the American Association for the Study of Mental Imagery, Toronto, 1986.

[xiii] Harlow,H.F., and Suomi,S.J. *Nature of Love-Simplified.* American Psychologist (1970) 25: 161-68.

[xiv] *The Rope Trick* well illustrates the phenomenon of symbolic encoding as a natural and normal part of human cognitive functioning. My experimental investigations very strongly indicated that the subjects' unconscious minds manifested conscious images whose very construction could be clearly seen to have some symbolic meaning which the creators did not consciously intend, or initially appreciate. It usually required carrying out specific but commonly employed clinical methodology to uncover the symbolic significance of their images.

[xv] A rather poignant yet humorous rendition of such a circumstances that, in spite of obvious drawbacks due to the Hollywood treatment of the subject, nevertheless contains enough truths to make the viewing worthwhile, is the

movie entitled *Fun with Dick and Jane,* starring Jane Fonda and Gerorge Segal. This 'married couple' turns to crime shortly after 'Dick' is fired from his substantial position with a high-tech company.

[xvi] I recall a theft offender who I asked whether there had been any meaningful losses that had occurred in her life just prior to her theft offense. She had replied "No, none!" . The following day I received a call from this woman who said that she had discussed our interview with her husband. He was dumbfounded that she had said that there had been no losses around the time of her offense. It turned out that her beloved grandmother and an uncle had died earlier in the week that her theft occurred. Let the interviewer beware of too readily accepting clients' answers to some of the questions asked.

It is usually not a matter of purposefully and consciously lying that is involved here. The offender seldom recognized the relevance of the question.

[xvii] Bowlby, J *Attachment and Loss, VolumeIII. Loss:Sadness and Depression,* Penquin Books, 1981

[xviii] I have found it to be only occasionally true that the nature of the items shoplifted have had such a blatant symbolic relationship to the precipitating cause. This makes the husband's impotence and his wife's stealing of lingerie all the more remarkable.

[xix] Fugere,R, D'Elia, A and Philippe,R *Considerations on the Dynamics of Fraud and Shoplifting in Adult Female Offenders*, Can J Psychiatry, Vol. 40, April 1995

[xx] James,M and Jongeward, D *Born to Win*, Addison Wesley, Reading, MA., 1971

[xxi] Cupchik, W, *Reintrojection Therapy: A procedure for Altering Parental Introjects*, Psychotherapy:Theory, Research, and Practice, Volume 21, Summer, 1984, #2

[xxii] Anderson, Robert, *I Never Sang for My Father*, Signet books, 1970, p.179

[xxiii] Fagan,J and Shephard,I, *Gestalt Therapy Now, Science and Behavior Books, Palo Alto, California, 1970*

[xxiv] Forward, Susan, *Toxic Parents*, Bantam Books, 1989

[xxv] Gannon, J.Patrick, *Soul Survivors*, Prentice Hall Press, 1989

[xxvi] Courtois, Christine, *Healing the Incest Wound: Adult Survivors in Therapy*, W W Norton, 1988, p.208

[xxvii] Yalom, Irvin, *The Theory and Practice of Group Psychotherapy, Fourth Edition*, Basic Books, 1995, p.5

LaVergne, TN USA
03 November 2010
203411LV00001B/135/A